ENGLISH CAMEO
GLASS

Vase, 13¼ inches, signed "T. & G. Woodall, Webb," W 2840. The Aurora Vase. *(Authors' collection)*

ENGLISH CAMEO GLASS

by
Ray and Lee Grover

CROWN PUBLISHERS, INC. New York

Also by Ray and Lee Grover

ART GLASS NOUVEAU
CARVED AND DECORATED EUROPEAN ART GLASS
CONTEMPORARY ART GLASS

Printed in the United States of America

Published simultaneously in Canada by General Publishing Company Limited

Library of Congress Cataloging in Publication Data

Grover, Ray.
    English cameo glass.

    Bibliography: p.
    Includes index.
    1. Cameo glass—England. I. Grover, Lee, joint author. II. Title.
NK5439.C33G76   1979   748.2'92   79-1443
ISBN 0-517-538156

Book design by Joan Columbus

TO OUR GREAT-GRANDCHILDREN

CONTENTS

ACKNOWLEDGMENTS

THE AUTHORS wish to express their grateful thanks to the collectors, dealers, and museum officials whose help has been of inestimable value in the compilation of this book. Officials of both Dema Glass, parent company of Thomas Webb and Sons, and Royal Brierley Crystal, formerly Stevens & Williams, Ltd., were of great help in facilitating our research. Christie's, Sotheby Parke Bernet, and Phillips Auction Galleries made available their transparencies and black-and-white glossy records from their past sales catalogs.

We particularly indicate our great indebtedness and deep appreciation to Herbert William Woodward, Brierley Hill Librarian and Curator in charge of Brierley Hill Glass Museum 1938–1966, and Dudley Museum Keeper of Glass and Fine Arts 1962–1966. He gave us extremely valuable and helpful suggestions and supplied us with material which we could not have found otherwise.

In addition, the following persons, in particular, deserve our gratitude and thanks: Kristin A. Amylon, Asst. Dir. Collections, Rockwell-Corning Museum; Mr. and Mrs. Jerome Ash; George Babcock; Keith R. Baker, Art Nouveau–Art Deco Department, Phillips Fine Auctioneers, London; Mae Belle Beith; Helen and George Bierly; Mrs. Mary Bowring, Sotheby's Belgravia, London; Mr. and Mrs. Philip Budrose; Peter Burford, Crown Publishers, Inc., Mrs. Lucille Catterson; Sander Davidson; Barbara Deisroth, Sotheby Parke Bernet, New York; Jessie McNab Dennis, Assistant Curator, Metropolitan Museum of Art; Paul Doros; Roger Dodsworth,

Museum Trainee, Dudley Museum, England; Alistair Duncan, Christie's, New York; Loraine E. Elferdink; Mr. and Mrs. Sam Feld; Stewart Feld; Derek Fontaine, Head of Fine Arts Department, Birmingham Public Library, Birmingham, England; Dr. and Mrs. Jesse B. Foote; Mr. and Mrs. James R. Freyermuth; Mr. and Mrs. Robert Frischmuth; Phillipe Garner, Head of Art Nouveau Department, Sotheby's Belgravia, London; Charles Hajdamach, Keeper of Glass and Fine Arts, Dudley Museum, England; Mr. David Hammond, Dema Glass Ltd., Chief Designer—Thomas Webb & Sons, Dennis Glassworks, Stourbridge, England; Billy and Becky Hitt; Barbara and Philip Hoover; Tom Jones, Design Department—Commemorative and Decorated Art Glass, Royal Brierley Crystal; J. Jonathan Joseph; Alan Kaplan, Leo and Ruth Kaplan; Susan P. Kaplan; Graham Knowles, Mrs. Marjorie Knowles; Joe and Eugenia Kolb; Mary and Jim Kux; Dwight P. Lanmon, Deputy Director, Corning Museum of Glass; Roger Mandle, Director Toledo Museum of Art; Jo Marshall, Specialist in Glass, Phillips Fine Auctioneers, London; Nancy O. Merrill, Curator of Glass, Chrysler Museum of Art at Norfolk; Barbara Morris, Victoria and Albert Museum; Robert D. Mowry, Milan Historical Museum, Milan, Ohio; Kenneth Northwood, Former Technical Director of Edinburgh Crystal Glass Company; Alice "Lal" Northwood; Dr. and Mrs. M. Nuckolls; Jenifer Oka, Museum Specialist, The Smithsonian Institution; William F. Pardoe, Stained Glass Artist and Photographer, Stourbridge, England; Nicola Redway, Sotheby's Belgravia, London; Robert Rockwell, Corning, New York; Minna Rosenblatt; Rita Rotman; Bill and Evelyn Runyon; Rachel Russell, Art Nouveau and Glass, Christie's, London; Colonel Reginald Silvers-Thomas, Chairman of the Board, Royal Brierley Crystal, formerly Stevens & Williams, Ltd.; M. B. Stauffer, Milan Historical Museum, Milan, Ohio; Penelope Hunter Stiebel, Assistant Curator, Metropolitan Museum of Art; Mr. A. E. Stott, Managing Director, Dema Glass, Ltd., Thomas Webb & Sons, Dennis Glassworks, Stourbridge, England; Sam Thompson, Caretaker of Museum, Royal Brierley Crystal, former manager of Etching and Processing Department; Alan Tillman; D. Leonard & Gerry Trent; Mr. R. S. Uffindell, Chairman of the Board, Dema Glass, Ltd., Thomas Webb & Sons, Dennis Glassworks, Stourbridge, England; Melvin E. Watts, Curator, Currier Gallery of Art, Manchester, New Hampshire; Harold Werner; Patricia Whitesides, Toledo Museum of Arts; Glennys Wild, Acting Keeper of Art, Birmingham City Museum & Art Gallery, Birmingham, England; Mr. David Williams-Thomas, Managing Director, Royal Brierley Crystal; Mr. Simon Williams-Thomas, Sales Director, Royal Brierley Crystal; Bertram Wolfson; Elliot and Enid Wysor.

FOREWORD

OUR PURPOSE in presenting this book is to expose glass collectors all over the world to the wide range of techniques and artistic achievement in the field of carved cameo decoration on glass produced in England.

Interest in the art of cameo glass carving was rekindled with the presentation to the British Museum in 1810 of the famous Portland Vase. Fifty years later, the desire of artist-craftsmen to emulate the ancient Greeks found expression in experimental processes in Stourbridge, England. We illustrate here, in color, outstanding examples of their work, much of it unique in the glass industry. Today, we find the artists' unusual confidence in carving such fine work on a material as fragile as glass a matter of astonishment and wonder.

The mythological subjects done by George Woodall after Greek themes have been researched and checked as to subject matter. We have tried to identify correctly all the immortals, major deities, and lesser gods and goddesses of Greece whose likenesses are carved in fine-detail cameo relief on the great vases and plaques. Floral subjects also have been subjected to a close botanical scrutiny and are, we hope, properly named and labeled.

We have personally examined the majority of pieces and, with a few exceptions, have done the actual photography ourselves.

Signatures, marks, and inscriptions are enclosed within quotation marks. The height of each piece illustrated is given to the nearest quarter-inch. In designating the illustrations, a "C" preceding a number refers to a color plate; an "S" indicates a sketch from the Woodall sketchbook:

C = Color plate
S = Sketch

We urge our readers to visit the various museums listed and acquaint themselves with the many fine collections to be found in them.

INTRODUCTION

The Stourbridge area of England still maintains the high distinction it has enjoyed since the seventeenth century as a center for the production of handmade quality glassware. The single word "Stourbridge" has come to stand for all the various glass factories in the region. Their excellence of production and the high quality of their glass brought fame and prosperity to the whole district.

The artistic results of the years of endeavor in the glass field from this particular area of England have played an important part in the world history of glassmaking. Today's products complement the distinguished records of accomplishment of the earlier years.

In our previous books, *Art Glass Nouveau* and *Carved and Decorated European Art Glass,* we mentioned the seventeenth-century beginnings by the men from Lorraine who settled in the parish of Kingswinford and started work in broad glass. Paul Tyzack, a master of the art, and his kinsmen, the Henzeys and the Titterys, came to England to work and resettle themselves. It was a propitious time, as a Royal Proclamation in 1615 had forbidden the import of glass and also the use of wood in the glass furnaces.

The Stourbridge area was extremely advantageous because of its natural resources—cheap pit coal and a great abundance of good clay and potash in the particular parish of Oldswinford. Materials necessary for building furnaces and making crucibles or small pots for melting the glass were at hand.

In 1618 Paul Tyzack was in possession of a "leasowe" called Colemans, with both clay and coal lying underneath at different depths. Here was built the first glasshouse recorded in the Stourbridge district. On the strength of Tyzack's prosperity, Lorrainers continued steadily to come into the district despite the Civil War of the next fifty years. Some of the most famous were the Dagnias, Rachettis, and Visitalias.

In the second decade of the seventeenth century, Admiral Sir Robert Mansell established a monopoly by organizing the glass industry on a national basis. He kept it under control for over forty years.

During the early part of the eighteenth century, the area developed a reputation for ornamental flint glass of high quality, and this gained wide recognition. Bristol, with fifteen glasshouses, became important for blue and white glass made in imitation of Chinese porcelain; Newcastle, for engraved and white enameled glass; Nailsea and Birmingham became known for polychrome decorative work and had many successful years. Glass companies flourished—they not only supplied England but exported worldwide.

During the early nineteenth century brilliant-cut lead crystal became important. It was joined by the colored Victorian art glass, most of which was beautifully decorated and ornamented. Finally, from 1870 through the 1920s, came the greatest period—that of the art of cameo carving.

To the present day, in the Stourbridge district, specialization in craftsmanship by the many artists has been the primary purpose of the factory owners. In fact, there has been not only a remarkable continuity of family management, but also a seemingly inherited artistic ability from one generation to the next.

Today the glass industry of the Stourbridge district is still healthy and thriving, serving a cultivated taste and sophisticated buying public.

As a foundation for using this book, *English Cameo Glass,* it is imperative for the reader to acquire a full knowledge of the basic processes used in the manufacture of this type of glass. John Northwood II, in a pamphlet called "Stourbridge Cameo Glass" from *News and Reviews of Society of Glass Technology* 1949, volume 33, pages 106–113, states it most concisely:

"The method of making a blank on which cameo designs can be worked consists first in producing a cup-shaped article of opal white glass of the size and thickness required for the ultimate shape and size of the finished article. This cup, while in the hot state, is completely filled up solid with molten transparent coloured glass gathered on the end of a glass blowing iron from the pot of glass in the furnace.

"The mass now attached to the blowing iron is rolled on an iron plate or 'marver' to weld thoroughly the two glasses together. It is then reheated in the pot mouth, thereby keeping it in a soft and ductile state for the glass blower to blow the solid mass into a hollow-shaped ball.

"The finisher or workman takes charge of it at this stage, and by his skillful manipulation forms it into the shape and size of the article required.

"This glass blank of transparent glass covered uniformly by opal is, after being well annealed, taken in hand by the decorator.

"He first draws his design on the opal glass surface, and then paints an acid-resisting varnish all over the subject of the design. After the varnish is thoroughly set and firm, the article is immersed in a bath of a mixture of hydrofluoric and sulphuric acids which dissolve all the opal glass which is unprotected by the varnish and so allows the transparent coloured underbody to be exposed round the design. The flat surface of opal relief on the article is now ready for the carver to commence his work.

"The tools used for hand-carving are very simple. Small size steel rods from one-sixteenth to one-eighth of an inch in diameter and carefully tempered, are held in a form of holder.

"Glass carving by hand is much more laborious than wheel engraving. The tool is held in the right hand by the thumb and first two fingers, while the thumb on the left hand is held and pressed against the side of the tool to form a fulcrum as it were, during the act of carving.

"If heavy or continuous work is being done a thumb-stall of leather is worn on the end of the left thumb to prevent soreness.

"The article while being worked is laid on a pad of ample size, filled with soft but firm material such as bran. With the steel point the carver proceeds to cut up the surface of the flat opal design. The process of carving in the early stages requires a fair amount of strength, particularly in the fingers and wrists.

"The tool is frequently dipped in a bath of paraffin oil to make it bite on the glass and keep it cool. To keep its sharp edge it is often rubbed up on an oil stone. Very often when one has to work on small and delicate details of a subject the aid of an adjustable magnifying lens is employed.

"Small files and rifflers can also be used with advantage for cleaning up the outlines of the design and where work has to be done on garments or hangings in shaping the folds of the drapery.

"Whilst the carving is being done the object is moved on the pad only intermittently; it is the hand tool which has to be continuously in motion. This contrasts with the engraving process, where the article itself has to be moved continuously in every direction under the engraver's wheel."

Inside the cover of the pamphlet from which the above is quoted there appeared the following inscription: "From Dad on his eightieth birthday, May 7, 1950, John Northwood II."

A Glassmaker's Song*

Bonny's backed the winner;
We're on the booze today,
We'll have a goose for dinner,
And drink whiskey in our "tay,"
We'll line our coats with five-pound notes,
And drink our noses blue,
For Bonny's backed the winner,
And we don't care what we do.

---

*Quoted from H. J. Haden's *Notes on the Stourbridge Glass Trade,* Libraries and Arts Committee, Brierley Hill, 1949.

ENGLISH CAMEO GLASS

A great triumph occurred in the last half of the nineteenth century for the glassmen and manufacturers of Stourbridge, for new tiny copper wheels and steel gravers made it possible for the glass engravers and sculptors to increase the extensive detail in their work. These infinitely patient and skillful artist-craftsmen were as important—perhaps more so—to the industry as the visionary manufacturers with their capital resources and great enthusiasm for their own products.

Among the first of the Stourbridge glass firms to be considered is that of Richardsons, first established in 1825 at Wordsley. Known as the "Father of the Stourbridge glass trade," Benjamin Richardson, born in 1802, began his career working for the Wordsley Flint Glass Works. On December 5, 1829, Ben Richardson, along with his brother William Haden Richardson and Thomas Webb, later of Dennis Glass Works, formed the firm of Richardson and Webb. Thomas Webb supplied half the capital for this enterprise, and the Richardsons each contributed a quarter share. Many years later the Richardson company, known then as Henry G. Richardson and Sons, Ltd., was bought by Thomas Webb & Sons and operated from the Dennis Glass Works.

During 1836 Thomas Webb left Richardson, and the name was changed again as another Richardson, brother Jonathan, joined the company. This union of three brothers prospered and achieved fame.

Ben Richardson had not only a love of art but a passion for glass. To him, glass was an exciting medium in which to work—delicate but strong, with infinite possibilities in shape, in applied or intaglio decoration, and particularly in color. He decided to improve on the glass colors being made by the Bohemians, producing a wide range not only in color, but in cutting, engraving, and etching. Every technique was employed—enameling, gilding, staining, frosting, and threading—as their advertisement of 1850 indicated. His complete devotion to the glass craft and his desire for perfection were both catalyst and inspiration for this remarkable period in glassmaking. In 1847, W. H. B. and J. Richardson Company received a gold medal from the Society of Arts for "specimens of enameled colours on glass"; in 1848 they were awarded a silver medal.

On May Day, 1851, the Great Exhibition was opened in Hyde Park by Queen Victoria and Prince Albert. Richardsons of Wordsley exhibited magnificent colored glass overlayed with enamel, on opal vases and jars. They received first prize with subjects drawn from "Aesop's Fables, Greek myths, Italian landscapes, Scotch lakes and marine views." This was but the beginning of the many awards won by the company in succeeding years. (One other award, in 1878, should be mentioned—the South African Exhibition Silver Medal.)

It was also at this time, 1852, that a Government School of Design was started in Stourbridge. All the men who later became famous in the glass world took advantage of the opportunity of learning the fundamentals of art—model drawing, perspective, and freehand drawing. It was not easy for these young men to work each day from 9:00 to 6:00 and then go to night school three nights a week, but the training they received was invaluable: it added to their appreciation of the qualities of the material they worked with every day.

We cannot minimize the inspiration that Ben Richardson brought to his trade. He attracted to his company many gifted young men—William J. Muckley, a fine painter of still lifes; Thomas Bott, uncle of the Woodalls, who later painted with Limoges-type enamel for Worcester Royal Porcelain Works; Philip Pargeter, subsequently owner of the Red House Glass Works; John Northwood the first, a pioneer of the glass trade; Joseph Locke, eventually of the New England Glass Co.; George Woodall, most prolific and famous cameo designer; and Alphonse Lechevrel, an eminent medalist. All these skilled artists added to the reputation of the Richardson firm and of Stourbridge glass.

In 1887, at eighty-five years of age, Ben Richardson died, leaving a legacy of achievement and originality. His son, Benjamin Richardson II, assembled a collection of glass that he bequeathed to the Stourbridge Town Council. Following his death in 1952 the Stourbridge Council House Museum was opened. A permanent collection was formed comprised of four fine cameo vases, two by George Woodall and two by Alphonse Lechevrel, given by Richardson with other examples of the work of the factory. This group of glass is most beautiful and imposing. In recent years the Lechevrel cameos have been moved to the Dudley Art Gallery in nearby Dudley. The gallery collection also includes pieces from the Stevens and Williams Works Museum, the Brierley Hill Collection, and the Wollescote Hall Collection.

By the end of the nineteenth century the term Stourbridge glass indicated the best possible quality of glass available to the buying public. Both table and fancy glass were produced in the general Stourbridge district running north to Wolverhampton. We had lunch at the old Talbot

Inn, which, through the many years, has been the general meeting place for the glass manufacturers and the place where many important decisions were made concerning the industry.

Alphonse Lechevrel, born in France in 1850, earned a reputation as a medalist and gem engraver. He was invited to come to Wordsley by Ben Richardson in 1877, and as he remained in England only two years, his work in cameo carving was limited although his influence on the many artists of the area was extensive. Six pieces that he created are most important in any discussion of cameo carving. The Grecian vases "Raising an Altar to Bacchus," dated 1878, and "Hercules Restoring Alcestis to Her Husband, Admetus," dated 1877, are shown in our book *Carved and Decorated European Art Glass*. They have the initials of the artist inscribed. When they were originally exhibited in the Paris Exhibition of 1878, a photograph was taken of them, and this shows that each had two handles rising upward from the shoulders to above the lip. The original identification in Paris was that of Lechevrel. Subsequently the handles were completely removed and George Woodall's signature appeared: in 1882 at the Worcestershire Exhibition, where the vases turned up, they were signed "Geo. Woodall." The plaque "Cupid on Panther" has George Woodall's signature; it is now at the Currier Art Gallery in Manchester, New Hampshire. "Venus" or "Birth of Venus," "Venus Arising," and "Bacchanalian Musician" are the three other pieces Lechevrel executed. The two Venus vases were also exhibited in the 1878 Paris Exhibition signed, with handles that were eventually removed.

Joseph Locke, who became one of the most famous and respected of American glassmen, began his career in England, where he was born on August 21, 1846, in Worcester. Edward Locke, his father, was a potter. At twelve years of age Joseph was apprenticed to the Royal Worcester china factory, where he was taught the rudiments of art by eminent painters. At the age of nineteen he won first prize in a competition for a fireplace design, which had been commissioned by the Czar of Russia from Guest Bros. of Brettell Lane, Staffordshire, etchers and decorators of glass. In their employment he learned all phases of the glassmaker's trade. Becoming acquainted with Joshua Hodgetts and then Benjamin Richardson, he decided to leave Guest's and work at the Richardson Company. Here he developed the art of engraving and cameo carving under the tutelage of the "Father of Glass." Alphonse Lechevrel was also his teacher, and Locke's natural ability and originality were encouraged and motivated.

When Ben Richardson decided to exhibit at the Paris Exhibition of 1878, he urged Locke to attempt a copy or second reproduction of the Portland

Vase for the exhibit. Forty to fifty blanks were made by the glassblowers, but only two survived the annealing. Locke started to work on one of them, but it shattered within three weeks. Then, with the one piece of glass left, Locke started his carving again. For twelve months he worked, engraving and sculpturing the relief design with great perseverance and care. When the vase was finally exhibited in Paris, it won a Gold Medal although it had not been completed. The final work was a great achievement and Locke received high praise from his contemporaries throughout the world.

At the opening of the Wordsley Art School in 1899, the Portland Vase by Locke and a plaque "Cupid Sailing on a Cockleshell" were exhibited. Another extremely fine piece created by Joseph Locke is the carved head of William Shakespeare, which is cemented on a four-inch square of cased gold-ruby glass. This masterpiece of carving can be seen today at Alfred Museum in Alfred, New York, a gift of Professor Alexander Silverman.

Locke left the employ of Richardson's, working first for Philip Pargeter of the Red House Glass Works, owner of the Northwood Portland Vase, and then for Webb and Corbetts. However, he was not satisfied in England, and decided to emigrate to the United States. In 1882 he arrived in Boston and was employed by the New England Glass Company of Cambridge, Massachusetts. Here, as the inventor of many new glass processes, a designer, and glass artist, he enjoyed great success. The Toledo Museum of Art, Toledo, Ohio, owns a Locke cameo vase, white on ruby, which he carved in the United States. At ninety years of age, still involved in glass etching, he died in Pittsburgh, Pennsylvania, on June 10, 1936.

Stevens & Williams, Royal Brierley crystal glassmakers by royal appointment, was formed as a partnership in 1847. The company, located in Moor Lane, Brierley Hill, originally had been the Brierley Hill Glass Works, founded about 1740 and owned then by the Honeybournes. They were related to the ancient Lorraine glassmaking family of Henzey, recorded in parish registers as "Gentlemen Glass Makers," very practical, skilled craftsmen. Early in the nineteenth century the works was leased to Joseph Silvers, who became joint owner with Mills and Stevens. William Stevens and Samuel Cox Williams both married daughters of Joseph Silvers, and they took control of the business, when its present name was adopted, in 1847. In 1870 a new works was built adjoining the obsolete factory; in 1949 the factory was again remodeled and streamlined.

From 1864 to 1933 Joseph Silvers Williams-Thomas was active, and then his son Hubert Silvers Williams-Thomas took charge of the works. Today Colonel Reginald Silvers Williams-Thomas is Chairman of the Board, with his two sons, David and Simon, as Managing Director and Sales Director respectively. The long association and continuity in this story of a company have resulted in a product with the highest standards. Stevens & Williams has supplied glassware for the royal family of England for a great many years. With foresight and energy, they have also created a world market for their product, developing the artistic side of glassmaking along with new scientific processes. Today, their factory is a model of fine planning and efficient management, producing beautiful high-quality crystal.

Besides John Northwood I and John Northwood II, whom we will discuss individually, other artists working for Stevens & Williams were exceptionally talented. Will Northwood, elder brother of John, was one whose ability has been overlooked in the past—a skilled photographer as well as a great carver, his plaque "Venus and Dancing Cupid" is now in the Dudley Gallery of Art, unfortunately damaged. Today he is recognized as being on a par with the best of his contemporaries. Charles Northwood, a son of Joseph Northwood, another brother of John's, was also talented, but he did only a small amount of carving, mostly sprays of flowers.

Joshua Hodgetts was employed by Stevens & Williams for over forty years. He had originally worked for J. & J. Northwood at their Wordsley decorating establishment, and learned intaglio engraving under the auspices of John Orchard. Hodgetts attended night school at the Stourbridge School of Art, where he was a prize pupil. His ability to draw floral designs that were botanically accurate gives him top place among the greats in glass carving. Truth to nature was typical of the Northwood School—Hodgetts even referred to the actual flower or leaf set in front of him as he carved.

Today it is interesting to compare those times with the present, and to realize that Stevens & Williams have kept their employees for many, many years. We were greatly helped by Tom Jones, a designer with the company for fifty-nine years, and Sam Thompson, etcher, who has fifty-seven years of service with the firm. This long tenure speaks well of the employer-employee relationship that is still pursued. Tom and Sam helped us identify some of the English flowers pictured in this book, many of them familiar to us but named differently.

5

Joshua Hodgetts, who was born in 1857 at Kingswinford, died on May 12, 1933. The amount and variety of the work he produced, carrying out final operations with the engraving wheel, cannot be counted—he was so prolific. He was the first worker on the intaglio lathe invented by John Northwood in the early 1890s.

Oscar Pierre Erard, a Frenchman, did unusual work in raised gold paste and enamel in the 1890s. His work today is avidly collected, being unusually striking with its rare and subtle designs.

James Hill, another fine artist, born March 5, 1850, also worked originally in the Northwood establishment, starting as a young boy. He was involved in cameo carving for some sixty-seven years. Under Northwood at Stevens & Williams in about 1880, he carved two plaques approximately twelve inches in diameter, one white on blue, the other white on ruby. He died on February 15, 1928.

We must mention here one of the greatest men in glassmaking history in the world—Frederick Carder, born on September 18, 1863, in Brockmoor, Kingswinford, Staffordshire. His achievements have been discussed in our book *Art Glass Nouveau,* but we will again recall his early English training. Starting as a potter working for his father, who owned Leys Pottery, he then went to school in the evenings at Dudley Mechanic Institute for classes in chemistry, electricity, and metallurgy as well as attending art classes at the Stourbridge School of Art. His time was spent most profitably. In 1878, after seeing John Northwood's "Portland Vase," Fred Carder decided he wished to learn the art of cameo carving. This decision changed his life.

In 1881 he started work for Stevens & Williams as a designer, eventually becoming assistant art director. The year 1888 found him winning a silver medal for a vase design, "Cupid and Psyche"; in 1889 he won a gold medal in the National Competition for "The Muses." In addition, about 1887 he had completed a great cameo plaque, "The Immortality of the Arts," which is now owned by The Corning Museum of Glass, Corning, New York.

Before going to the United States in 1902, Fred Carder had visited Germany and Australia. In a report to the Staffordshire County Council, which had sponsored the tour, Carder commented on the widespread use of gas furnaces in the two countries. He mentioned that a German glasshouse was quite bearable—"free from the vile, the insufferable temperature, and the still worse effects of sulphur which are always in evidence in English glasshouses."

His career in the United States was unprecedented in achievement. Cofounder in 1903, with T. G. Hawkes, of the Steuben Glass Company, Corning, New York, Carder became sole owner and headed that company until 1918, when his company became the Steuben division of Corning Glass Works, owned today by the family that acquired it then, the Houghtons. Carder continued his association with the company, having his own studio laboratory at the plant. Today all his glass is avidly collected—a few of his special types were Aurene, Cire Perdue, Diatreta, Florentia, and Intarsia. He lived to be one hundred years of age, still active, agile, and interested in his first love, glass.

Jim Millward did some beautiful carving in the period of 1920 to 1951, using factory blanks that had been in storage for many years. Others who were most prolific were Frank Schreibner, W. O. Bowen, Percival Cartwright, Benjamin Fenn, Daniel Beech, Samuel Phipps, Joseph Hill, Anton Anzel, and Benjamin Price.

All the men we have mentioned, from 1881 when John Northwood became Works Manager and Art Director of Stevens & Williams, produced great quantities of cameo glass. They were all capable artistic artisans working under the guiding light of John Northwood I and then for his son, John Northwood II—leaders in knowledge and expertise.

Edwin Grice, born in 1839, was employed by J. & J. Northwood as a glass engraver for eighteen years. A skilled patternmaker and inventor of new movements in the machines, he worked on the Dennis Vase, helping Northwood rough out the horsehead handles and the Pegasus finial. Files and drills dipped in paraffin were the means used to cut the glass. A great deal of early time and effort was saved by Grice's working on the piece. When Northwood's closed, Grice moved to Guest Bros., where for twenty-five years his activity in various departments was important to the Brettell Lane company. Grice also made the box in which Northwood carried the Portland Vase. In 1913 he died, after being in retirement for nine years.

We show a photograph of Her Majesty Queen Elizabeth taken April 23, 1958, with John Northwood II and H. S. Williams-Thomas, owner of Stevens & Williams. The goblet that the Queen is examining is one of a pair made for the use of Queen Victoria and the Prince Consort at the opening of the Royal Exchange on October 28, 1844. One picture of John Northwood II, posed carving a bowl, was taken in his later years; another shows him with the Mayor of Stourbridge on the occasion of the presentation of his collection and the opening of the Council House Museum.

Photographs of several of the pieces from the Royal Brierley Crystal (Stevens & Williams) Museum give pictorial evidence of the skill and meticulous knowledge of the great carvers who sculptured the details on the cameo vases. One large ruby rose vase decorated with exotic birds and horse-chestnut leaves and flowers now in the museum was purchased from a great-granddaughter of Joshua Hodgetts and finished off in minor detail in 1972. The same shaped vase is shown in the Stevens & Williams Description Book—a pattern from 1887—as No. 12674, which sold for £45. Factory prices in 1885 varied from about £5 to £17 for vases 10 inches to 16 inches high. These would have sold in London for £15 to £45 and for double that in New York. Unfortunately Stevens & Williams did not have their glass pieces artist-signed; some were not even trademarked with the famous "S & W" on either side of a "fleur de lis" set in a round, deep acid-etching.

Of course, John Northwood I had a great deal to do, not only with the development of new machinery for the glasshouse, but with his Northwood group of designers; he did not neglect the artistic side of the industry.

"Dolce Relievo" was the soft-sounding name given to beautiful vases with an ivory body and an outer casing of different colors, generally light purple or cream. They were decorated in low relief by the various etchers. Colored casings were used on light backgrounds, with the ground "peckled" or "chipped" and the design in relief in color. Silver mounts were used on many pieces, done by silversmiths of Sheffield and Birmingham.

John Northwood was the most famous individual who worked for Stevens & Williams. A pioneer in the glass trade, he designed and developed numerous machines and processes. Not only was he a great cameo artist; he was also a skilled technician.

In any account of the achievements of the glass industry of Stourbridge, one must go back to the ancient art of cameo glass carving. The first example we have is the original Portland Vase, which is preserved in the British Museum in London, England. Probably made by Greek craftsmen from Alexandria, the glass center of ancient times, it was possibly done before the birth of Christ (the exact date is under contention, as well as where it was discovered in Italy). Brought to light in the early seventeenth century, supposedly taken from a sarcophagus near Rome, it was called then the Barberini Vase because of its association with the Italian family of that name. Eventually it was purchased by the Englishman Sir William Hamilton, Ambassador to Italy, who sold it to the Duchess of Portland, an important collector and connoisseur of art, upon which it became known as the Portland Vase. This vase is cased in opal glass, with sculptured figures carved with genius and creativity around the whole piece. A different style of decoration on the base with a separate disk or plate most probably was made at a later time.

Copies of the piece are familiar to the collecting public because the great potter, Josiah Wedgwood, reproduced it in jasperware, the body being done in black with figures in relief in white jasper, cut to a wonderful degree of sharpness and finish by the Sealand gem engravers. It took Wedgwood three years of constant work and perseverance to produce the replicas. The original numbered series is extremely rare and collectible. It has been most interesting to obtain from Kenneth Northwood, grandson of John Northwood I, letters written from the firm of Josiah Wedgwood & Sons, Etruria, Stoke-upon-Trent, to Kenneth's grandfather. Their dates range from 1877 through 1880, during which time Northwood polished the pottery editions of the Portland Vase. He was the first man to apply the art of glass engraving to pottery, and his etchers and engravers decorated a large quantity of Wedgwood Rockingham ware. We reproduce the correspondence, which surely will be of interest to both Wedgwood and glass collectors.

In addition, we have been fortunate enough to examine, in a private collection, a copy of a cameo vase unearthed in Pompeii in 1834. A similar one in the Naples Museum is described in *Curiosities of Glass-Making* (London, 1849) by Apsley Pellatt. The vase has a one-form body with cylindrical neck that is flared at the lip; it is made with white overlay on a royal blue ground. This extremely rare object is described as the "Ingathering of the Vintage Harvest." The body of the vase is covered with an intricate design depicting Sylvanus and Pan with the fruits of the harvest and vine. Two birds are carved near the top, and two mask heads at the base. Beautifully harmonizing Bacchanalian figures with arabesque scrolls cover the vase, and an inch-high frieze at the base of the body has carved animals on it. A silver base used for support and display purposes only was obviously made at some later date.

John Northwood was born in 1836 in Wordsley in Staffordshire, England. His father owned a general grocery shop in the village. John was one of seven children, of whom only three boys survived to adulthood. William, the oldest, John, and Joseph all eventually became involved in the glass trade. At twelve years of age John started work at W. H. B. and J. Richardson's glass factory, learning to decorate glass by painting, gilding, and enameling. From the beginning he evinced a great aptitude and proficiency in all aspects of the glass trade. Under Ben Richardson's guidance he not only attended, and eventually taught at, the Stourbridge School of Art, but won prizes—a Bronze Medal in 1855 at the age of eighteen, and many others. Visiting many museums in England and France, which gave him a background in art, Northwood accumulated a wealth of material from every possible source.

His inventiveness was backed by skill and craftsmanship, and many improvements in glass-decorating techniques are credited to his name. The tools of glassmakers were efficient, but simple and old, and John Northwood was not satisfied with them. He introduced new, totally different automatic ways to etch glass, the template etching machine being one of his early inventions. Northwood was one of the first men since antiquity to produce cameo glass and train others in the art. The idea of overlaying a glass of one color with one or more layers of different colors, and then carving the desired design, had been practically forgotten or overlooked for almost eighteen hundred years. Many of the tools were newly developed by Northwood for easier carving of the glass. He made gravers of thin steel rods set in wooden handles. The ground ends cut away the glass surfaces, and then a sculptor's mallet and chisels were used.

John worked for Richardson's for many rewarding years, and then in 1860 he and his brother Joseph formed a partnership and opened a small decorating shop of their own. Joseph was responsible for the office, price books, warehouse, packing, and other business aspects. John was the art director, designer, and the innovator of new techniques. Their name, J. and J. Northwood, became known throughout the glass business as a successful operation for decorating and etching. Some of the young men who worked for them are known to us—James Hall, E. Grice, George and Tom Woodall, and Charles and Will Northwood.

At about this time a small vase with a relief cameo of St. George and the Dragon, composed of two layers of glass, was carved by John Northwood. It was damaged and then broken. Subsequently, Northwood started his first important work. This was a flint glass vase called the "Elgin," named after the Elgin Marbles in the British Museum, which had a frieze based on scenes from the Greek Parthenon in Athens. It was commissioned by J. B. Stone (later Sir Benjamin Stone) of the Birmingham glass firm, Stone, Fawdry, and Stone, in 1864. Stone was a lover of fine glassware, familiar with many of the great collections of art, and a noted photographer as well.

This work took all Northwood's extra time for nine years, but it was a remarkable achievement in glass carving, exquisite and elegant "accurately delineated figures displaying the marvelous skill and patience of the artist." Signed and dated on the base, it is about 15½ inches high. Eventually this vase was donated by Stone to the Birmingham Art Gallery, where it can be seen today. It is looked upon as the first successful carved piece of glass in

10

modern times, its completion leading the way not only to the major achievement of reproducing the Portland Vase, but to the whole gamut of cameo carving which followed.

For many years John Northwood had admired the Portland Vase. When his cousin, Philip Pargeter, owner of the Red House Glassworks, Wordsley, approached him about making a reproduction of the vase, the time was propitious for achieving a successful replica. To digress for a moment: Philip Pargeter, born in Wordsley on February 13, 1826, was a nephew of Ben Richardson. He had worked for his uncle, and had become thoroughly knowledgeable about the manufacture of glass. His specialty was engraving, in which he excelled. Pargeter was able to start and finance the whole endeavor, finally paying the huge sum, for that day, of over a thousand guineas for the completed work.

Numerous opal cased blanks were produced at the Red House Glass-works before they felt they had an accurate replica, made by Daniel Hancox, factory worker; Joseph Worral, servitor; Charles Hancox, foot-maker; and Benjamin Downing, taker-in for annealing. Perfection was required—and achieved.

This was an important project, and the preparations—getting drawings together, copying details from the original vase, and finding a place for privacy in which to work—occupied Northwood's time initially. The carving took three years to complete. It is a masterpiece of art. On several occasions Northwood took the incomplete vase to the British Museum, in a specially lined box made by Edwin Grice, to compare it with the original. On one of these visits the heat of his hands on a cold morning cracked the vase. One crack encircles it and cuts through two figures, extending up into the shoulders.

When he had finished in 1876, John Northwood had carved a perfect reproduction of the original, not only in material but in every minute detail of design, with microscopic accuracy. The sides show a continuous frieze said to depict Peleus and Thetis; carved on the base is a figure wearing a Phrygian cap and billowing cloak beneath spreading foliage, and at the base of each handle is a lion's mask support. This vase marked the auspicious beginning of an epoch in which artist-workmen outdid themselves: cameo carving at its most difficult and most beautiful. The vase remains today in a private collection, a unique example, far in advance of anything else that has been produced, the foundation in glass art for all artists to emulate.

The results were so gratifying to both Pargeter and Northwood that a decision was made to make another vase with an original design, and they chose a scene from Milton's *Paradise Lost.* "Expulsion from the Garden of

Eden" became a most effective subject. Shaped in the classic form that was most popular in the late 1800s, the vase has figures of Adam and Eve on one side and the Archangel Michael on the other, with a variety of tropical plants and flowers. It has great delicacy and grandeur of concept combined with perfection in the carving of the human figure. Obviously Northwood put heart and soul into this project. Every detail was carried out with the utmost patience and skill. The result was a vase of original design, excellent composition, unique characteristics, and superb workmanship. This piece is also in a private collection.

After finishing the Milton Vase, Northwood executed for Pargeter three tazzas representing "Art," "Literature," and "Science." Each one has a carved portrait medallion of white opal in the center: "Flaxman," "Shakespeare," and "Newton" respectively. Around the edge each tazza has a different design—oak for Shakespeare, hawthorn for Newton, and holly for Flaxman. In 1881 Northwood won a Silver Medal at the Plymouth Art and Industrial Exhibition for two of the tazzas that had been completed. A fourth tazza of James Watt, the engineer, was supposed to have been made, and a sketch was drawn that is shown in the book *John Northwood,* but this was never completed.

The last great art work by John Northwood I was the "Dennis Vase." Also called "The Pegasus Vase," this was instigated by Mr. Wilkes Webb of Thomas Webb and Son, Dennis Glass Works, in 1876. He had been an admirer of Northwood's work and career, and decided to sponsor the carving of a great vase. Now one of the major works of art at The Smithsonian Institution in Washington, this vase was originally sold to Tiffany's of New York, then to Mary Morgan, then auctioned, and finally donated in the John Gellatly gift to the museum in 1929.

The Dennis, or Pegasus, Vase, 21½ inches high, was made in three parts; foot, body, and cover. The stories depicted on it were taken from a vase the frieze of which was designed by John Flaxman; that vase was presented to the British Museum by Josiah Wedgwood in 1786. The glass blank was probably made by Tom Hill. The body of the Pegasus Vase has two handles of opal glass carved into horses' heads. On one side is a sculpture of Aurora, Goddess of the Dawn, scattering flowers as she rides a chariot in the clouds with her attendants. Carved on the other side is Venus, Goddess of Love, surrounded by cherubs and figures, standing in a large shell-shaped chariot drawn by seahorses. The lid is carved in the shape of Pegasus, the flying horse, with encircling laurel leaves. The base, carved with a large flange, has a steel bolt fastening it to the body and stem and the large red velvet cushion on which it stands.

Probably one of the largest pieces of carved cameo glass, the vase took John Northwood six years to complete. He finished it in 1882, but it was exhibited at the Paris Exhibition of 1878 in its unfinished state. Even so, it won a Gold Medal. The cover and body of the vase are dated 1882 and signed "John Northwood." This monumental work of art attests to the unsurpassed skill and great genius of one man.

About 1882, after the completion of the Dennis Vase, Northwood decided to give up his business and work for Stevens & Williams as Art Director and Works Manager. For twenty years he and Mr. J. S. Williams-Thomas, director of the company, formed an ideal partnership. Working together, they made the reputation of Stevens & Williams a respected one in the glass world. The high quality of production in Brierley Hill continues to the present day.

Many different techniques were developed by Northwood in the last twenty years of his life: stone engraving, silver threading, intaglio engraving, and the pull-up machine. In February 1902, after a short illness, John Northwood died in Wallheath. His burial place is Wordsley Churchyard, Staffordshire. In the short sixty-four years of his life he accomplished a giant's work, leaving a legacy of dedication, devotion, and accomplishment to the glass trade that is hard to equal.

It was interesting to walk into the home of John Northwood in the yard of the Stevens & Williams glass factory. This dwelling, on the factory grounds, is used by the company today as a museum for glass display. It was in this house that John Northwood II, born on May 7, 1870, spent his early youth, surrounded on all sides by examples of artistic ability and practical know-how in the glass field. He was educated at King Edward VII Grammar School, Stourbridge, and at the age of fifteen he started working in the cameo department at Stevens & Williams.

At seventeen, in 1888, at his father's instigation John II started the large 16-inch plaque, "Aphrodite and Attendants," which is shown in our book *Carved and Decorated European Art Glass*, page 53, Plate 47. He did not finish it until he was thirty-three years old, after the death of his father, in honor of his father's memory. Unfortunately, after it had been completed, it fell by accident and has since been mended. The opal blank may possibly have been made by Tom Cartwright, one of Stevens & Williams's fine glass artists; he worked for the firm until he died in July 1930. The plaque was carved with a mythological subject popular at that time. Joshua Hodgetts helped in the final polishing of the plaque, using wooden wheels, polishing powders, and high-speed lathes. The transparent poppy-colored ground with opal overlay was chiseled away to disclose darker glass beneath as a

---

background. A second plaque, for which a sketch was drawn in 1907, was never completed. Ken Northwood showed us this fine drawing, which was called by two titles, "Morning" and "To Wake the Morn," from Shakespeare's poem *Lucrece*. This drawing was made for a 16-inch-diameter sculptured glass plaque, with the central figure, Dawn, bringing with her figures representing Life, Light, and Sonnet.

John Northwood II followed the methods adopted by his father. Hydrofluoric acid was used to remove unwanted glass, but the work on more delicate detail was done with hand tools. When acid was considered too drastic, some of the heavier sculpturing was executed with the engraving wheel. Natural brightness and gloss were brought out not only by hand but by mechanical means.

Following his father's footsteps, John Northwood II also became a Director and Technical Manager at Stevens & Williams. He traveled extensively in the United States and Europe, studying the methods used everywhere he went. At Brierley Hill cameo glass became transformed from a luxury technique to one of mass production, various processes being streamlined so that a cheaper product could be made. New colors were concocted for the bodies of the pieces, and the white outer layer was made thinner to save time and labor in removing unwanted areas. There was a speedup of production, which was a lucrative achievement for the company. During recent years the emphasis has been wholly on crystal glass, with no colored glass being manufactured.

In 1947 John Northwood II was made a Fellow of the Society of Glass Technology. His informative book recording the activities of his famous father, titled *John Northwood,* written in 1958, is a great contribution to the history of Stourbridge glass. He was responsible for collecting and organizing the group of Stourbridge glass now displayed at the Council House, and donated 143 pieces from his own extensive collection. In addition, he prepared a meticulous catalog. Northwood was also very active in the 1951 Festival of Britain Exhibition of Glass, for which he made a fine catalog as well.

John Northwood II died at the age of ninety, in 1960. The Northwood School, as it is known, played an important role in the progress and success of glass art and manufacturing in England.

A major name in the long history of glassmaking in the Stourbridge area is that of Thomas Webb & Sons, known as "the Crystal King of England." For the last 150 years, the name Webb has been associated with business in

14

the parishes of Wordsley and Amblecote, England.

One signature commonly used on the glass is "Thomas Webb & Sons," or "Thos. Webb & Sons," impressed underfoot in the form of a circular or semicircular ribbon with or without the word "cameo." A registry number often appears on the scent bottles carved in the opal. The words "Gem Cameo" are found on many of the pieces deemed most important. A butterfly frequently appeared in the designs of both Thomas Webb & Sons and Stevens & Williams, Ltd., but it is in no sense a signature. It is difficult at times to tell whether a piece of glass was made at one factory or at another if a mark is not used, since the craftsmen worked at various companies during their long careers.

The first Thomas Webb, born in 1804, founded the firm in 1837, but it was not until 1842 that the name T. Webb & Co. was adopted. Having previously been in the glass business with the Richardsons, and also in another glassworks known as the White House, which was owned by his father, John Webb, Thomas had gained valuable experience in the complexities of glass manufacturing. He was also involved in an ironworks, first at Wordsley and then at Brettell Lane.

England at this time was in a period of expansion, technological advances, and prosperity. There was an increasing demand for good-quality glass, which Thomas Webb determined to supply. Having become affluent, he bought the Dennis estate at Amblecote in 1856, and the handsome Georgian mansion became the family home. A new glasshouse was built at the rear of Dennis Hall, and this remains the place where an astonishing amount of high-quality beautifully colored crystal glass is produced. In recent years the glassworks has been extended and the Hall utilized as showroom and offices.

Three sons of Thomas Webb—Thomas Wilkes Webb, Charles Webb, and Walter Wilkes Webb—became directors of the company upon his death in 1869 at the age of sixty-five. Under their management, standards of workmanship were improved immeasurably and the master craftsmen-artists were encouraged and inspired. In 1878 their decorated glass, crystal and colored, won the Grand Prix at the International Exhibition in Paris. Thomas Wilkes Webb knew the glass trade technically and artistically, and gave his men marvelous encouragement for their accomplishments. He himself became a Chevalier of the Legion of Honor, and the company was acclaimed as "the best makers of crystal glass in England."

During the Franco-British Exhibition in 1905, an impressive display of their products—cut and engraved glass of the finest quality; carved cameo glass created by George Woodall, an acknowledged master of the art of glass; rock crystal decorated by William Fritsche; and enameled examples by Jules Barbe—in all shapes and sizes was exhibited. "Dance," a 20-inch plaque by George Woodall, priced at forty guineas, was one of the pieces displayed. Two years later, this piece and one other, "Diana and Endymion," were destroyed by fire at the Brussels Exhibition. It is interesting to consider the number of other expositions that Thomas Webb & Sons appeared in throughout the world: 1851, Crystal Palace, London; 1862, International, London; 1878, Paris; 1879, Sydney; 1880, Melbourne; 1882, Adelaide; 1884, Inventions, London; 1887, Edinburgh; 1889, Paris; 1908, Franco-British, White City. Another Grand Prix was won at the 1889 Paris Exhibition.

A novelty type of cameo glass in imitation of old carved ivory was made by a process patented November 30, 1887, by Thomas Wilkes Webb. An American patent was issued in Washington, D.C., on February 19, 1889.

In 1891 Thomas Wilkes Webb, the driving force of the company, died, but his two brothers continued producing fine examples of crystal and a range of gorgeous colored glass. Fancy names like Pearl Satin, Queens Burmese, Venetian Filigree, Tapestry, Silver Deposit, Iris, Bronze, Allsontes, or Sidonian were given to the novelty lines being produced. In 1887, as already mentioned, a simulation of old carved ivory was produced. Finished carved cameo vases were tinted with brown or other suitable color, which was applied more darkly in some parts than in others and then fixed in a kiln like a piece of pottery. Unfortunately there was a slow, steady decline in sales volume because of foreign competition until the onset of the First World War.

The Dennis Glassworks managed to keep going during the depression years; then it was sold to new owners and modernized. World War II was extremely hard on the glass business, but Webbs' famous lead crystal is still being produced and new designs created. Today the company is part of a group comprised of Dema Glass, Ltd., of Chesterfield; Dema Glass (trading as Thomas Webb & Sons, Amblecote near Stourbridge, West Midlands); Edinburgh Crystal Glass Co. of Pencuik; and Jones Glass of Haverhill, Suffolk.

To go back to the days of Thomas Wilkes Webb: It is important to mention the various distinguished glass artists who were employed by Dennis Glassworks. In 1878 Thomas Wilkes Webb saw the work of Jules Barbe in Paris, and invited him to come to Webb's in Stourbridge, where he worked exclusively for twenty-one years. His specialty was gilding and enameling, employing a remarkable technique for which he had received awards in France. It has been said: "The gold he used in a dissolved state looks like a brownish paste painted on. It was fired in specially constructed muffles two, three or four times, then burnished with spun glass bristles and afterwards with agate or bloodstone."

Bohemian glassworkers Frederich Engelbert Kny, William Fritsche, and Franz Joseph Palme were employed by Webb. F. E. Kny came to Amblecote in 1860 and had his own workshop at the Dennis Glassworks. His engraving and intaglio work became famous. In 1879, for the first time, the words "rock crystal" appeared in a Thomas Webb pattern book, referring to table crystal engraved with animal scenes by Kny. Kny was one of the most superior engravers of that era; his importance cannot be overstressed. The crystal glass claret jug, 14½ inches high and 16 inches in width, known as the "Elgin Jug," is one of his finest accomplishments. It took over two years to engrave and was completed in 1873; it was exhibited at the Paris Exhibition of 1878. This jug is engraved with a frieze of Greek horsemen around both the body and stopper; footmen march around the neck.

Many of Kny's pieces were copied primarily from Flaxman's illustrations for the *Iliad* and *Odyssey*. Kny generally signed his work F. E. K. Many pieces were regularly made in art nouveau and neo-classical styles, not only by Kny but by his three sons. Ludwig, the most talented, did cameo carving as well as engraving; the "Kny Brothers" were well known in the Stourbridge area. Harry died young, but William worked for many years at Webb and Corbetts. The cameo work they did was limited and cannot be identified properly because it was rarely signed.

Franz Joseph Palme, who joined Webb in 1882, signed his work. Like Kny, he also specialized in engraving animals, but is less well known.

The forefathers of William Fritsche had been glassmakers and engravers for many generations in the village of Meistersdorf, Bohemia. Born in 1853, he came to Stourbridge as a very young man in 1868 and entered the employ of Thomas Webb & Sons, where he worked for some forty years. He carved rock crystal glass with designs in high, bold relief, and he designed his own work. Particularly with the piece called the "Fritsche Ewer," 16 inches in height, his absolute mastery of this medium is evident; the engraving is so deep it could be termed glass sculpture. The "Fritsche Ewer" represents the sea, the ornamentation including a mask of Neptune under the lip, waves and fish on the body, and shells on the foot. The time involved in this carving was some two and one-half years. This unique piece, signed by Fritsche, can be seen at The Corning Museum of Glass, Corning, New York. Another exquisite work is at the Dudley Museum in Dudley, England. Fritsche died March 24, 1924, having lived a very constructive and rewarding life.

Another prominent artist at Thomas Webb & Sons during the Woodall period was F. Kritschman. His name appears often in Woodall's price book, and he seems to have been second only to Woodall in the amount of work he accomplished. A cameo portrait thought to be that of Bismarck, dated 1885, was signed by him. Numbered cameo pieces that have the capital letter "K" can reasonably be attributed to Kritschman, and possibly he did the Queen Victoria plaque currently in the Currier Gallery of Art, Manchester, New Hampshire. In an article in the September 1936 *Antiques Magazine* Homer Eaton Keyes showed a picture of a "Cameo Gourd Vase in Chinese Style" cut by Kritschman and colored by Jules Barbe that certainly shows the artistic talent and aptitude of this member of the "Woodall Team."

Daniel and Lionel Pearce, father and son, joined Webb in 1884 after giving up their decorating business interests in London. Daniel received considerable recognition at the International Exhibition in 1862 as an engraver. The design details and flawless carving on many ivory carved vases are attributed to their particular and unusual artistry. In Webb's price book we have the design (dated May 9, 1908) for the Polar Vase engraved by Lionel Pearce. Daniel Pearce, the father, was born in 1819; his son Lionel was born in 1852.

John Thomas Fereday became one of the most talented cameo specialists and engravers to work for Thomas Webb & Sons. Born on March 18, 1854, and retiring in 1922 after about forty years with the company, Fereday was a great friend of George Woodall and became executor of his will. Much of the geometric carving was Fereday's work and many details and borders are attributed to his skill. Fereday was the designer of the crystal tableware of Egyptian theme called "Dynasty," which was given as a wedding gift to Her Royal Highness, The Princess Royal, in 1922. He was in retirement for twenty years before he died at Llandudno on February 28, 1942.

A writer and critic as well as an artist was James M. O'Fallon, of Irish descent. Art Director of Thomas Webb & Sons for many years, he planned their display at the 1878 Paris Exhibition. He was expert in the carving of fruits and flowers. His article in the *Art Journal* for December 1885, called "Glass Carving," discussed the Milton and Dennis vases in a most critical fashion. He, with George and Tom Woodall, created many of the designs we see today on the commercial cameos of Thomas Webb & Sons.

Other names found in references without specific information, and difficult to trace, are those of Jabez Facer, whose name appears frequently in Webb's price book; Hanke Keller; Shuker; T. Guest, and Joseph Muckley; the names Charles Nash and Burke, William Mullett, G. Round,

C1. Vase, 10½ inches, signed "G. Woodall, Thomas Webb & Sons, Gem Cameo," with cabbage roses, Canterbury bells, carnations, sweet peas, pansies, verbena, lilies of the valley, and jonquils. *(Private collection)*

C2. Vase, 8¾ inches, signed "G. Woodall, Painting" GW 22. *(Private collection)*

C3. Vase, 12 inches, signed "Stevens & Williams, Art Glass, Stourbridge, England." Decorated with nasturtiums. *(Private collection)*

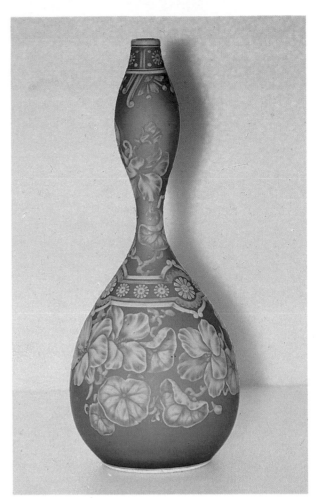

C4. Vase, 9¾ inches, signed "Thomas Webb & Sons, Gem Cameo," with bird, dragonfly, and iris against a carved red background. *(Private collection)*

C5. Vase, 14¾ inches, signed "Thomas Webb & Sons, Gem Cameo." Geranium decoration. *(Private collection)*

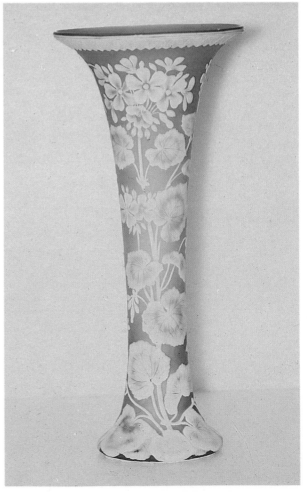

C6. Vase with roses, 11¾ inches, signed "Theodore B. Starr, New York." *(Private collection)*

C7. Vase, 5½ inches, signed "Thomas Webb & Sons." *(Collection of Howard and Paula Ellman)*

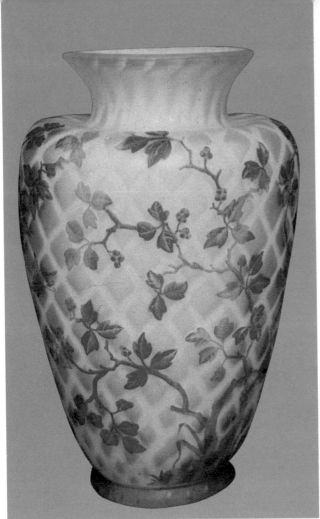

C8. Vase, 9½ inches, rainbow cameo on white on white mother-of-pearl. *(Private collection)*

C9. Vase, 11¼ inches, signed "Tiffany & Co., Paris Exhibition 1889—Thomas Webb & Sons, Gem Cameo"; pink on blue on white. *(Private collection)*

C10. Vase, 8¾ inches, signed "Thomas Webb & Sons," with poppies and trumpet vine. *(Private collection)*

C11. Vase, 6 inches, with daisies, signed "Webb." *(Collection of Leo Kaplan Antiques, courtesy of Alan Kaplan)*

C12. Decanter, 9½ inches. *(Collection of Leo Kaplan Antiques, courtesy of Alan Kaplan)*

23

C13. Vase, 7½ inches, with morning glories. *(Collection of Rockwell-Corning Museum)*

C15. Vase, 4¾ inches, signed "Webb"; prunus blossoms, white on raisin ground with mica flakes. *(Private collection)*

C14. Vase, 6 inches, with honeysuckle. *(Private collection)*

C16. Stick vase, 9¾ inches, with wild roses. *(Private collection)*

C17. Plaque, 6½ inches, colored enamels on white cameo, on tan ground. *(Authors'
collection)*

C18. Vase, 9 inches, signed "Thomas Webb & Sons." *(Collection of Leo Kaplan
Antiques, courtesy of Alan Kaplan)*

C19. Bowl, 7 inches, decorated with marine scene, seaweed, and shells. *(Private collection)*

C20. Vase, 11 inches, signed "Thomas Webb & Sons, Gem Cameo, Theodore B. Starr, New York." *(Private collection)*

26

C21. Covered jar, 13 inches, with Cupid and Psyche, attributed to Alphonse Lechevrel, signed "Tiffany & Co., Paris Exhibition 1889." *(Authors' collection)*

27

C22. Vase, 7 inches, with giraffes; signed "G. Woodall, Thomas Webb & Sons, Gem Cameo." *(Private collection)*

C23. Vase, 9¼ inches, with foxgloves; signed Thomas Webb & Sons, Gem Cameo. *(Private collection)*

C24. Two place-card holders, 3 inches, attributed to Thomas Webb & Sons. *(Collection of Leo Kaplan Antiques)*

C33. Vase, 11 inches, signed "Geo. Woodall, Autumn." W 3160. *(Private collection)*

C34. Vase, 19 inches, signed "Tiffany & Co., Paris Exhibition 1889, Thomas Webb & Sons, Gem Cameo." *(Private collection)*

C35. Vase, 8¼ inches, with lilies of the valley; attributed to Stevens & Williams; the artist, Joshua Hodgetts. *(Brierley Hill Glass Collection, courtesy of the Dudley Art Gallery)*

34

C36. Vase, 6½ inches, signed "Thomas Webb & Sons"; simulated jeweled ivory. (Private collection)

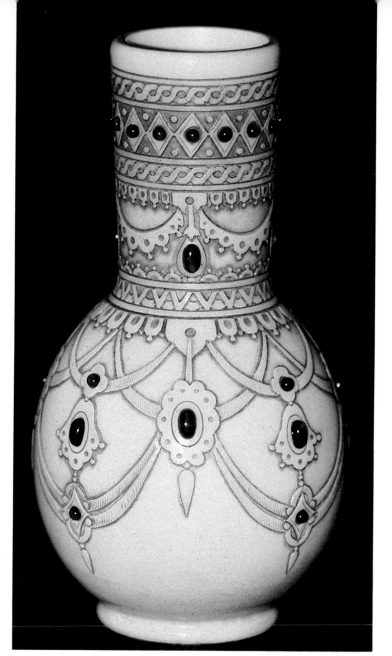

C37. Oil lamp, 21½ inches, attributed to Thomas Webb & Sons. (Collection of Leo Kaplan Antiques, courtesy of Alan Kaplan)

C38. Vase, 4¾ inches, signed "Thomas Webb & Sons"; gold fired on celery-color cameo. (Private collection)

C39. Vase, 8¾ inches, with stylized floral motifs. *(Collection of The Chrysler Museum of Art at Norfolk)*

C40. Vase, 10¼ inches; chrysanthemum decoration, stippled foot. *(Private collection)*

C41. Vase, 10 inches, with iris; signed "Thomas Webb & Sons." *(Private collection)*

C42. Vase, 7 inches. Apple-blossom decoration done with enamel on cameo in the mother-of-pearl technique. *(Private collection)*

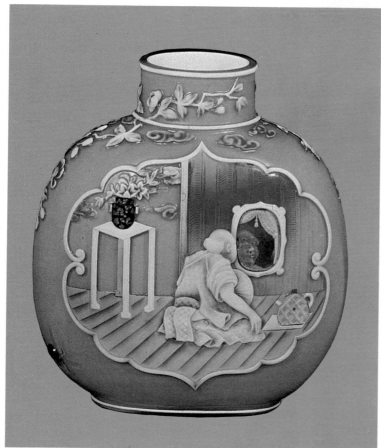

C43. Curio vase, 6 inches, signed "Thomas Webb & Sons." *(Collection of Leo Kaplan Antiques)*

37

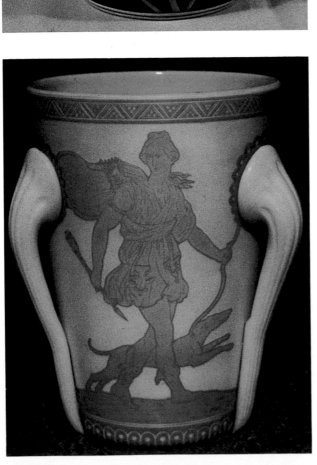

C44. Vase, 10 inches, with columbine decoration; signed "Thomas Webb & Sons." *(Collection of Leo Kaplan Antiques)*

C45. Vase, 10¾ inches, signed "Thomas Webb & Sons"; white cameo on diamond-quilted mother-of-pearl.

C46. Dolce Relievo vase, 4¼ inches, attributed to Stevens & Williams. *(Private collection)*

C47. Vase, 10½ inches, with cover; signed "G. Woodall 1890 Night, Webb." W 2567. *(Private collection)*

39

C48. Vase, 13¾ inches, signed "Paris Exhibition 1889, Thomas Webb & Sons, Gem Cameo." Dahlias, bumblebees, sunflowers, and dragonflies. *(Private collection)*

C49. Vase, 18 inches, attributed to the Woodall team. *(Collection of the Currier Gallery of Art)*

C50. Vase, 7½ inches; iris in white cameo on yellow mother-of-pearl ground. *(Private collection)*

C51. Vase, 10 inches, with sunflowers. *(Collection of Leo Kaplan Antiques)*

C52. Vase, 8 inches, signed "Thomas Webb & Sons, Gem Cameo." White on blue on emerald-green stippled ground. *(Private collection)*

C53. Vase, 12 inches, signed "Thomas Webb & Sons, Gem Cameo." *(Private collection)*

C54. Vase, 9 inches, signed "Thomas Webb & Sons, Gem Cameo." *(Private collection)*

C55. Vase, 6 inches, signed "Thomas Webb & Sons." Novelty decoration of enamels fired on cameo. *(Private collection)*

C56. Vase, 12 inches, signed "Stevens & Williams, Art Glass, Stourbridge." Motifs include lilies and Christmas rose. *(Collection of The Chrysler Museum of Art at Norfolk)*

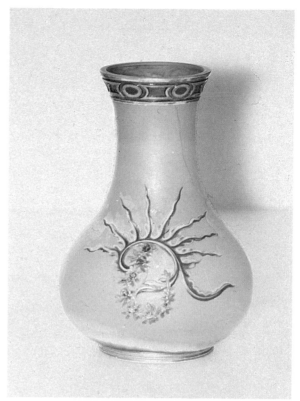

C57. Vase, 8 inches, with intricately carved neck. *(Private collection)*

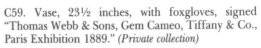

C58. Vase, 6½ inches, signed "Thomas Webb & Sons, Gem Cameo." Honeysuckles. *(Private collection)*

C59. Vase, 23½ inches, with foxgloves, signed "Thomas Webb & Sons, Gem Cameo, Tiffany & Co., Paris Exhibition 1889." *(Private collection)*

C60. Vase, 11½ inches, signed "Thomas Webb & Sons, Gem Cameo." Passion flowers with a stippled background on the top border. *(Private collection)*

C61. Vase, 6½ inches, white on cinnamon. Attributed to Stevens & Williams. *(Collection of J. Jonathan Joseph)*

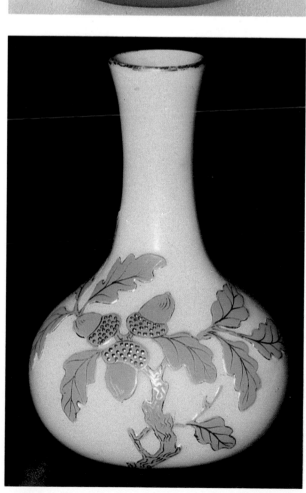

C62. Vase, 24½ inches, with foxgloves; white on pink on blue. Attributed to Thomas Webb & Sons. *(Collection of The Chrysler Museum of Art at Norfolk)*

C63. Vase, 5 inches. Dolce Relievo ground with gold fired on the cameo oak leaves and acorns. *(Authors' collection)*

C64. Handled vase, 8½ inches, signed "Ceres receiving from Bacchus a restorative cup. Thomas Webb & Sons, Gem Cameo." W 2510. *(Authors' collection)*

C65. Vase, 9¾ inches, signed "Thomas Webb & Sons, Gem Cameo." *(Private collection)*

C66. Vase, 8¾ inches, with grape design, signed "E. 204." Attributed to Thomas Webb & Sons. *(Collection of The Chrysler Museum of Art at Norfolk)*

C67. Vase, 6½ inches, with wild roses; green on blue on a stippled raisin ground. *(Private collection)*

C68. Vase, 6½ inches, attributed to Richardson Glass Co., and decorated by Joseph Locke according to Mr. Horace Richardson. *(Brierley Hill Glass Collection, courtesy of the Dudley Art Gallery)*

C69. Vase, 7½ inches. *(Collection of Rockwell-Corning Museum)*

C70. Vase, 9½ inches, signed "Thomas Webb & Sons, Gem Cameo." *(Private collection)*

C71. Venus plaque, 4½ inches. *(Collection of Leo Kaplan Antiques, courtesy of Alan Kaplan)*

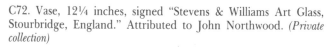

C72. Vase, 12¼ inches, signed "Stevens & Williams Art Glass, Stourbridge, England." Attributed to John Northwood. *(Private collection)*

C73. Finger bowl and saucer, 6 inches, attributed to Stevens & Williams. *(Authors' collection)*

C74. Vase, 8¼ inches, signed "G. Woodall, Thomas Webb & Sons Gem Cameo." *(Private collection)*

C75. Vase, 8½ inches, with stylized fish and mythological beast. Signed "Thomas Webb & Sons Gem Cameo." *(Private collection)*

J. Reynolds, Beddard and Francis Smith are those of glass engravers. Members of the "Woodall Team" were Harry Davies (1862–1937), Tom Farmer, and William Hill, about whom we have found no information except their identification in the photograph working on the punch bowl now in a private collection. This picture is from a glass plate developed by George Woodall, who was also a fine photographer when the art was in its infancy. Great quantities of high-caliber commercial cameo glass were produced by this large group of capable artists.

Today the glass collecting world is very conscious of cameo glass. Wide varieties of mythological and natural floral subjects, scrupulously executed, appeal to a sophisticated and discerning public. Although the period for the production of cameo glass was comparatively short, the pieces produced can be termed masterpieces of art and craftsmanship. They also demonstrate that glass can be a perfect medium of expression for the artist.

The most widely sought-after and collectible cameo glass is that carved by George Woodall, the "Rembrandt" of glass. So beautiful and exquisite was his work that even in his lifetime he was acclaimed by connoisseurs as the equal—even the superior—of the original Greek artists. Since his death the full realization of his genius has become apparent, and now, many years later, his prolific and outstanding work is a supreme testimonial to one of the greatest artists who ever lived.

George Woodall was born in Kingswinford on August 15, 1850, and baptized at Wordsley Church on October 6, 1850; he came from a family of artistic people. His maternal uncle, Thomas Bott, who worked at Richardson's for a time, was extremely well known for his work at the Royal Worcester Porcelain Co. He painted figures and natural subjects in Limoges-type enamel; his pâte-sur-pâte is today invaluable. Tom Woodall, born on June 25, 1849, was a year older. The two brothers underwent thorough training in drawing and painting under the guidance of their uncle, and attended the Stourbridge School of Design. George went to grammar school in Wordsley, but at the age of twelve he became an apprentice in the J. and J. Northwood decorating shop with brother Tom. John Northwood recognized George's latent talents, gave him drawing lessons, and encouraged his attendance at the Stourbridge Government School of Design. Here, both brothers did extremely well, Tom eventually teaching and both of them winning various prizes during the years they attended the school. George Woodall married Pamela Parks and had two sons and four daughters. Tom Woodall married Martha Patience Newman. They had a family of two sons and five daughters.

About 1875 Tom moved to Thomas Webb & Sons; George quickly

followed as an apprentice draftsman. His ability was early acknowledged by Thomas Wilkes Webb, who even sent George to Europe several times to study in the various museums the works of art he had seen and wished to emulate in glass.

Early in their career at Dennis Glassworks, both Woodalls, William Fritsche, and T. Wilkes Webb were involved in the manufacture of fine flint and rock crystal engraving, copying the real rock crystal—taking the glass and polishing it with acid in such a way as to make it resemble the natural product. The first twenty pieces they reproduced, with Chinese and Indian motifs, were purchased by Queen Victoria; they were also shown at the 1878 Paris Exhibition.

The natural successor to rock crystal carving was cameo carving. At first, George Woodall worked with hand tools of the type Northwood had designed, but George outstripped his master, making improvements in techniques, designing his own tools, and developing a style all his own. Patient handwork with a delicately manipulated chisel was his chief method, and no type of design was too difficult. George Woodall introduced backgrounds for his figures; the tremendous detail and the perspective were achieved with extreme meticulousness and sensitivity.

George was a tireless worker, constantly improving his skill as etcher, sculptor, and engraver of cameo glass. His ingenuity, patience, and practiced skill cannot be stressed enough—the naturalistic aspect of his cameo work, the delicately cut leaves and flowers, the female figures with their symmetry of form and beauty of feature, have seldom been equaled.

Some details of the poses came from the works of Antonio Canova (1757–1822), a Venetian sculptor, in the book entitled *The Works of Antonio Canova* (London, 1876). Other sources were books on mythology, the sculptures of such artists as Flaxman, who designed for Wedgwood, and paintings such as Guido Reni's "Aurora," which was an inspiration for Woodall's Aurora Vase.

Exquisite decorative details characterize Woodall's work—the soft perspective and bold relief of rounded limb, the gossamer drapery, the light and shade effects, were achieved with technical virtuosity, outdistancing the work of ancient cameo glassmakers. Immense care was taken by Woodall to be realistic, certainly in the carving of figures of dancers. He attended local theaters to study attitudes and poses until he had mastered a knowledge of the dancing suited to his carving.

Though the majority of his subjects were classic or pseudo-classic, he did not hesitate to execute realistic portraits of individuals who sat for him. William Thomson, Lord Kelvin (1824–1907), an eminent scientist, posed

52

for a cameo portrait, which was carved in six months, through sketches and photography. When finished, it was purchased in 1905 by the American Society of Scientists, the equivalent of the Royal Society of England, as a memento of Kelvin's American visit. This plaque, measuring 14 inches in diameter, cost 100 guineas. It was subsequently presented to Burlington House, London. Others completed were cameo reliefs of "Mr. and Mrs. Winans"; "Mrs. Martin," wife of a Stourbridge doctor; "Armenian Girl," believed to be a carving of his daughter Alice Woodall; and "William E. Gladstone."

George Woodall was never a copyist; he always worked out his own designs. He was affiliated with Thomas Webb & Sons at Dennis Glassworks for thirty-four years.

Tom Woodall's skill in the design and cutting of borders on plaques and vases was so complicated and refined that one false move would have meant ruin. The striking regularity of his scallop borders and the graceful lightness of the border cupids often carved on the vases are superb. Tom Woodall was awarded a Bronze Medal at the International Health Exhibition in London, and in 1888 both brothers won a Gold Medal at the Melbourne Exhibition in Australia. In 1893 Webb's exhibited George Woodall's work in Chicago, Illinois, where it had an immediate impact and many pieces were sold.

The astounding variety and abundance of commercial cameo produced by Webb at the end of the nineteenth century was fostered by the motivation of the two Woodalls. "The Woodall Team," as it became known, was assisted by as many as seventy other craftsmen artists who designed and worked on the various pieces of glass, all of them well skilled in engraving and cameo carving.

Among George Woodall's best works is "Moorish Bathers," which was sold to the Australian millionaire banker, the Honorable George Brookman, a member of the Australian legislature, and eventually loaned to the Adelaide Museum. It cost 800 guineas and took four years to complete. Sold in 1960 by Mrs. Brookman for $2,500, it is now in a private collection.

Woodall's work was shown in 1908 at the Franco-British Exhibition, and again in 1910 at the Brussels-Turin Exhibition. A fire in Brussels not only destroyed two Woodall plaques ("The Dance," 20 inches in diameter, with four dancers carved on it, and "Diana and Endymion," from which a fragment was recovered in the debris), but the complete Thomas Webb & Sons exhibit, valued at between two and three thousand pounds.

"The Attack" and "Cleopatra" show, in their carving, the perspective attained by thinning down the opal glass to show a white with blue tinge.

George Woodall perfected as his material a metal, white with blue cast, which when carved down upon the brown background became a translucent, delicate shade of blue. The scope of his ability to carve perspective in a cameo picture was shown in his scenic effects and reproductions of architecture, which are completely true to life. He used not only his steel instruments but he introduced the cutting wheel, which saved considerable time and labor, reducing the cost of production. In addition, a big help was the discovery of Roentgen's X ray in 1895, which could detect flaws in the opal blanks before the blanks were carved. In the past it had been common for these to shatter while work was being done on them.

George and Tom Woodall quarreled, for reasons unknown, and George continued alone. The brothers had signed their pieces jointly "T. & G. Woodall" from about 1880 to 1895. Subsequently, Tom's name was removed from some early cameo pieces. From then on, George signed "G. Woodall" or "Geo. Woodall" generally on the opal-colored surface of the glass, rather than on the dark ground of the piece or underfoot. Titles of Woodall vases and plaques were often incised under the foot of vases or on the reverse side of plaques, occasionally with a date. The name T. Woodall rarely appears alone, but we have observed it on carved rock crystal. Later in George Woodall's career, after his breakup with his brother, he worked on many pieces with his contemporaries, but a great many were done almost single-handed.

At the end of 1911 George Woodall retired from the Dennis Glassworks of Thomas Webb & Sons. He did some traveling and worked in a studio at the rear of his house on Market Street, Kingswinford. Some of his finest cameo work was done in his home studio in his later years. He died after a short illness on February 27, 1925, and is buried in Kingswinford. Tom Woodall died June 2, 1926, and is buried at Wordsley.

The amazing variety and amount of cameo glass that George Woodall produced in his lifetime brought him worldwide fame, not only in his own time but today. He is recognized by private collectors and leading museums throughout the world.

RECORDED TITLES

GEORGE WOODALL

	Adam and Eve	18″ plaque, signed "Geo. Woodall"
GW 2	Airborne November 1899	vase
GW 33	Andromache October 1902	panel, signed "Andromache Geo. Woodall"
	Andromeda	16½″ vase, white on brown
GW 141	Antarctic	16½″ vase
	Antarctic, February 1915	16½″ vase, signed "Antarctic"; white on blue on brown; Fereday worked on this second piece
W 3058	Antony and Cleopatra, 1897	18″ plaque, white on brown, signed "Geo. Woodall"
GW 113	Aphrodite November 1904	plaque on marble
	Aphrodite	plaque, seashell border
GW 146	Aphrodite, August 1910	11″ plaque; Turin Exhibition 1910; a presentation piece sold in Leipzig
GW 2732	Aphrodite	13⅛″ plaque, signed "G. Woodall 1892, Aphrodite, Thomas Webb & Sons, Gem Cameo, Webb"; white on brown; exhibited in Chicago 1893

GW 160	Aphrodite September 1914	10⅝″ plaque, white on brown, sea-shell-ribbon border; signed "Aphrodite, Geo. Woodall"
	Aphrodite	plaque; signed "Geo. Woodall"; exhibited Franco-British Exhibition 1908
	Aphrodite	8¼″ plaque, signed "Geo. Woodall"; white on brown; Stourbridge Festival 1951, Stourbridge Council House Collection
	Aphrodite	4½″ by 5¾″ plaque
	Aphrodite	vase
	Aphrodite	plaque, white on blue
	Armenian Girl	4¾″ portrait plaque in frame, signed "The Armenian Girl, Geo. Woodall"
W 2822	At the Portal	10″ vase, signed "Woodall, Thomas Webb & Sons, Gem Cameo"; white on brown; goddess under portico feeding doves, formal key-and-scroll designs on top and foot
	The Attack	18″ plaque, white on red; signed "T. & G. Woodall"
W 2840	Aurora	13″ vase, white on brown; signed "T. & G. Woodall"
	Aurora	8¾″ vase; signed "Aurora, Thomas Webb & Sons, Geo. Woodall"
	Aurora	jar and cover, white on brown; signed "Aurora"; from Guido Reni's painting; piece was destroyed during Melbourne Exhibition, 1880
GW 9	Aurora	7″ vase, white on brown
W 3160	Autumn	11″ vase, white on brown; flat-sided; companion piece to "Spring"
GW 2	Autumn	a vase
	Autumn	13″ vase, white on light brown;

		signed "Geo. Woodall, Thomas Webb & Sons"
	The Bather	12″ vase, white on blue; signed "G. Woodall, Thomas Webb & Sons, Gem Cameo"
W 2043	Before the Race	12″ vase, white on brown
	Before the Race	12½″ vase; signed "T. & G. Woodall, Webb. Before the Race"
	Blue Sea Foam	12″ two-handled vase, white on blue; also titled "Wild Waves"
GW 32	Calypso October 1902	12½″ panel; signed "Calypso, Geo. Woodall"; sold February 1917
GW 16	The Captive, July 1907	6½″ vase, white on brown; companion piece to The Chase
GW 152	Caught, July 29, 1913	7½″ vase, white on brown
GW 21	Ceramia	6¼″ case, white on brown, "Ceramia, Geo. Woodall"
W 2510	Ceres	vase, two-handled; white on light brown; signed "Ceres receiving from Bacchus a restorative cup, Thomas Webb & Sons, Gem Cameo"
GW 15	The Chase	6½″ vase, white on brown; companion piece to The Captive
	Cherub and Putti	12½″ vase, white on brownish red; signed "T. Woodall, Thomas Webb & Sons, Gem Cameo"; "Cupid" on a vine
	Children on Panther	10½″ unfinished vase, white on blue; possibly carved by Alphonse Lechevrel
W 2848	Cleopatra (or The Egyptian Princess); made November 15, 1915	11″ vase
GW 4	Cleopatra	small panel
W 2832	Cleopatra March 1896	10″ vase; signed "T. & G. Woodall"
	Cleopatra	18″ plaque; signed "T. & G. Woodall"; exhibited in Paris in 1899

W 2803	Cloelia	7½" vase, white on brown
W 2801	Corinna	10¼" vase, white on brown; signed "T. & G. Woodall, Thomas Webb & Sons, Gem Cameo"
	Crane and Palm (also known as The Stork)	11¾" two-handled vase; signed "Geo. Woodall"; flying bird on one side, stork and fish on the other; exhibited at Stourbridge Festival 1951
	Cupid	9" two-handled vase; signed "Thomas Webb & Sons"
W 2796	Cupid Dancing	3" vase, white on brown
W 2734	Cupid in Disgrace	plaque; signed "G. Woodall 1892"; exhibited in Chicago 1893
W 2660	Cupid and Figure	12" covered jar
	Cupid and Flute	3½" perfume bottle, white on brown; signed "Woodall"
	Cupid on Panther	Vase
	Cupid on Panther	7¾" plaque; signed "Geo. Woodall"
W 2609	Cupid and Psyche	15½" two-handled vase, white on brown; signed "G. Woodall, Tiffany & Co., Paris Exhibition 1889, Thomas Webb & Sons, Gem Cameo"
	Cupid and Putto at Play	8" vase, white on brown; signed "Geo. Woodall, Thomas Webb & Sons, Gem Cameo"
	Cupids	10" vase
	At Cupid's Shrine May 12, 1908	18" plaque

(See also *Cherubs*)

GW 30	The Dance (also called "The Dancing Hours")	20" plaque with three figures; signed "Geo. Woodall"; exhibited in Brussels in 1910, and destroyed there by fire
	Dancing Girl	pair 12¾" vases, white on blue on brown; arms of Capel Cure of London; signed "T. & G. Wood-

		all, Thomas Webb & Sons, Gem Cameo"
W 2828	Dancing Girl	7½" vase, white on brown
W 2579	Dancing Girl	8" vase; white, topaz, and light blue on a red ground; spray on the obverse
W 2578	Dancing Girl	8" vase; white on blue, on red ground; spray on the obverse
W 2714	Dancing Girl	9" vase, opal on dark brown
W 2710	Dancing Girl	vase, opal on dark brown
	Dancing Girl	12" vase, white on blue; signed "G. Woodall, Thomas Webb & Sons, Gem Cameo"
	Dancing Girl	plaque, white on brown
W 1753	Dancing Girls	12" vase, white on pink on yellow; signed "G. Woodall"
	Dancing Girls	14" covered jar; signed "T. & G. Woodall, Webb, Dancing Girls"
W 733	Dancing Girls	13¼" plaque, white on brown; signed "G. Woodall 1886, Thomas Webb & Sons"
GW 20	Dawn	7½" vase, white on brown
GW 158	Diana	7⅜" vase with oval top; signed "Geo. Woodall"; exhibited in London 1899
GW 26	Diana	7" vase, white on blue
GW 26a	Diana	7¼" vase, white on blue
W 2786	Diana and Endymion	17½" plaque, white on brown; signed "T. & G. Woodall"; exhibited in Chicago 1893, and in Brussels 1910, where it was destroyed by fire
GW 28	Diana and Endymion	17½" plaque, white on brown
W 2718	Diana and Nymph	10" covered vase, white on brown
GW 137	Dolphin	6" vase
	Dolphin and Cupids	13" plaque, white on brown; authenticated and attributed to T. & G. Woodall, circa 1885, by Frederick Carder in November 1937
GW 142	Edin	9" plaque

GW 2832	Euterpe (the muse of music)	8″ vase, white on brown
W 2848	Egyptian Princess (or Cleopatra)	11″ vase
W 2514	Fairies' Spring	6″ vase
	The Favourite	13″ plaque, white on light brown; signed "T. & G. Woodall 1882"; exhibited in the Stourbridge Festival 1951
	Feathered Favourites	6″ plaque; signed "Geo. Woodall"
W 2759	Feathered Favourites	12″ plaque; signed "T. & G. Woodall 1892"; exhibited in Chicago 1893
W 2731	Feathered Favourites	13″ vase, white on brown; signed "T. & G. Woodall"
GW 131	Feathered Favourites	7″ vase
	Feathered Favourites	pair of vases
W 2760	Flora	9″ panel, white on brown; signed "T. & G. Woodall"
W 2785	Flora	11¾″ panel, white on brown; signed "T. & G. Woodall, Thomas Webb & Sons, Gem Cameo, Webb"
GW 116	Flora	vase
GW 10	Flora	7½″ vase, white on brown on flint
GW 143	Flora Captive	8″ vase
GW 144	Flora Surprise	8″ vase
W 2733	Floralia	13″ plaque; signed "G. Woodall"
W 2716	The Flower Gatherer	7½″ vase, flat-sided; white on light brown; signed "Thomas Webb & Sons, Gem Cameo, G. Woodall"
W 2513	Flower Girl	6″ vase
W 2335	Frogs	vase, white on blue
	Fruit and Flower Girls	12½″ vase, white to deep red; signed "Webb," "Fruit and Flower Girls"
	Fruit Gatherer (companion piece to "At the Portal")	10″ vase, white on brown
W 2403	Fruit Seller	15¾″ two-handled vase, white on brown; signed "G. Woodall, 1889, Thomas Webb & Sons, Gem Cameo"

60

W 3220	Flying Against the Storm	11″ vase, amber shaded to ruby-red; curio
	Ganymede	vase; sold to Phillips in 1910
	Girl in the Clouds	13″ plaque, white on red
	William E. Gladstone	2½″ plaque; signed "William E. Gladstone, G. Woodall, Thomas Webb & Sons, Gem Cameo"
W 2797	Greek Girl March 1894	7½″ x 5″ oval plaque, white on brown
	Happy Childhood and Unhappy Childhood	ivory with red, brown, green, and gold; signed "Webb"
W 2831	Harmony	10″ vase, white on brown
W 2827	Hebe	9¼″ vase, white on brown; sold to Finnigan November 15, 1915
GW 27	Hebe	7½″ vase, white on blue
W 2872	Hebe	9½″ vase
GW 148	Idle Moments	5″ plaque, white on red; signed "Geo. Woodall"; exhibited in Turin 1911
	Industry	two-handled vase; signed "G. Woodall"
W 2724	Inspiration	12″ vase, white on brown; signed "Geo. Woodall, Inspiration, Thomas Webb & Sons, Webb"
W 2794	Intruders	16½″ plaque, white on brown; signed "T. & G. Woodall"; exhibited in Chicago 1893
W 3111	Iris	11″ two-handled vase, opal on brown; exhibited in London 1907
GW 18	Juno	8″ vase, white on brown
	William Thomson, Lord Kelvin (1824–1907)	14″ plaque; signed "Geo. Woodall"; 1900
	The Lovers	10″ vase, white on blue; signed "G. Woodall, Thomas Webb & Sons, Gem Cameo"
	The Lovers	10″ vase, white on blue
	Loves Areo	7½ vase, white on blue; signed "Geo. Woodall"

61

W 2660	Love's Awakening	12″ vase with cover, white on blue on brown; signed "G. Woodall"
GW 8	Luna	9″ vase, white on brown; signed "Geo. Woodall"
W 2722	A Maid of Athens	10½″ vase, white on brown
W 2723	A Maid of Athens	10½″ vase, white on brown; signed "T. & G. Woodall, A Maid of Athens, Webb"
	Mrs. Martin (wife of Stourbridge doctor)	plaque; signed "Geo. Woodall"
W 2811	Mermaid	8″ vase, white on green on flint
GW 130	A Message August 1912	7″ vase
GW 14	The Message	7″ vase
W 1776	The Milkmaid	12″ two-handled vase; light blue ground, dark blue and white outside; obverse decorated with flowers
	Minerva	ewer, Thomas Webb & Sons, white on brown
W 2720	The Minuet	two-handled vase, white on brown; signed "Thomas Webb & Sons"
	The Minuet	11″ vase, white on amethyst; signed "Geo. Woodall 1891"
	Mischief	8½″ vase, white on brown; signed "Mischief" and "Geo. Woodall"
W 3139	Moorish Bathers	18″ plaque, white on brown; signed "Geo. Woodall"; exhibited in Paris 1898; Phillips, London, June–July 1899; Adelaide Museum 1901
GW 5	Morning February 22, 1900	10″ vase, white on brown
GW 24	Morning	8½″ vase, white on blue; sold to Tiffany, New York, June 13, 1901
GW 139	Morning August 1909	7″ vase
W 2807	The Muses	8″ vase, white on red; cut with five of the nine muses; inscribed

		"Erato, Euterpe, Thalia, Cleo, Terpsichore, T. & G. Woodall, Des & Sculps Thomas Webb & Sons, Gem Cameo"
	Music	12″ x 9½″ plaque, in a velvet frame
	Narcissus August 3, 1907	10¾″ two-handled vase, opal on brown
W 2728	Nature's Mirror	11″ vase, white on brown; signed "Nature's Mirror, T. & G. Woodall"
GW 150	Nautilus	4″ red slab; exhibited in Turin 1911
GW 136	Nautilus	6″ vase
	Night	8½″ vase, white on brown; signed "Night, G. Woodall"
GW 3	Night February 22, 1900	10″ vase, white on brown
GW 23	Night	8½″ vase, white on blue; sold to Tiffany, New York, June 13, 1901
GW 140	Night August 1909	7″ vase
GW 189	Night	7″ vase
W 2567	Night	10½″ covered vase, white on brown; signed "G. Woodall 1890, Night, Webb"
	Night	10¾″ lamp base; signed "Thomas Webb & Sons, Gem Cameo"
	Night	plaque, white on brown; with owls and bats
W 2805	Nymph of the Sea	8″ x 5¾″ plaque, white on brown; signed "Geo. Woodall"
W 2805	Nymph of the Sea	8″ x 5½″ plaque, white on russet; signed "The Nymph of the Sea, Geo. Woodall"
GW 132	Ocean Gems	7¾″ vase
W 2834	On the Terrace	12¼″ x 8½″ panel, white on brown; signed "T. and G. Woodall"
GW 163	Origin of the Harp February 7, 1918	7″ oval-bodied vase (5¼″ x 4½″); sold to Phillips on May 28, 1918; subject from Moore's Irish Melodies; harp on one side

W 1797	Origin of Painting	9¼″ vase, white on brown; signed "Geo. Woodall, Origin of Painting"
GW 145	Origin of Painting September 29, 1910	11″ plaque, white on brown; signed "Geo. Woodall"; sold January 1913
	Origin of Painting	9½″ vase; signed "G. Woodall 1887"
	Origin of Painting	9½″ vase; signed "G. Woodall"
GW 22	Painting	9″ vase, white on blue; sold to Tiffany, New York, June 13, 1901
	Pandora	vase, white on brown
W 2730	Pandora	13½″ vase, white on brown; signed "T. & G. Woodall"
	Pandora	8½″ vase, white on brown; signed "G. Woodall, Paris Exhibition 1889, Thomas Webb & Sons"
W 2792	Pandora	panel, white on claret brown; alternative title "Psyche"; signed "Geo. Woodall"
GW 155	The Pearl Necklace	6¼″ x 4⅜″ oval panel; signed "Geo. Woodall"
GW 12	Penelope February 1901	7″ flat-sided vase
W 2765	Penelope	flint jar, white on brown; signed "T. & G. Woodall." Presented to Mrs. Parker by the Liberals of Wordsley and the district in recognition of the gallant attempt made by her husband, Thomas Parker, Esq., to win for the popular cause the Kingswinford Division of Staffordshire at the parliamentary election of 1892. Designed and executed by T. & G. Woodall.
GW 7	Pharaoh's Daughter September 1900	11″ vase, white on brown
	Phyllis	10″ vase, white on blue; signed "Geo. Woodall"
W 2817	Phyllis	8″ vase, white on brown

W 2722	Phyllis at the Fountain	10″ vase, white on brown; signed "Phyllis at the Fountain, T. & G. Woodall, Thomas Webb & Sons"
GW 11	Pluvia	7″ vase, white on brown on flint
GW 1	Poetry November 1895	12″ panel; signed "Geo. Woodall"
	Poetry	12″ x 9½″ plaque in a velvet frame
	Polar Vase, May 9, 1908	16″ vase, white on green
	Polar Vase	16″ vase
GW 29	Pomona	7″ vase, white on blue
W 2795	Pomona	10″ vase, white on brown
W 3172	Pompeian	18″ plaque; Italian panorama with figures
W 2806	A Pompeian Girl July 1894	9″ vase, white on brown
W 2685	Pompeian Maidens	covered vase
	Portrait Plaque	signed "Geo. Woodall"
	Proserpina	4½″ x 6″ plaque, framed in ormolu with a marble base; signed "Geo. Woodall"
W 2721	Psyche	10″ vase, white on brown
W 2792	Psyche	panel, white on claret brown
W 2804	Psyche	10″ vase, white on brown
W 2831	Psyche	7½″ vase, white on brown; signed "Psyche, T. & G. Woodall, Thomas Webb & Sons"
GW 13	Psyche	6¾″ vase, white on brown
GW 13a	Psyche	7½″ vase, white on blue
	Putti and Butterflies	5½″ vase, "Geo. Woodall"
	Queen Victoria	5″ x 6½″ plaque, white on red
	Queen Victoria	plaque similar to the preceding one
	Queen Victoria	vase, white on red
W 2726	A Quiet Nook	9″ covered jar, white on brown; signed "Geo. Woodall"; back depicts a Grecian urn, fruit supported in formal scroll and acanthus-leaf design; finial is the opening lotus bud; additionally signed "A Quiet Nook, Thomas Webb & Sons, Art Cameo"

W 2179	The Race	12″ vase, white on brown; companion piece to "Before the Race"
	Reindeer	8″ vase, white on light brown, signed "G. Woodall, Thomas Webb & Sons, Gem Cameo"
	Marion Roberts	portrait plaque
	The Roman Bath	18″ plaque
W 2402	The Rose 1895	16″ two-handled vase; signed "G. Woodall"
W 2790	Sappho	12½″ x 7½″ panel mounted in a satinwood frame; white on brown; signed "T. & G. Woodall, Sappho"
GW 154	Sappho	6¼″ x 4⅜″ panel, white on brown; signed "G. Woodall"
	Sappho	6½″ x 4¼″ panel; signed "G. Woodall"
GW 6	Sea Foam	10″ flat-sided vase, white on brown; signed "Geo. Woodall"
GW 153	Sea Gulls July 1913	7½″ vase
W 2767	Sea Nymph	13″ x 10″ panel; signed "Geo. Woodall"
W 3218	Sea Nymph–Fishes– Seaweed (not officially titled)	8″ vase; blue, green, brown, Burmese on flint
G 2719	Sea Scene	15″ vase, white on sea green
	Sea Shell and Nymph	panel
GW 147	Sea Shells March 1911	5″ slab, white on red; exhibited in Turin 1911
GW 133	Seaweed March 1909	7¾″ vase; signed "Geo. Woodall"
GW 149	Seaweeds	4″ slab, white on red; signed "Geo. Woodall"; exhibited in Turin 1911
GW 19	Serpentina	7½″ vase, white on brown
	A Siren	8″ vase, white on brown; signed "Geo. Woodall, A Siren"
W 25	Sirene	12″ vase; signed "Geo. Woodall"
GW 114	Sirene	plaque on a green marble base
GW 115	Sirene	plaque on a green marble base
GW 25	Sirene	8½″ vase, white on blue

	Song of the Sea (or Sirene)	6¼" plaque, white on brown; signed "Geo. Woodall"; signed on the case, "Alice Woodall, A Song of the Sea"
GW 134	Soppa	7" vase, white on brown; companion piece to "Tambourina"
	Spring (Proserpina)	4½" x 6" plaque, white on brown, framed in ormolu on marble; signed "Geo. Woodall"
W 3160	Spring	11" flat-sided vase, white on brown; companion piece to "Autumn"
	Spring	8½" vase, white on blue; signed "G. Woodall, Thomas Webb & Sons, Gem Cameo"
GW 151	Springtime	7" vase; signed "G. Woodall, Thomas Webb & Sons, Gem Cameo"; Turin Exhibition 1911
W 2842	Surprise November 1895	17" plaque, white on brown
GW 161	Syrene	10¾" plaque, white on brown
GW 162	Syrene	9½" plaque, white on brown
GW 157	Syrene	8¼" vase, white on purple
	Syrenea	8" vase, white on brown; signed "Syrenea, Geo. Woodall"
GW 135	Tambourina	7" vase, white on brown; companion piece to "Soppa"
GW 17	Terpsichore	7½" vase, white on brown; June–July Exhibition at Phillips, Ltd., 1899
	Toilet of Venus	covered jar
W 3185	Toilet of Venus 1898	18" plaque; sold to Tiffany, New York, June 1901
GW 2793	Un jour d'été	8¼" plaque, white on brown
GW 159	Undine	11½" x 6" vase, white on brown; sold to Phillips, October 14, 1918
GW 31	Undine October 1902	6" framed panel signed "Geo. Woodall"; sold February 1917
GW 156	Venus 1913	7½" vase; signed "Geo. Woodall"
	Venus	8" vase, white on brown; signed "Venus, Geo. Woodall"

	Venus Arising from the Sea	13″ plaque, white on red
	Venus and Cupid	vase
	Venus and Cupid	18¼″ plaque; signed "G. Woodall"
W 2830	Vestal April 1895	9″ vase, white on brown; signed "T. & G. Woodall"
W 2802	Wandering Stars	panel; sold 1901
W 2805	Water Nymph (also known as "Nymph of the Sea")	8″ x 5½″ panel, white on brown; signed "G. Woodall"
W 2720	Water Nymph	two-handled vase, white on dark brown
	Wild Waves	12″ two-handled vase
	(Mr. & Mrs.) Winans	pair of portrait plaques, each 11″ x 8½″; signed "G. Woodall 1885"; Mr. & Mrs. Winans were residents of Cleveland, Ohio, U.S.A.

UNTITLED RECORDED PIECES

W 2812	animals	opal on light brown
	Ares (Mars) in armor on horseback in clouds	8″ vase, white on brown; signed "Thomas Webb & Sons"
W 1346	bird with blossoms	plaque
W 2477	birds	6½″ vase
W 3236	birds and sunset	10″ vase; aqua, white, and ruby on flint
W 2604	black boy on ivory	6½″ vase; curio
	boy skating on pond; with sprays of holly and mistletoe	4¼″ ovoid bottle, white on blue; gold neck and cover have hammered finish and are set with five diamonds
W 2815	cameo head	4″ bowl, white on blue on light green
W 2576	Chinese dogs October 1890	vase, white on brown
	Cloelia	8¼″ vase, white on blue; signed "G.

		Woodall, Thomas Webb & Sons, Gem Cameo"
W 2582	cupids	10″ vase, white on brown
	dogs of Fo	15″ vase, white on sea green
	dragon	15″ vase, white on sea green
W 2715	fish	15″ vase, white on sea green
	girl, holding branch of flowers	8¼″ vase; signed "G. Woodall, Thomas Webb & Sons, Gem Cameo"
	masque and griffins	16¼″ vase; white, pink, and opal; signed "G. Woodall Thomas Webb & Sons Gem Cameo Tiffany & Co. Paris Exhibition 1889"
W 3186	mice and trellis	6½″ vase; opal, ruby, and topaz
W 2428	mouse and gourd	vase, jade flat rim
W 2580	nude holding spray	8″ vase, white on blue on red; spray on obverse
	putti fishing	6″ plaque, white on brown; signed "T. G. Woodall"
W 2581	woman holding branch	8⅜″ vase, white on red on light blue; signed "G. Woodall, Thomas Webb & Sons, Gem Cameo"
W 2725	(untitled)	15¼″ two-handled vase, white on blue; signed "G. Woodall, Thomas Webb & Sons, Gem Cameo"; foot filled in and fitted on. Nash and D.P. (probably Daniel Pearce) attached foot and body.
	(untitled)	10″ vase, white on blue; signed "Geo. Woodall"

ALPHONSE LECHEVREL

Bacchanalian Musician	
Birth of Venus	11⅛″ vase signed "Geo. Woodall." Earlier pictures of this piece indicate that "A.L. 1877" has been

69

obliterated. Formerly, the vase had two handles, which were removed; engraved on the base was "'The Birth of Venus' Wordsley." It is accepted that the original blank was made by Richardson & Co., with Woodall possibly doing additional cutting early in the 1920s.

Hercules Restoring Alcestis to Her Husband Admetus	14¼" vase, white on blue; signed "A.L. 1877"
Jupiter and Ganymede	6" covered vase, white on deep purple; attributed to Lechevrel
Jupiter and Hebe	6" covered vase, white on deep purple; attributed to Lechevrel
Raising an Altar to Bacchus	15½" vase, white on blue; signed "A.L.–78"
Two Children on Panther	10½" vase; possibly Lechevrel
Venus Rising from the Sea	11¼" vase, white on blue; signed "A.L. 1877"; another signature also appears: "Geo. Woodall"

JOHN NORTHWOOD

The Dennis Vase (also known as "The Pegasus Vase")	signed "John Northwood"
The Elgin Vase	signed "John Northwood"
The Milton Vase	13⅜" two-handled vase, white on blue; signed "John Northwood 1878"; the fine carving depicts the angel Raphael sent by God to instruct Adam and Eve, who are seen on the obverse
The Portland Vase	10" two-handled vase, white on blue; signed "John Northwood 1876." Said to depict the myth of Peleus and Thetis, this fine copy of the original Portland vase, which dated from the inception of the Christian era, was the most

	important milestone in great English cameo carving.
Saint George and the Dragon	Vase, two layers, ca. 1860
Tazza (portrait of Newton)	7⅜″ two-section piece, white on blue; signed "J. Northwood 1878." This portrait of Isaac Newton, symbolic of Science, has a star behind his head, an ivy-bordered rim, and a flower and acanthus-leaf border.
Tazza (portrait of Flaxman)	7⅜″ two-section tazza, white on blue; signed "JN 1880." The low-relief carving of John Flaxman, symbolic of Art, has a border of hawthorn leaves. Tazza has a detachable footed stem.
Tazza (portrait of Shakespeare)	7⅜″ sectional tazza, white on blue; carved about 1882. Portrait of William Shakespeare, the symbol of Literature, has border of oak leaves and acorns.

JOHN NORTHWOOD II

Aphrodite and Attendants	15″ plaque, white on brown; signed "John Northwood II"
To Wake the Morn ("The Coming of Dawn")	sketch for a plaque, inspired by Shakespeare's *The Rape of Lucrece;* the plaque was never carved, but the sketch was authenticated by Northwood's son Kenneth, who supplied the photograph.

JOSEPH LOCKE

Cupid Sailing on a Cockleshell	exhibited in the Paris Exhibition 1878; attributed to Locke
Happy Childhood	9″ vase, white on blue; signed "J.L. 1887"
head	portrait plaque, attributed to Locke

The Portland Vase	9⅞″ two-handled vase; signed "Joseph Locke 1878"
Shakespeare	2⅛″ x 1⅝″ plaque, attributed to Locke
Unhappy Childhood	9″ vase, white on blue; signed "J.L. 1877"; companion piece to Happy Childhood

WORK OF OTHER ARTISTS

Bismarck	7½″ plaque, white on red, in velvet frame; signed "F. Kritschman 1886"
Boxing Day Meet	16″ plaque, white on dark amber; signed "H. J. Boam"; circa 1885. The scene depicted shows hounds, five riders, including a woman riding sidesaddle, and one rider being thrown at a hedge; clouds are overhead, and there is a white rim.
The Elgin Vase	8″ crystal vase; signed "Frederick Kny." Around the center is a broad band of Grecian warriors and horses; ears of corn are carved around the edge.
Horse and Rider	11¾″ vase; signed "J. Millward, Stevens & Williams"
The O'Fallon Vase	11″ stoppered jug. Carved in neo-Egyptian style by J. M. O'Fallon, art director at Thomas Webb; he was instrumental in carrying Webb to a high peak of artistic conception.
Joseph Silvers	8¾″ plaque; carved by Joshua Hodgetts in 1926
The Two Muses	vase, white on amber; attributed to William Northwood
Venus and Dancing Cupid 1888	plaque, white on rose ground; signed "W. Northwood"
Venus Instructing Cupid	plaque by W. Northwood

MYTHOLOGICAL AND HISTORICAL SUBJECTS

Andromache: the devoted wife of Hector of Troy in Homer's *Iliad.*

Andromeda: daughter of Cepheus and Cassiopeia, king and queen of Ethiopia. Chained to a rock for a monster to devour, she was saved by Perseus, who slew the Medusa.

Antony and Cleopatra: a tragedy by Shakespeare, written 1607, published 1623. Marcus Antonius, orator, Senator General, and friend of Julius Caesar; husband of Cleopatra, the Egyptian queen.

Aphrodite (Greek); *Venus* (Roman): goddess of love, beauty, and life and the planet Venus. She arose from the foam of the sea and is often pictured in a large shell surrounded by dolphins and other sea creatures. Her son was Eros or Cupid; Ares or Mars, god of war, was her husband. A major goddess, she was worshipped by many cults. One of G. Woodall's most popular subjects. Also subject of famous painting by Botticelli and sculpture by Praxiteles.

Ares (Greek); *Mars* (Roman): god of war.

Artemis (Greek); *Diana* (Roman); *Selene:* goddess of varied attributes in myth and art, most typically the virgin huntress, the goddess of wild nature, who is associated with the moon as her twin brother, Apollo, is with the sun. Goddess of the lakes, rivers, woods, and the wildlife of these places, especially the boar, stag, and faun.

Athena (Greek); *Minerva* (Roman): goddess of wisdom and civic virtue; goddess of health and politics, pictured fully armed with distaff in one hand.

Aurora (Roman); *Eos* (Greek): goddess of the dawn. Aurora appeared in a fresco painting by Guido Reni in the Palazzo Rospigliosi, in which she was represented as strewing flowers before the advancing chariot of Phoebus, the sun, attended by the Hours.

Bacchus (Greek); *Dionysus* (Roman): god of wine and vegetation. Called "Twice Born" because his father Zeus snatched the unborn child from the womb of his mother, Semele, and sewed him into his own thigh. In due course he opened the stitches and removed the infant. Dionysus was worshipped as a type of fertility god with rites of mystical communion.

Calypso: goddess of silence. A sea nymph in the *Odyssey* who kept Odysseus seven years on her island of Ogygia.

Ceramia: goddess of pottery. In ancient Athens "ceramicus" was the potters' quarters.

Ceres (Roman); *Demeter* (Greek): ancient goddess of corn and of the earth. Presided over the crops, particularly all the grains. Mother of Persephone, goddess of the underworld, Hades. Symbol of fertility, Ceres was Mother Earth.

Clio: the Muse of History (see "Muses").

Corinna: a noted poetess who defeated Pindar five times in poetic contests and won poetic crown.

Cupid (Roman); *Eros* (Greek): son of Aphrodite (Venus). The god of Love, represented as a winged youth or boy carrying a bow and arrow; identified with swans, dolphins, the lyre, and mussel shells.

Diana: an ancient Italic goddess. Originally a deity of the Latins or Sabines, Diana was a patroness of wild things and of birth, both human and animal. Apparently a fertility goddess of the "mountain-mother" type, she was easily identified with the Greek Artemis.

Diana and *Endymion:* Endymion was a beautiful youth loved by the moon goddess Selene, who threw him into a sleep so that he would be unconscious of her caresses.

Dike: goddess of justice, one of the Horae or goddesses of the seasons, hence of orderliness in both nature and society.

Euterpe: the Muse of music. Her name means "delight" and she is often associated with the flute and flute music.

Flora: goddess of flowers or of blooming vegetation whose festival was celebrated on April 28 with games, mimes, and dances.

Floralia: the festival of Flora, celebrated April 28.

Ganymede: son of Tros of Ilion; borne aloft by Zeus in the form of an eagle for his beauty's sake that he might become an immortal and cupbearer to the gods. He stands for the health, beauty, and joy of youth.

Harmonia: wife of Cadmus of Thebes in Greek legend. As a wedding gift she was given a costly garment and a necklace that had the property of stirring up strife and bloodshed, so bringing evil to every possessor. She was also a goddess of order and harmony.

Hebe: the goddess of youth, daughter of Zeus and Hera, and cupbearer of the gods. She became the wife of the deified Hercules and was believed to have the power of restoring youth.

Hermes (Greek); *Mercury* (Roman): herald or messenger of the gods, conductor of souls to the lower world, god of eloquence.

Homnis—Nox (night): goddess of the night (also "Nyx").

Iris: goddess of the rainbow and the swift-footed messenger of Zeus and Hera. She was thought of as the link between Olympus and the mortals below, as she touched both earth and sky.

Juno (Roman); *Hera* (Greek): chief goddess and wife of Jupiter (Zeus), a deity of light and the sky as represented with crown and scepter; the goddess of marriage and childbirth, and patroness of women.

Jupiter (Roman); *Zeus* (Greek): the chief god, title meaning "Heavenly Father." He was a sky-god who had control of the weather and whose weapon was the thunderbolt.

Luna (Roman); *Selene* (Greek): the goddess of the Moon.

Muses: nine goddesses, daughters of Zeus and Mnemosyne, who preside over song, different kinds of poetry, and the arts and sciences. Their names are Calliope, Clio, Erato, Euterpe, Melpomene, Polymnia, Terpsichore, Thalia, and Urania.

Name	Domain	Symbol
Calliope ("Sweet-Voiced")	Heroic Epic	Writing-tablet
Clio ("Praise")	Historical Epic	Scroll or writing-tablet
Urania ("Heavenly")	Astronomical Epic	Globe
Erato ("Loveliness")	Love lyric	Zither
Terpsichore ("Delight in the Dance")	Choral lyric	Lyre
Euterpe ("Delight")	Flute music	Flute
Melpomene ("Song")	Tragedy	Tragic mask
Thalia ("Luxuriant Beauty")	Comedy	Comic mask
Polymnia ("Many Hymns")	Religious hymns and pantomime	No definite device

Nymph: one of the minor divinities of nature, represented as a maiden dwelling in the mountains, forests, meadows, and waters.

Pandora: the first woman (the all-gifted), to whom Zeus gave a box enclosing all human ills. They escaped over the earth when she opened it out of curiosity. Hope was all she prevented from escaping. Another version states that the box contained all the blessings of the gods, which were lost when she opened it.

Penelope: a weaver, the faithful wife of Odysseus. When importuned by numerous suitors, she postponed deciding among them until she had finished a funeral pall for her father-in-law, Laertes. Every night, however, she unraveled what she had woven during the day, and thus put off the suitors.

Persephone: daughter of Ceres; she was the wife of Hades, king of the Underworld, and kidnapped by him.

Phyllis: a Thracian princess betrothed to Demophon, son of Theseus. When he failed to return to marry her at a set time, she thought herself deserted and hanged herself, and was transformed by the gods into an almond tree. Literally, the name means "a green bough."

Pluvia: the rain goddess.

Pomina: apple orchard, fruit garden.

76

Pomona: goddess of the fruit of trees, one of a class of minor female divinities—a wood nymph excelling in gardening and the culture of fruit. Her right hand bore a pruning knife as its weapon.

Psyche: a lovely maiden, the personification of the soul; usually represented with the wings of a butterfly, emblematic of immortality. She became the bride of Cupid and was raised to Olympus, the home of the gods.

Sappho: Greek poetess (circa 600 B.C.) of Lesbos, famous for beautiful love lyrics.

Selene (Greek); *Luna* (Roman): goddess of the moon; she loved Endymion, King of Elis, and had fifty daughters by him.

Serpentina: a sinuous, serpent-like woman.

Siren: one of a group of minor divinities associated with death, sometimes represented with heads and busts of women or in the form of birds or mermaids. Said to be so fascinating they lured men to destruction.

Spring: time of first beginnings, growth, and progress. Associated with Ceres, the earth mother.

Syrene: same as Siren.

Tambourine: represents goddess of music.

Terpsichore: the Muse of dancing and choral song; daughter of Jupiter and Mnemosyne, usually shown wearing a laurel wreath and holding a musical instrument.

Thalia: the Muse of comedy and bucolic poetry. Her name signifies "Luxuriant Beauty."

Undine: fabled female water spirit who could receive a human soul by intermarrying with a mortal.

Venus: the goddess of love.

Vesta: goddess of the hearth and its fire and the patroness of household activities in general; eventually regarded as the guardian of the home, the family, and the community. Associated with the large family; worshipped as the mother of the city of Rome.

GLASS SCULPTURE,

DESIGNED & EXECUTED

BY

GEORGE WOODALL.

THOS. WEBB & SONS LTD.,
DENIS GLASS WORKS,
STOURBRIDGE. ENGLAND.

1. *(Courtesy of the Dudley Art Gallery)*

2. "Honeylane," lived in by John Northwood, is still standing in the factory area of Stevens & Williams; it is used as the company museum. *(Courtesy of the Dudley Art Gallery)*

3. John Northwood, in a photo made from a George Woodall glass photographic plate. *(Courtesy of the Dudley Art Gallery)*

STEVENS & WILLIAMS,

MANUFACTURERS OF ALL KINDS OF

**TABLE AND DECORATIVE
ART GLASS.**

Brierley Hill Glass Works, near Stourbridge.

Large exhibits of our Newest Designs, suitable for the Home and Foreign Markets, can always be seen at our

London Offices and Show Rooms: 47, HOLBORN VIADUCT, E.C.

AND AT WORKS.

N.B. Specialities in cheap and effective lines as well as High Class. Inspection from Buyers invited.

4. From a glass photographic plate. *(Courtesy of the Dudley Art Gallery)*

5. The house at the left was John Henzey's "Hallstons"; it is now the office of Webb & Corbett, who have made glass on that site since 1898. The furnaces pictured indicate a date of 1800. *(Courtesy of the Dudley Art Gallery)*

7. William Fritsche. *(Courtesy of the Dudley Art Gallery)*

6. Benjamin Richardson: March 9, 1802–November 30, 1887. *(Courtesy of the Dudley Art Gallery)*

8. Joshua Hodgetts at work. *(Courtesy of the Dudley Art Gallery)*

9. Joshua Hodgetts, 1857–1933. *(Courtesy of the Dudley Art Gallery)*

CARVING CAMEO GLASS

10. John Northwood II in a photograph taken in 1958. *(Courtesy of his son Kenneth Northwood)*

11. Photographed in the showrooms of Stevens & Williams, with his plaque in the background, John Northwood II was being presented to H.M. Queen Elizabeth, April 23, 1958. On the left is H. S. William-Thomas. The goblet being held by the Queen was made for the use of Queen Victoria and the Prince Consort at the opening of the Royal Exchange October 28, 1844. *(Courtesy of Kenneth Northwood)*

12. John Northwood II and the Mayor of Stourbridge. *(Courtesy of Kenneth Northwood)*

81

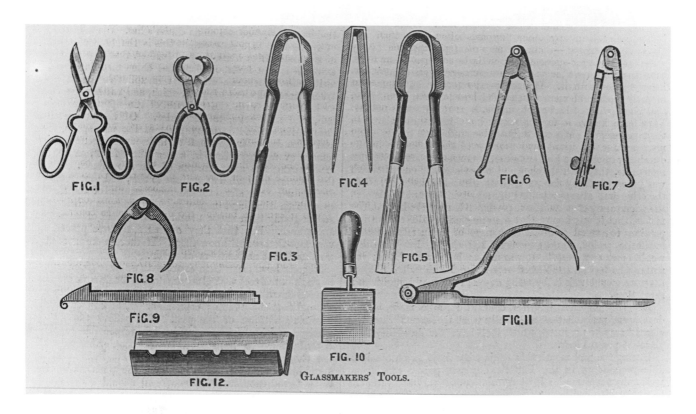

GLASSMAKERS' TOOLS.

Fig. 1: A pair of strong steel scissors used for cutting away any superfluous metal when making an article.

Fig. 2: A pair of parrot-nose shears specially used for cutting through a round rod of glass whilst in a soft state without destroying its roundness at the point of cutting.

Fig. 3: The pucellas, or what the glassmaker calls his iron tools, although, in reality, they are made of the finest steel.
These are the principal tools used by a glassmaker, being those with which he fashions the glass to whatever shape he requires. By inserting the two blunt steel blades into a hollow body of glass whilst in a soft state, he can open it out wider; or, by rubbing the blades on the outside of the glass, he can make it narrower; or he can cut off, elongate, or turn it into any shape required, as might be done in a lathe.

Fig. 4: A pair of steel pincers or tongues, used for taking hold of pieces of hot glass, which may have to be attached to the body of an article, such as handles for jugs, etc.

Fig. 5: The glassmaker calls these his wooden tools which resemble very much the pucellas, the only difference being that instead of having the two steel blades like the pucellas, two peartree-wood prongs are fitted into sockets just below the handle.
These tools are used chiefly for shaping hollow bodies of glassware, whose surfaces are required to be absolutely free from scratches or tool marks, the two wood prongs, when rubbed on the hot glass not being so liable to scratch its surface as the steel blades of the pucellas.

Fig. 6: A pair of iron compasses for measuring the length or depth of an article having a hollow body, such as the bowl of a wine glass, the small hook on the one end of the compasses being to hook on to the rim of the glass, and so prevent the compasses from slipping.

Fig. 7: A similar pair of iron compasses to the above, but with an arrangement at the one end for holding a small bit of French chalk with which hot glass can be marked. These are called the wax-markers, and are used for marking a line round the top of an article to guide the glassmaker in shearing away the superfluous metal when finishing it.

Fig. 8: A pair of ordinary steel callipers, used for measuring the diameter or thickness of an article.

Fig. 9: A flat strip of plain steel about twelve inches long called the measure stick, on which the glassmaker marks, with chalk, the size across the top of the article he is making, so that by applying the measure stick to the top of the unfinished article occasionally as he goes along, he can see when he has arrived at the correct measurement.

Fig. 10: The palette, which is a flat piece of steel about four inches square, with a wood handle attached to it. This is used for flattening glass generally.

Fig. 11: A large pair of iron compasses used for measuring the depth of large bowls, such as salad bowls, etc.

Fig. 12: A pair of footboards, used for forming the feet of wine glasses and other articles; they consist of two flat pieces of peartree-wood boards about eight or nine inches long, with two bits of leather nailed on to the outer edges, so as to form hinges, by which they can be opened or closed like a book.
In making the foot of an article with these tools, the glass in a soft state is squeezed flat between the two wood boards whilst rotating it on the chair-arm.

13. Glassmakers' tools. *(Courtesy of the Dudley Art Gallery)*

TO

ALL WHOM IT MAY CONCERN.

Several parties in Brettell Lane and Wordsley having advertized for a number of Boys, from 14 to 16 years of age, under the pretence of learning them the Art of FLINT GLASS CUTTING: we,

THE
GLASS CUTTERS

feel it to be our duty to inform the Public that our Members left those Shops, being satisfied that the system under which they were working was detrimental to the interests of the Trade at large, and calculated finally to produce most ruinous consequences; our Members only desired to Work by the Piece, which the Employers thought proper to refuse, thereby causing the present dissatisfaction. The Employers alluded to are termed *Middle Men*, or *Small Masters*, standing between the Manufacturer and the Workman in our Trade, more especially in some of the Shops connected with the Manufactories of this District; the men have suffered most severely from this state of things, and we consider it to be our bounden duty to put an end to such a ruinous system, and we trust that the Working Men of other Trades will not aid or assist in any way to encourage any system that is injurious to the Rights of Labour.

BY ORDER OF THE COMMITTEE
OF THE UNITED FLINT GLASS CUTTERS' SOCIETY,

July 2nd, 1857. WORDSLEY BRANCH.

THOMAS MELLARD, PRINTER, STOURBRIDGE.

14. A notice by the United Flint Glass Cutters' Society. *(Courtesy of the Dudley Art Gallery)*

16. The "Woodall Team," from a Woodall glass photographic plate. *Standing, from left to right:* Tom Hill, Harry Davies, Tom Woodall; *seated,* William Mullett, George Woodall, J. T. Fereday. *(Courtesy of the Dudley Art Gallery)*

15. Thomas Woodall, 1849–1926. *(Courtesy of the Dudley Art Gallery)*

17. Webb Advertisement. *(Courtesy of the Dudley Art Gallery)*

18. George Woodall, 1850–1925. *(Courtesy of Philip T. Budrose)*

19. George Woodall in a photograph taken about 1885. *(Courtesy of the Dudley Art Gallery)*

21. Beatrice Alice Woodall, from a glass negative taken by her father, George Woodall. *(Courtesy of the Dudley Art Gallery)*

23. Thomas Woodall. *(Courtesy of Philip A. Budrose)*

22. Advertisement dated June 10, 1899. *(Courtesy of the Dudley Art Gallery)*

20. Advertisement. *(Courtesy of the Dudley Art Gallery)*

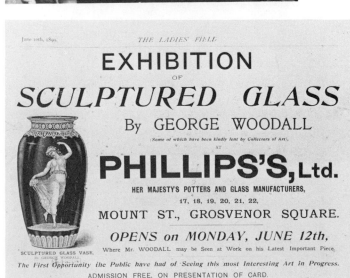

24. Workers posed at a furnace. Photograph was made from a Woodall glass plate. *(Courtesy of the Dudley Art Gallery)*

25. Photograph made from a Woodall glass plate. *(Courtesy of the Dudley Art Gallery)*

26. Stylized floral plaques. *(Courtesy of a private collector)*

27. Stylized floral plaque. *(Courtesy of a private collector)*

28. Queen Victoria portrait plaque. *(Courtesy of a private collector)*

GOLD MEDAL PARIS EXHIBITION, 1878.
MEMORANDUM.

FROM *Josiah Wedgwood & Sons, Etruria, Stoke upon Trent.*

TO Mr Northwood

Ap. 1879

Sir

We have complaints from the person we sent the last Portland you cut for us — that the leg of the man going through the doorway was badly modelled it appeared he said as if too much had been cut away — do you remember whether such was the case please to take the greatest care in doing those that are coming on that the modelling in cutting away is faithfully executed to the original design

Wedgwood & Sons

29. Letter from Wedgwood & Sons to John Northwood concerning Northwood's finishing of Portland vases for Wedgwood—complaints about Northwood's work. *(Courtesy of John Northwood's grandson Kenneth Northwood)*

GOLD MEDAL PARIS EXHIBITION, 1878.
MEMORANDUM.

FROM *Josiah Wedgwood & Sons, Etruria, Stoke upon Trent.*

TO M^c J. Northwood

May 19 1880

Dear Sir

We send you today a Portland vase polished by you & painted but which came out of Kiln dirty all over. Can you polish the dirt off the white unpainted parts & make it look really well. Please try a small portion of it first & then let us know whether you think it will be best to proceed with it, or whether it is hopeless & we must then sell it as it is.

J W & S

88

30. Letter from "J W & S" (Josiah Wedgwood & Sons) regarding what might be done by Northwood to improve a Portland vase and make it saleable. *(Courtesy of Kenneth Northwood, grandson of John Northwood)*

Gentlemen

I am sorry to say in cutting
the cupids foot, it was so hollow under
that the piece came off, I was quite aware
of it being hollow and used the greatest
care, but off no avail, I return the
base with the piece in small box in side
that came off. I do not know if you
have any means of fluxing it on, I think
I should have succeeded in making the
feet passable.

I am Your Obediently,
John Northwood

To.
Mess. I. Wedgwood & Son

31. Letter from John Northwood, dated September 26, 1879, to Wedgwood about the difficulties encountered in his work on their Portland vases. _(Courtesy of Kenneth Northwood, grandson of John Northwood)_

34. William Thomson, Lord Kelvin, 14-inch portrait plaque, 1900; signed "Geo. Woodall." Photo made from a Woodall glass plate. *(Courtesy of the Dudley Art Gallery)*

32. Plaque Idle Moments, GW 148, 5 inches; signed "Geo. Woodall." *(Courtesy of the Dudley Art Gallery)*

33. The O'Fallon vase, by J. M. O'Fallon, Art Director at Thomas Webb & Sons during the 1878 period. Exhibited at the Paris International Exhibition in 1878; 7 inches. *(Courtesy of Phillips Fine Art Auctioneers)*

42. Aphrodite, signed "Geo. Woodall." *(Courtesy of the Dudley Art Gallery)*

43. Sea Nymph, W 2767; 13 inches by 10 inches; signed "Geo. Woodall." Photograph made from a Woodall glass plate. *(Courtesy of the Dudley Art Gallery)*

44. Penelope, W 2765, white on brown on flint jar; signed "T. & G. Woodall." This was presented to Mrs. Parker by the Liberals of Wordsley and the district, in appreciation of her husband's work in their behalf. *(Courtesy of the Dudley Art Gallery)*

45. Diana and Nymph, W 2718; 10-inch covered vase, white on brown. *(Courtesy of the Dudley Art Gallery)*

47. Sea Foam, white on brown vase, 10 inches, GW 6; signed "Geo Woodall." *(Courtesy of the Dudley Art Gallery)*

46. Adam and Eve plaque, 18 inches; signed "Geo. Wood-all." *(Private collection)*

48. Mrs. Martin; signed "Geo. Woodall." *(Courtesy of the Dudley Art Gallery)*

49. Armenian Girl, 4¾-inch plaque; signed "Armenian girl, Geo. Woodall." *(Courtesy of the Dudley Art Gallery)*

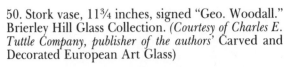

50. Stork vase, 11¾ inches, signed "Geo. Woodall." Brierley Hill Glass Collection. *(Courtesy of Charles E. Tuttle Company, publisher of the authors'* Carved and Decorated European Art Glass*)*

51. Feathered Favourites, W 2759, a 12-inch plaque; signed "T. & G. Woodall 1892." *(Courtesy of the Dudley Art Gallery)*

52. Penelope, GW 12; 7-inch vase, signed "Geo. Woodall," February 1901. *(Courtesy of the Dudley Art Gallery)*

53. Pomona, W 2795; 10-inch vase, white on brown; signed "T. & G. Woodall." *(Courtesy of the Dudley Art Gallery)*

54. Wandering Stars, W 2802. *(Courtesy of Thomas Webb & Sons)*

55. Venus and Cupid. *(Courtesy of the Dudley Art Gallery)*

57. Undine, W 159, white on brown vase. *(Courtesy of the Dudley Art Gallery)*

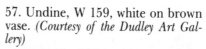

56. The Elgin Vase, 8 inches. The design is after the frieze of the Elgin marbles. Signed "Frederick Kny" *(Courtesy of Phillips Fine Art Auctioneers, London)*

96

58. Night, 8½ inches, white on brown vase, GW 23; signed "Geo. Woodall," February 1900. *(Courtesy of the Dudley Art Galley)*

59. Morning, GW 24, white on brown vase, 8½ inches, February 1900. *(Courtesy of the Dudley Art Galley)*

61. Portrait plaque, signed "Geo. Woodall." *(Courtesy of the Dudley Art Gallery)*

60. Dancers plaque. *(Courtesy of Philip A. Budrose)*

62. The Muses, 8-inch vase, white on red; signed in cameo "Erato / Euterpe / Thalia / Clio / Terpsichore; T. & G. Woodall; Des & Sculps; Thomas Webb & Sons, Gem Cameo." *(Copyright Sotheby Parke Bernet, Inc., New York)*

63. Birds plaque, white on brown. *(Courtesy of Philip A. Budrose)*

65. Vase, signed "Geo. Woodall." *(Courtesy of the Dudley Art Gallery)*

64. The Intruders, W 2794; 16½-inch plaque, white on brown; signed "T. & G. Woodall." Picture was made from a Woodall glass plate. *(Courtesy of the Dudley Art Gallery)*

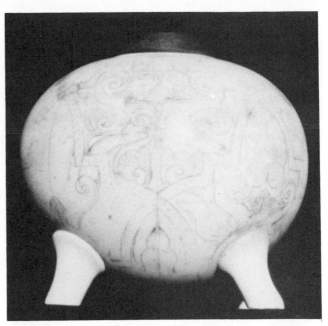

67. Cased opal blank with sketched design prior to cutting. *(Authors' collection)*

66. Cased opal blank with sketched design prior to cutting. *(Authors' collection)*

68. Cased opal blank with sketched design prior to cutting. *(Authors' collection)*

69. Covered cased opal jar prior to cutting. *(Authors' collection)*

71. Sappho, 17 inches in frame, signed "T. & G. Woodall, Sappho." *(Courtesy of Charles E. Tuttle Company, publisher of the authors' Carved and Decorated European Art Glass)* ⟶

⟵ 70. Venus and Cupid plaque, 18¼ inches, signed "G. Woodall." *(Courtesy of Philip A. Budrose)*

72. Spring, white on brown vase, 11 inches. *(Courtesy of the Dudley Art Gallery)*

73. Autumn, W 3160, white on brown vase, 11 inches; companion piece to Spring. *(Courtesy of the Dudley Art Gallery)*

74. Pair of opal plaques on bright, translucent blue ground, 5¾ inches; attributed to Thomas Webb & Sons. *(Courtesy of Phillips Fine Art Auctioneers)*

75. Putti and Butterflies, 5½-inch vase signed "Geo. Woodall." Morning, GW 139; 7-inch vase signed "Geo. Woodall." Ceramia, GW 21, 6¼-inch vase, white on brown, signed "Ceramia, Geo. Woodall." *(Courtesy of Thomas Webb & Sons)*

101

76. Group of five pieces made by Stevens & Williams. *(Courtesy of Kenneth Northwood)*
1—designed by W. Northwood, engraved by B. Fenn, 1887
2—designed and carved by J. Northwood II, 1887
3—designed by W. Northwood, engraved by Joshua Hodgetts, 1887
4—designed and worked by Charles Northwood, 1881, unfinished
5—engraved by Joshua Hodgetts, 1888

77. The Dance, GW/30, 20-inch plaque, signed "Geo. Woodall." Picture was made from a Woodall glass plate *(Courtesy of the Dudley Art Gallery)*

78. Aphrodite, signed "Geo. Woodall." Picture was made from a Woodall glass plate. *(Courtesy of the Dudley Art Gallery)*

102

79. Origin of Painting, GW 145, white on brown plaque, 11 inches; signed "Geo. Woodall." Picture was made from a Woodall glass plate. *(Courtesy of the Dudley Art Gallery)*

80. Syrene, GW 161, white on brown plaque, 10½ inches; signed "Geo. Woodall." Picture was made from a Woodall glass plate. *(Courtesy of the Dudley Art Gallery)*

81. Night, GW 140; 7-inch vase signed "Geo. Woodall." *(Courtesy of the Dudley Art Gallery)*

82. Morning, GW 139, 7-inch vase, signed "Geo. Woodall." *(Courtesy of the Dudley Art Gallery)*

103

83. The Moorish Bathers, in an unfinished preliminary state. Picture was made from a Woodall
glass plate. *(Courtesy of the Dudley Art Gallery)*

84. The Roman Bath, in a preliminary, unfinished state. Picture was made from a Woodall
glass plate. *(Courtesy of the Dudley Art Gallery)*

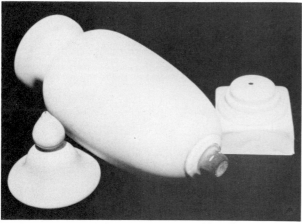

85. Three-piece uncut vase, white over brown lining.
(Authors' collection)

86. *Left:* Narcissus, W/3111, opal on brown vase, 11 inches; partially cut, but
unfinished. Picture was made from a Woodall glass plate. *(Courtesy of the
Dudley Art Gallery) Right:* Iris vase, W 3111, a companion piece; opal on
brown, 11 inches. Picture was made from a Woodall glass plate. *(Courtesy of
the Dudley Art Gallery)*

87. Anthony and Cleopatra, W 3058, white on brown plaque, 18 inches; signed "Geo. Woodall," 1897. Picture was made from a Woodall glass plate. *(Courtesy of the Dudley Art Gallery)*

88. Cleopatra, an 18-inch plaque exhibited in Paris in 1889; signed "T. & G. Woodall." Picture was made from a Woodall glass plate. *(Courtesy of the Dudley Art Gallery)*

89. Syrene, a plaque, signed "Geo. Woodall." *(Courtesy of Elliot and Enid Wysor)*

90. Calypso, GW 32, panel, 12½ inches; signed "CALYPSO, Geo. Woodall." *(Courtesy of the Dudley Art Gallery)*

91. Feathered Favourites, GW 131, a 7-inch vase. *(Courtesy of the Dudley Art Gallery)*
←

92. A Message, GW 130, companion vase to Feathered Favourites, 7 inches. *(Courtesy of the Dudley Art Gallery)*

93. Terpsichore—Dancing Girl. *(Courtesy of the Dudley Art Gallery)*

94. Floralia plaque, W 2733; 13 inches; signed "G. Woodall." *(Private collection)*

96. Polar vase, 16 inches, white on green. Picture was made from a Woodall glass plate. *(Courtesy of the Dudley Art Gallery)*

→

←

95. Polar vase, 16 inches, white on green. Picture was made from a Woodall glass plate. *(Courtesy of the Dudley Art Gallery)*

98. A Quiet Nook, W 2726, covered jar, white on brown; 9 inches; signed "Geo. Woodall." *(Courtesy of the Dudley Art Gallery)*

97. Underwater fish vase. *(Courtesy of the Dudley Art Gallery)*

107

99. Ivory vase in a Persian motif. (*Courtesy of Christie's, London*)

100. Cupid in Disgrace, W2734, signed "G. Woodall, 1892." Exhibited in Chicago in 1893. (*Courtesy of the Dudley Art Gallery*)

101. Tambourina, GW 135, a 7-inch vase, companion piece to Soppa; signed "Geo. Woodall." (*Courtesy of the Dudley Art Gallery*)

102. Soppa, GW 134; 7-inch vase. (*Courtesy of the Dudley Art Gallery*)

103. White on amethyst bottle, decorated with nesting birds; 10¾ inches. *(Courtesy of Phillips Fine Art Auctioneers)*

104. Bottle attributed to the Woodall Team. *(Courtesy of Christie's, New York)*

105. Before the Race, W 2043, white on brown vase, 12 inches; signed "Before the Race, Webb, T. & G. Woodall." *(Courtesy of Charles E. Tuttle Company, publisher of the authors'* Carved and Decorated European Art Glass)

106. The Race, W 2179, white on brown vase, 12 inches; signed "T. & G. Woodall, The Race, Webb." *(Courtesy of Charles E. Tuttle Company, publisher of the authors'* Carved and Decorated European Art Glass)

109

107. Sappho, oval plaque, 6½ inches by 4½ inches; signed "G. Woodall." (*Courtesy of the Dudley Art Gallery*)

108. The Pearl Necklace, GW 155; signed "Geo. Woodall." (*Courtesy of the Dudley Art Gallery*)

109. Industry, two-handled vase, signed "Geo. Woodall." (*Courtesy of the Dudley Art Gallery*)

110. Aphrodite, 13½ inches; signed "Aphrodite, G. Woodall 1892, Webb, Thomas Webb & Sons, Gem Cameo." (*Courtesy of the Dudley Art Gallery*)

110

111. Minerva, ewer, white on brown. *(Photo courtesy of Thomas Webb & Sons, Stourbridge, England)*

⟵

⟶

112. The Rose, W 2402, two-handled vase, 16 inches; signed "G. Woodall." *(Courtesy of the Dudley Art Gallery)*

113. Feathered Favourites, W 2731; 13-inch white on brown vase; signed "T. and G. Woodall." *(Courtesy of the Dudley Art Gallery)*

⟵

114. Inspiration, W 2724, white on brown vase, 12 inches; signed "Geo. Woodall, Inspiration, Thomas Webb & Sons, Webb." *(Courtesy of the Dudley Art Gallery)*

⟶

115. Pompeian Maidens, W 2685, covered jar. *(Courtesy of the Dudley Art Gallery)*

116. Pandora, W 2792, white on claret brown; signed "Geo. Woodall." *(Courtesy of the Dudley Art Gallery)*

117. Original Aurora jar and cover, signed "Aurora"; design copied from Guido Reni's painting. Melbourne Exhibition 1880; destroyed by fire.

118. Origin of Painting, white on brown vase, 9¼ inches; signed "Geo. Woodall, Origin of Painting." Stourbridge Glass Collection. *(Courtesy of Charles E. Tuttle Company, publisher of the authors'* Carved and Decorated European Art Glass*)*

112

119. Psyche. *(Courtesy of the Dudley Art Gallery)*

120. A Maid of Athens, W 2723; 10⅛ inches; signed "T. & G. Woodall, Webb." *(Courtesy of the Dudley Art Gallery)*

121. Diana, GW 26, white on brown, 7 inches; signed "Geo. Woodall." *(Courtesy of the Dudley Art Gallery)*

122. A Message, GW 14; 7-inch vase. *(Courtesy of the Dudley Art Gallery)*

123. *Top center:* Two-handled vase, W 2510, signed "Ceres receiving from Bacchus a restorative cup"; 8½ inches. *Bottom row, left to right:* The Fruit Seller, W 2403, two-handled vase, 15¾ inches; signed "G. Woodall 1889, Thomas Webb & Sons, Gem Cameo." Hebe, W 2892, 9½ inches. Ceramia, GW 21, white on brown, 6½ inches; signed "Ceramia." Cupid and Psyche, two-handled vase, W2609, white on brown; 15½ inches. Picture was made from a Woodall glass plate. *(Courtesy of the Dudley Art Gallery)*

124. Pharaoh's Daughter. GW 7, white on brown vase, 11 inches. Picture was made from a Woodall glass plate. *(Courtesy of the Dudley Art Gallery)*

125. Night, GW 3, white on brown vase, 10 inches; signed "Night, G. Woodall." *(Courtesy of the Dudley Art Gallery)*

126. Morning, GW 5, white on brown, 10 inches; signed "G. Woodall." *(Courtesy of the Dudley Art Gallery)*

C76. Clock, 7 inches, signed "British United Clock Ltd., Birmingham, England"; wild roses. *(Private collection)*

C77. Vase, 10½ inches, signed "Tiffany & Co., Paris Exhibition 1889, Thomas Webb & Sons, Gem Cameo." Pink on white on blue, with engraved ground. *(Collection of Leo Kaplan Antiques, courtesy of Alan Kaplan)*

C78. Vase, 6¾ inches, signed "Tiffany & Co., Paris Exhibition 1889, Thomas Webb & Sons, Gem Cameo." Chrysanthemums. *(Private collection)*

C79. Vase, 10 inches, signed "Thomas Webb & Sons, Limited." *(Private collection)*

C80. Unfinished pedestal bowl, 8¾ inches; formerly in the collection of Beatrice Alice Woodall, daughter of George Woodall. *(Private collection)*

C81. Vase with hibiscus, 8 inches, signed "Thomas Webb & Sons, Gem Cameo, Paris Exhibition 1889, Theodore B. Starr, New York." *(Private collection)*

116

C82. Plaque, 9¼ inches, signed "Thomas Webb & Sons, Gem Cameo." *(Private collection)*

C83. Morning glory vase, 11¾ inches. *(Collection of Leo Kaplan Antiques)*

117

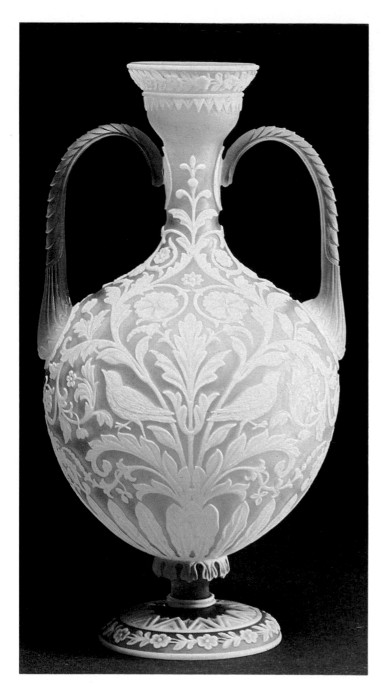

C84. Two-handled vase, 7½ inches, Thomas Webb & Sons, designed by Thomas Woodall and executed by J. T. Fereday. Manufactured in 1884; acquired by the Victoria and Albert Museum in 1885 at the International Health Exhibition.

C85. Candlesticks, 7½ inches, attributed to Thomas Webb & Sons. *(Private collection)*

118

C93. Vase, 9 inches, attributed to Stevens & Williams; roses on a trellis with hammered topaz ground. *(Collection of Leo Kaplan Antiques)*

C94. Vase, 6¼ inches, signed "Thomas Webb & Sons, Gem Cameo." *(Private collection)*

121

C95. Vase with dahlias, 8½ inches, signed "Thomas Webb & Sons, Gem Cameo." *(Private collection)*

C96. Two-handled 9-inch vase signed "Thomas Webb & Sons, Gem." *(Private collection)*

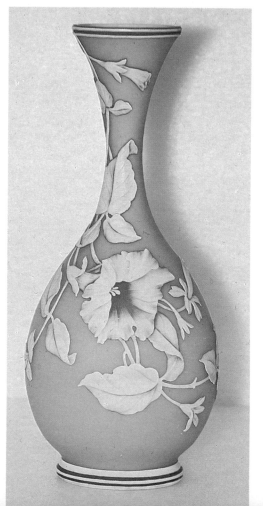

C97. Vase with morning glories, 12 inches, signed "Thomas Webb & Sons, Gem Cameo." *(Private collection)*

C98. Vase, 10 inches, with currants, cherries, plums, and raspberries on scroll-carved background. Attributed to Jules Barbe. *(Private collection)*

C99. Vase with a fish-scale background, 10 inches; three panels have various carved fruits. *(Private collection)*

C100. Vase, 8½ inches, signed "Thomas Webb & Sons." *(Private collection)*

C101. Curio vase, 4½ inches, signed "Thomas Webb & Sons." *(Collection of Howard and Paula Ellman)*

C102. Decanter, 9½ inches. *(Collection of Leo Kaplan Antiques)*

C103. Vase, 11¾ inches, attributed to Stevens & Williams, a typical Frederick Carder design. *(Collection of The Chrysler Museum of Art at Norfolk)* ⟶

124

C104. Plaque, 18 inches, signed "T & G Woodall," The Attack. *(Private collection, photo courtesy of Alan Kaplan)*

C105. Vase, 8 inches, signed "G. Woodall, Thomas Webb & Sons, Gem Cameo." *(Private collection)*

C106. Vase and cover, 12 inches, signed "G. Woodall, Loves Awakening, Thomas Webb & Sons, Gem Cameo, Webb." W 2660. White on blue on brown; top is white on brown. *(Private collection)*

C107. Eight-inch vase signed
"Webb." W 2579. Dancing girl is
white against red background.
Top and foot, white on blue on
red. *(Authors' collection)*

C108. Vase, 12 inches, signed "Stevens & Williams Art Glass. Stourbridge"; ornithogalum lily and dog rose. *(Collection of The Chrysler Museum of Art at Norfolk)*

C109. Parrot-tulip vase, 10½ inches, white on topaz. *(Collection of the Currier Gallery of Art)*

C110. Ten-inch lamp, attributed to Thomas Webb & Sons, with gloxinias. *(Collection of Leo Kaplan Antiques)*

C111. Vase, 7¼ inches, attributed to George Woodall, Thomas Webb & Sons. *(Authors' collection)*

C112. Panel, 12¼ inches, signed "T & G Woodall." On the Terrace, W 2834. *(Private collection)*

C113. Vase, 8 inches, signed "Thomas Webb & Sons, Gem Cameo, G. Woodall." Cameo cutting on blown-out neck. (*Private collection*)

C114. Vase, 13½ inches, signed "Thomas Webb & Sons, Gem Cameo." (*Private collection*)

C115. Curio vase, 8½ inches, with birds, fish, and waves on a sea-green ground. Attributed to Thomas Webb & Sons. (*Private collection*)

C116. Vase, 10½ inches, with figs and cherries; signed "Paris Exhibition 1889, Thomas Webb & Sons, Gem Cameo." Attributed to Jules Barbe. *(Private collection)*

C117. Lamp base, 13¾ inches, with morning glories. *(Private collection)*

C118. Vase, 6¼ inches, with seashells and coral motif. *(Collection of Minna Rosenblatt Antiques)*

133

C119. Vase, 7¾ inches, with morning-glory decoration. *(Authors' collection)*

C120. Tall vase, white on pink on chartreuse. *(Private collection)*

C121. Eleven-inch vase signed "Thomas Webb & Sons, Gem Cameo, Tiffany & Co., Paris Exhibition 1889." *(Private collection)* →

C122. Two-handled vase, 8¾ inches, signed "Unhappy childhood J L [for Joseph Locke, superimposed] 1877." Made at Richardson Glass Co. *(Collection of The Chrysler Museum of Art at Norfolk)*

C123. Two-handled vase, 8¾ inches, signed "Happy childhood," with the initials "J L" superimposed on each other for "Joseph Locke." Made at Richardson Glass Co. in 1877. *(Collection of The Chrysler Museum of Art at Norfolk)*

135

C124. Perfume bottle, 4¼ inches, signed "Thomas Webb & Sons, Gem Cameo"; primula decoration. *(Private collection)*

C125. Vase, 9 inches, signed "Thomas Webb & Sons, Gem Cameo"; with achimenes. *(Private collection)*

C126. Vase, 8½ inches, with stylized floral and geometric design, signed "Thomas Webb & Sons." *(Private collection)*

C127. Pair of apple-blossom vases, 7¼ inches in height. *(Collection of Currier Gallery of Art)*

C128. Dolphin perfume bottle, 4½ inches. Attributed to Thomas Webb & Sons. *(Private collection)*

C129. Ten-inch vase signed "Tiffany & Co., Paris Exhibition 1889, Webb." Known as The Lovers. *(Private collection)*

C130. Vase, 9 inches, signed "Thomas Webb & Sons, Gem Cameo." *(Private collection)*

C131. Vase, 6¼ inches, signed "Thomas Webb & Sons, Gem Cameo." Motifs are stylized clouds, berries, and waves. *(Private collection)*

C132. Vase, 11¾ inches, signed "S & W, England"; wine and green cameo over intaglio. *(Private collection)*

C133. Four-layer vase, 3¾ inches, white on blue on chartreuse with a white lining. *(Authors' collection)*

C134. Vase, 7¾ inches, signed "Thomas Webb & Sons, Gem Cameo," with jasmine decoration. *(Private collection)*

C135. Vase, 7¾ inches, signed "Stevens & Williams, F. Carder." *(Collection of Rockwell-Corning Museum)*

C136. Vase, 8 inches, with convolvulus decoration; signed "Webb." *(Authors' collection)*

C137. Vase, 7½ inches, signed "Webb," with sweet Williams. *(Private collection)*

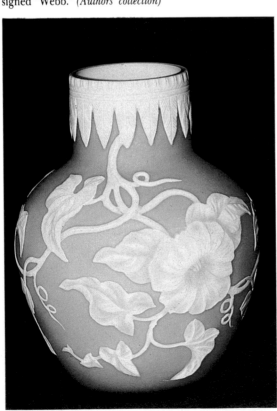

C138. Vase, 8 inches, signed "A Siren, Geo. Woodall"; white on brown.

C139. Vase, 4½ inches, with cinerarias; two shoulder appliqués. *(Collection of Minna Rosenblatt)*

C140. Vase, 6¾ inches, with passion-flower decoration; signed "Thomas Webb & Sons, Tiffany & Co., Paris Exhibition 1889." *(Private collection)*

C141. Vase, 6½ inches; signed "Thomas Webb & Sons, Gem Cameo"; anemone decoration. *(Private collection)*

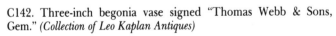

C142. Three-inch begonia vase signed "Thomas Webb & Sons, Gem." *(Collection of Leo Kaplan Antiques)*

C143. Two-handled vase, 15¼ inches, white on blue. Signed "G. Woodall, Thomas Webb & Sons, Gem Cameo." W 2725. *(Private collection)*

C144. Eight-inch vase signed "Thomas Webb & Sons, Gem Cameo"; attributed to Jules Barbe. *(Private collection)*

C145. Ten-inch vase signed "Paris Exhibition 1889, Thomas Webb & Sons"; clematis motif. *(Private collection)*

C146. Vase, 12½ inches, with cyclamen decoration. *(Collection of Leo Kaplan Antiques)*

144

C147. Plaque, 12½ inches; Cupids and Dolphin, attributed to George Woodall, by Frederick Carder in 1937. *(Authors' collection)*

C148. Two-handled vase, 16 inches, signed "Thomas Webb & Sons, Gem Cameo"; completely decorated on all sides. *(Private collection)*

C149. Vase, 5½ inches, signed "Webb." *(Collection of Leo Kaplan Antiques, courtesy of Alan Kaplan)*

C150. Vase, 12 inches, with prunus blossom decoration on ground of rose duBarry color. Attributed to Stevens & Williams. *(Private collection)*

C151. Vase, 2½ inches, with stylized floral and fruit decoration; signed "Thomas Webb & Sons, Gem Cameo." *(Private collection)*

147

C152. Pitcher, 6½ inches, with maidenhair-fern decoration. *(Private collection)*

C153. Vase, 15½ inches, signed "Thomas Webb & Sons"; foxglove motif. *(Private collection)*

C154. Vase, 4 inches, signed "Thomas Webb & Sons, Gem Cameo." *(Private collection)*

C155. Curio vase, 9½ inches, signed "Thomas Webb & Sons, Gem Cameo." Fish and lion masks; gold and platinum fired on ivory ground. *(Private collection)*

C156. Vase, 17½ inches, attributed to Thomas Webb & Sons; additional scene on other side. *(Authors' collection)*

149

C157. Clematis-decorated cologne with matching stopper, 5¾ inches. (*Private collection*)

C158. Vase, 14½ inches, signed "Thomas Webb & Sons, Gem Cameo"; shells, coral, and seaweed. (*Private collection*)

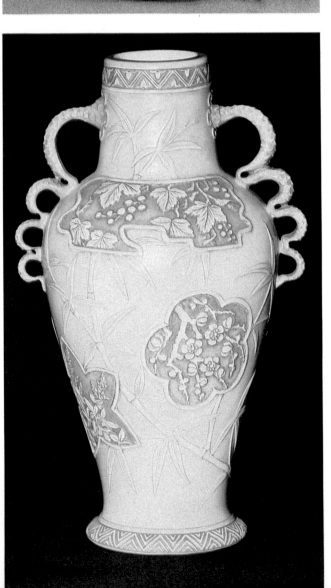

C159. Vase, 6 inches, signed "Thomas Webb & Sons"; prunus blossoms. (*Collection of D. Leonard and Gerry Trent Antiques*)

C160. Vase, 8¾ inches, hibiscus decoration; attributed to Thomas Webb & Sons. *(Collection of The Chrysler Museum of Art at Norfolk)*

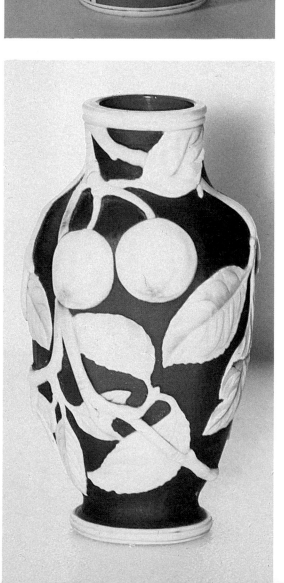

C161. Vase, 13¾ inches, unusual double-gourd shape; attributed to Stevens & Williams. *(Brierley Hill Glass Collection, courtesy of the Dudley Art Gallery)*

C162. Cherry-decorated cameo on blown vase, 4¼ inches; attributed to Thomas Webb & Sons. *(Authors' collection)*

C163. Blue and white fern vase, signed "Stevens & Williams"; rosebowl and tumbler, signed "Thomas Webb & Sons." The rosebowl is decorated with clematis; the tumbler is cassia decorated. Tallest piece, 4 inches. *(Private collection)*

C164. Mullein-decorated vase, 7½ inches. *(Private collection)*

C165. Epergne with fairy lamps, 12 inches in diameter, signed "Thomas Webb & Sons." *(Collection of Leo Kaplan Antiques, courtesy of Alan Kaplan)*

C166. Vase, 8½ inches, signed "Thomas Webb & Sons, Gem Cameo"; stylized fish decoration. *(Private collection)*

C167. Vase, 4¼ inches; dogwood decoration in low-relief cameo. *(Authors' collection)*

153

C168. Vase, 12¾ inches, signed "T. & G. Woodall, Thomas Webb & Sons, Gem Cameo"; subject is a dancing girl. Arms of the Capel Cure family of London on obverse. *(Collection of The Toledo Museum of Art)*

C169. Vase, 12¾ inches, with dancing girl; signed "T. & G. Woodall, Thomas Webb & Sons, Gem Cameo"; made for the Capel Cure family. *(Collection of The Toledo Museum of Art)*

C170. Vase, 12¾ inches, signed "T. & G. Woodall, Thomas Webb & Sons, Gem Cameo"; arms are those of the Capel Cure family of London. This coat of arms also appears on the obverse sides of the two vases on the opposite page. (Collection of The Toledo Museum of Art)

C171. Fairy lamp, 5½ inches, signed "Thomas Webb & Sons"; verbena decoration. (Private collection)

C172. Vase, 6¾ inches; decorated with the Christmas rose. (Private collection)

C173. Vase, 7 inches, signed "Thomas Webb & Sons, Gem Cameo"; motif is flowering cactus. (Private collection)

C174. Vase, 8 inches; celadon color to simulate jade. *(Private collection)*

C175. Vase, 9¼ inches, signed "Aquatic Life, Geo. Woodall"; similar marine life motifs appear on other examples in this book. *(Collection of The Pilkington Glass Museum)*

156

C176. Vase, 5 inches, signed "Paris Exhibition 1889, Thomas Webb & Sons." *(Private collection)*

C177. Vase, 4 inches, with rose decorations, signed "Thomas Webb & Sons, Gem Cameo." *(Private collection)*

C178. Anemone vase, 7¼ inches, signed "Thomas Webb & Sons, Gem Cameo." *(Private collection)*

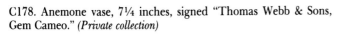

C179. Vase, 5 inches, signed "Thomas Webb & Sons"; fish and seaweed motifs. *(Collection of Leo Kaplan Antiques, courtesy of Alan Kaplan)*

C180. Vase, 7½ inches, signed "T. & G. Woodall, Thomas Webb & Sons, Gem Cameo."

C181. Plaque, 7½ inches in diameter, Cupid on Panther, set in a 15½-inch-diameter roundel with rose, poppy, violet, and dahlia in the spandrels. *(Collection of The Currier Gallery of Art)*

C182. Vase, 8½ inches, with sunflowers, signed "Thomas Webb & Sons, Gem Cameo." *(Private collection)*

C183. Peony vase, 10 inches; note spider and web in the decoration. *(Private collection)*

C184. Camphor-footed goblets, 10 inches. *(Collection of Leo Kaplan Antiques)*

C185. Vase, 8 inches, cameo on mother-of-pearl background; orchid motif. *(Private collection)*

C186. Vase, 3 inches, signed "Tiffany & Co., Paris Exhibition 1889, Thomas Webb & Sons, Gem Cameo." *(Private collection)*

160

C187. Vase, 7 inches, signed "Thomas Webb & Sons–RP 8016." *(Private collection)*

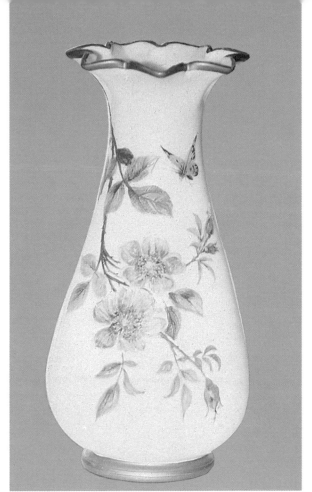

C188. Vase, 9 inches, signed "Thomas Webb & Sons, Gem"; basket-weave pattern. *(Private collection)*

C189. Bottle, 7½ inches, signed "Thomas Webb & Sons. Gem Cameo"; convolvulus decoration. Underneath, base is carved as a flower. *(Private collection)*

C190. Plaque, 12½ inches, signed "Geo. Woodall." Music; W 2824. *(Collection of Leo Kaplan Antiques, courtesy of Alan Kaplan)*

162

C191. Plaque, 6 inches, signed "Geo. Woodall." Note similarity of subject in the plaque above. *(Collection of Leo Kaplan Antiques, courtesy of Alan Kaplan)*

127. *Top row:* Flora, 7½-inch vase, GW 10; white on brown; signed "Geo. Woodall." Psyche, 7½-inch vase, GW 13; possibly the figure represents Pandora, although price book identifies it as "Physche." *Bottom row:* Iris vase, W/3111, opal on brown, 11 inches; signed "Geo. Woodall." Sirene, GW25, 8½ inches; signed "Geo. Woodall." Cleopatra, W 2843, 10 inches; signed "Geo. Woodall." Picture was made from a Woodall glass plate. *(Courtesy of the Dudley Art Gallery)*

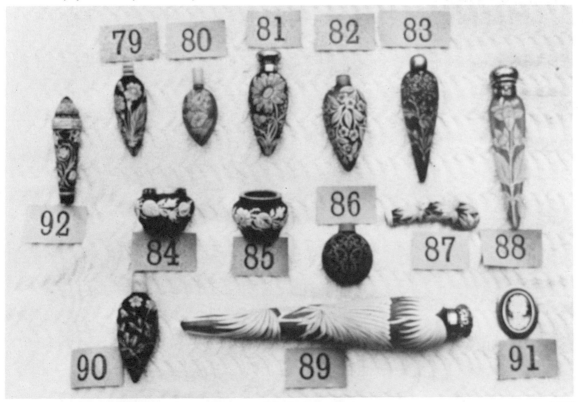

128. Perfume and other miniatures. *(Private collection)*

163

129. The Minuet, 11-inch vase, W 2720; signed "Geo. Woodall, 1891." *(Courtesy of Elliot and Enid Wysor)*

130. Aphrodite, 8¼ inches; signed "Geo. Woodall." *(Courtesy of Charles E. Tuttle Company, publisher of the authors'* Carved and Decorated European Art Glass)

131. Hunting Scene, 11¾ inches, white on brown; signed "J. Millward 12, Stevens & Williams." *(Courtesy of Charles E. Tuttle Company, publisher of the authors'* Art Glass Nouveau)

132. Pandora, W 2730, white on brown; signed "T. & G. Woodall." *(Courtesy of the Dudley Art Gallery)*

133. Group of five pieces, as shown on a George Woodall glass photographic plate. *(Courtesy of the Dudley Art Gallery)*

134. Group of six pieces, as shown on a George Woodall glass photographic plate. *(Courtesy of the Dudley Art Gallery)*

165

136. Oil lamp, 18 inches, white on blue; attributed to Thomas Webb. *(Courtesy of Phillips Fine Art Auctioneers)*

135. Andromache, GW 33, panel, October 1902; signed "Andromache, Geo. Woodall."

137. *Left:* Ivory bowl with stylized floral decoration; attributed to Thomas Webb. *(Courtesy of the Dudley Art Gallery)*
138. *Right:* Elephant-handled ivory bowl with stylized flowers. *(Courtesy of the Dudley Art Gallery)*

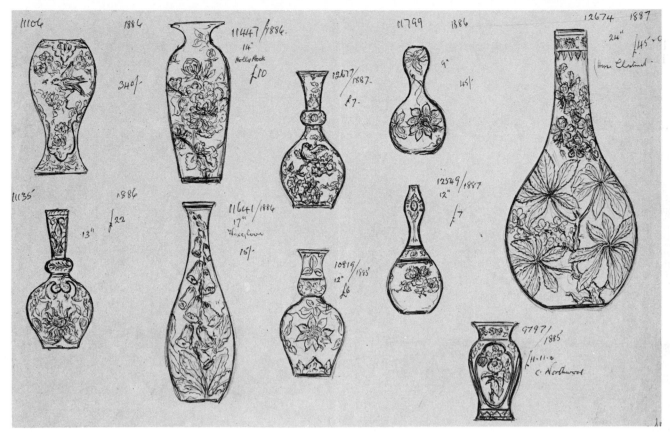

139. From the records of Stevens & Williams. *(Courtesy of Stevens & Williams, Brierley Hill, England)*

140. Fruit and Flower Girls, opal on deep claret ground; 12½ inches; signed "Fruit and Flower Girls." *(Courtesy of Sotheby's Belgravia, Inc., London)*

141. Claret jug in foxglove pattern, 12¼ inches. Silver mark 1884. *(Copyright Sotheby's Belgravia, Inc., London)*

143. Aphrodite plaque, 15 inches, carved by John Northwood and signed "John Northwood II, Aphrodite and Attendants." 1905. (*Courtesy of Kenneth Northwood, son of John Northwood II*)

→

←

142. This is a sketch by John Northwood II, 16 inches in diameter, titled "To Wake the Morn" (from Shakespeare's poem *The Rape of Lucrece*) and signed "JNII." Central figure is the coming of the dawn, bringing with her light, life and sound. (*Courtesy of Kenneth Northwood, son of John Northwood II*)

144. Undine, 12-inch vase, signed "Geo. Woodall." (*Courtesy of the Currier Gallery of Art, Manchester, New Hampshire, the Albert and Sophie Murray Collection*)

145. Ivory vase with applied insects and birds. *(Courtesy of Christie's, London)*

146. Vase with strawberry cameo decoration, white on red; 8 inches. *(Courtesy of Christie's, London)*

147. Raising an Altar to Bacchus, 15½ inches; signed "A.L.–78, Raising an Altar to Bacchus." Brierley Hill Glass Collection. *(Courtesy of Charles E. Tuttle Company, publisher of the authors'* Carved and Decorated European Art Glass)

148. Hercules Restoring Alcestis to her Husband Admetus, 14¼ inches; signed "A.L. 1877, Hercules Restoring Alcestis to her Husband Admetus." Brierley Hill Glass Collection. *(Courtesy of Charles E. Tuttle Company, publisher of the authors'* Carved and Decorated European Art Glass)

169

149. Aphrodite, signed "Geo. Woodall." Picture was made from a Woodall glass plate. *(Courtesy of the Dudley Art Gallery)*

150. Psyche, 7½-inch vase, white on brown; signed "Psyche, T. & G. Woodall, Thomas Webb & Sons." Picture was made from a Woodall glass plate. *(Courtesy of the Dudley Art Gallery)*

151. Diana and Endymion, W 2786; 17½ inches, white on brown plaque; signed "T. & G. Woodall." Picture was made from a Woodall glass plate. *(Courtesy of the Dudley Art Gallery)*

PRICE BOOK

Thomas Webb & Sons Price Book, which we reprint in this volume, refers specifically to work that was done in great part by George Woodall and the "Woodall Team." The book measures 6¼ by 7¾ inches.

It is the manufacturer's record of the name of the aritst, the number and size of the piece, the artist's cost in hours spent, and the selling price of the article. Sales prices of course reflect the value placed on the glass at that time. Details are concerned with the titles of the more important cameo figure plaques and vases, as well as a group of ivory cameo and floral pieces. Names were given by George Woodall to most of the significant glass carvings, though these were not always signed with a title.

Sometimes George Woodall did a series of similar subjects, though no two would be absolutely identical; many were unsigned by him.

SKETCH BOOK

The Sketch Book, approximately 1½ feet by 2 feet, has Woodall's original designs in it, with occasional names of the Woodall Team.

Frequently the Price Book contains the notation "T & Co.," which can be assumed to be Tiffany & Co., a valued customer of Webb's. Names that continually appear are "Barbe," "Facer," "Nash," "Fereday," "Guest," "Kritschman," and "Kny."

There were generally only two signatures used by Woodall: "G. Woodall" and "Geo. Woodall." We have seen "Woodall" in block letters on a plaque of Sappho, but this is rare. With few exceptions, Woodall signatures appear on the opal part of the glass, worked into the design. "T. & G. Woodall" appears primarily on early pieces; seldom is "T. Woodall" seen alone. Only on occasion does the date appear, and then with the signatures. Titled pieces frequently have engraving underfoot, or on the back of plaques. "Thomas Webb & Sons" was used extensively, frequently with the addition of "Gem Cameo," as well as the mark "Webb" by itself.

MARKS AND SIGNATURES

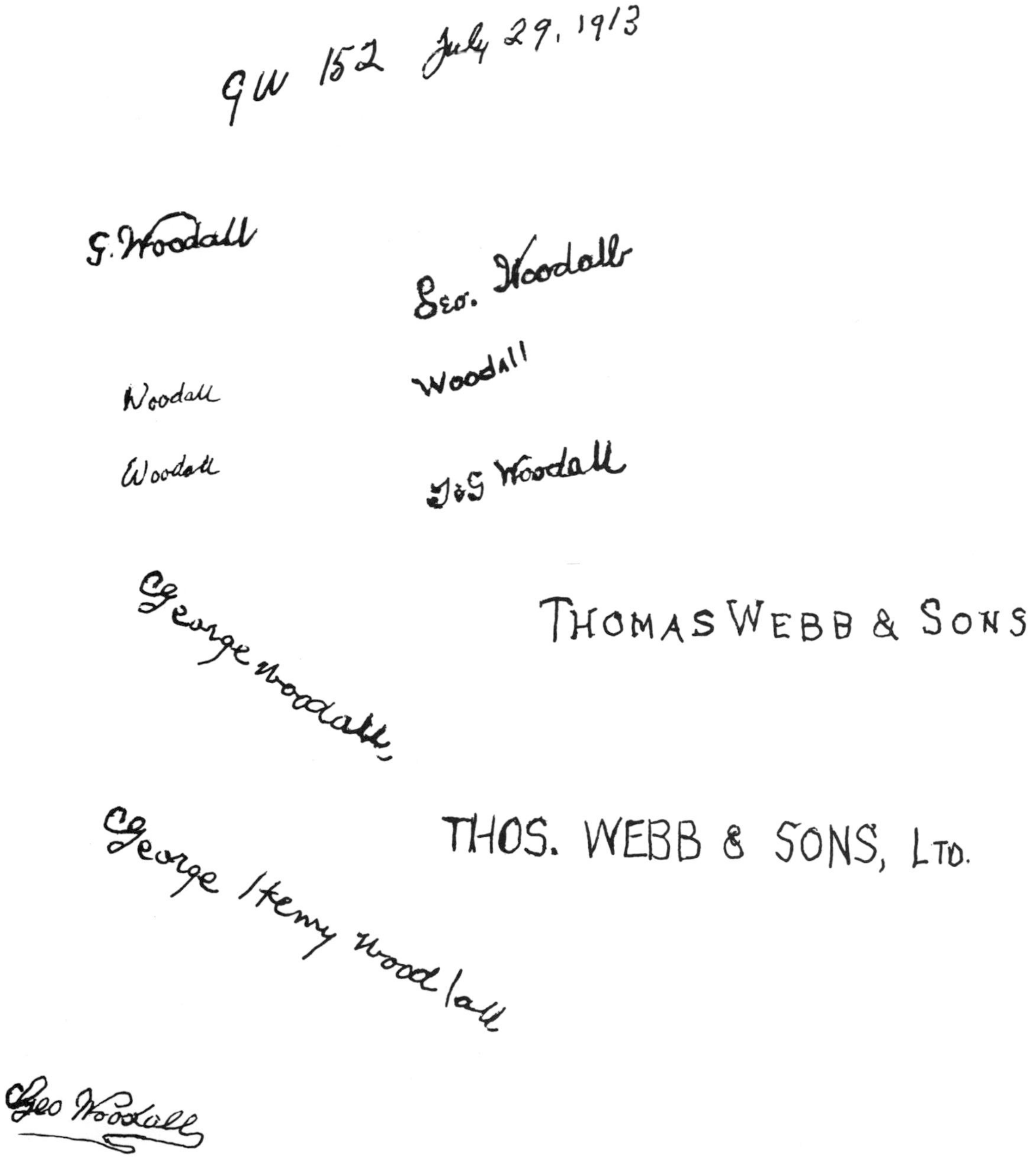

GW 152 July 29, 1913

G. Woodall

Geo. Woodall

Woodall

Woodall

Woodall

J&G Woodall

George Woodall

THOMAS WEBB & SONS

George Henry Woodall

THOS. WEBB & SONS, LTD.

Geo Woodall

Woodalls inch Price
for Cameo

4 inch 3/-
5 "   3/6
6 .   4/6
7 .   6/6
8 -   10/
9 —   13/6
10 —   16/3
11 —   18/6
12 —   21/-

TELEPHONE Nº 811. HOLBORN.

Telegrams { "CASSOCK, LONDON."
           "WILKES, STOURBRIDGE."

FROM

MANUFACTORY
GLASS WORKS
STOURBRIDGE

THOMAS WEBB & SONS, LIMITED.
Glass Manufacturers.
11, CHARTERHOUSE STREET.
HOLBORN CIRCUS.
LONDON E.C.

London. Managing Directors.
CONGREVE JACKSON.

April 23ʳᵈ 1908

Cameos

1.	Vase	"Morning" (damaged)		£60. 0. 0
1.	D.	"Phyllis"	W. 2817	16. 16. 0
1.	D.	"Diana"	G.W. 26	18. 10. 0
1.	D.	"Hebe"	W. 2827	18. 18. 0
1.	D.	"Seaform"	G.W. 6	42. 0. 0
1.	D.	"Ganymede" × sold to Phillip 1910		15. 0. 0
1.	D.	"Sirene"	G.W. 25	×22. 10. 0
1.	D.	"Dawn"	G.W. 20	14. 0. 0
1.	D.	"Flora"	G.W. 10	14. 0. 0
1.	Plaque	"The Dance" ×		350. 0. 0
1.	D.	"Diana Endymion"	G.W. 28	125. 0. 0
1.	Panel × "Calypso"		G.W. 32	63. 0. 0
1.	D. × "Undine"		G.W. 31	63. 0. 0
1.	Claret decanter × "Elgin marbles"			125. 0. 0

| Please return |

×. reduced to £20/-/. Oct. 27/08.

173

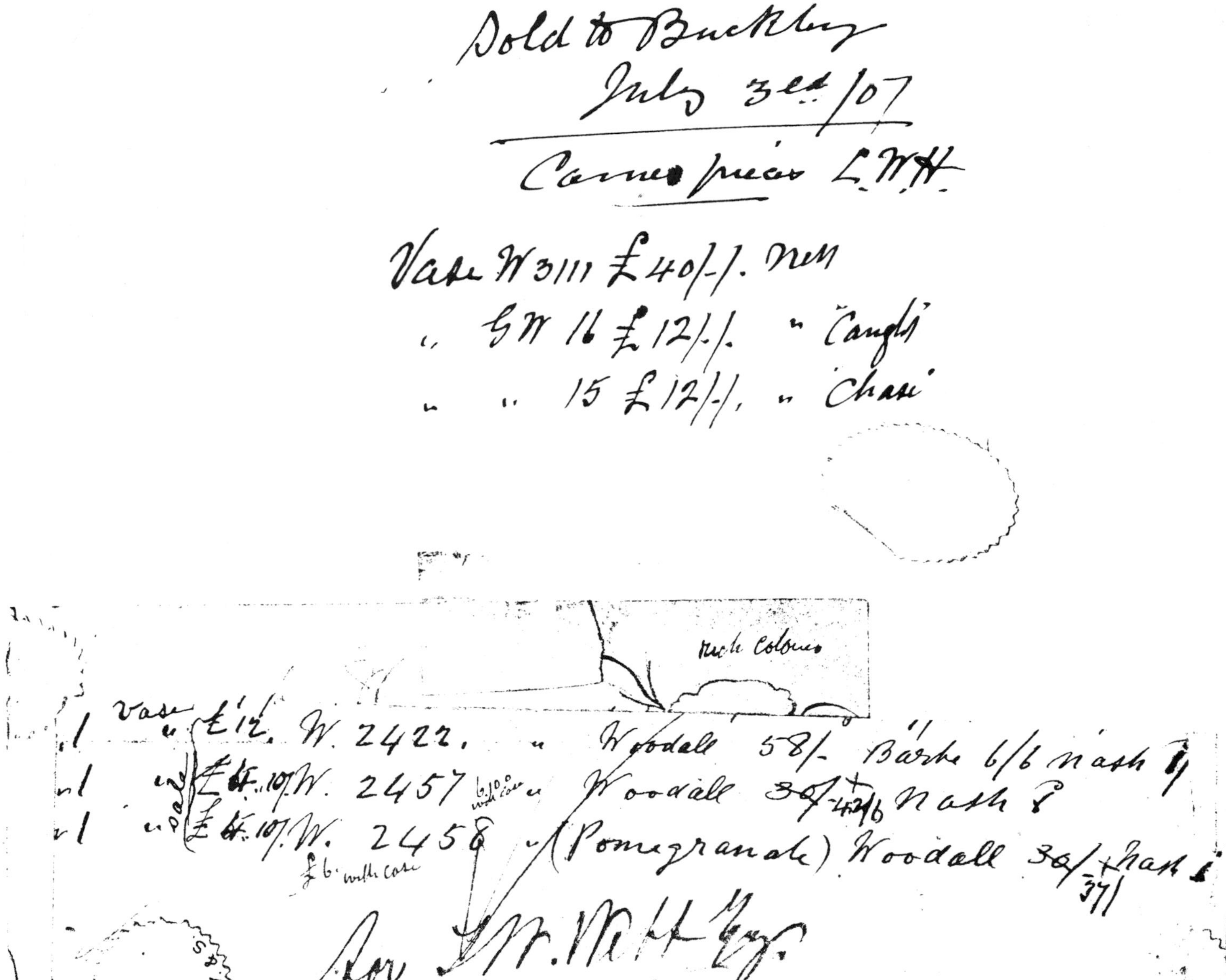

Sold to Buckley
July 3rd/07
Cameo pieces L.W.H.

Vase W 3111 £40/-/. nett
" GW 16 £12/-/. " Caught
" " 15 £12/-/. " Chase

rich colours

1 vase £12. W. 2422. " Woodall 58/- Barke 6/6 nash 1/
1 " £4.10/. W. 2457 £6.10.0 with case " Woodall 30/- 42/6 nash ?
1 " £4.10/. W. 2458 " (Pomegranate) Woodall 30/- 37/ nash
£6. with case

For L.W. Webb Esq.

2411 9" Vase Cameo on [illegible] 8.0

Cost of Moore Vases sent to day

No.	Number	Etching	rough	Painting	Brushing	Total Cost	Value
J. 134	30	3/-	10/6	3/-	2/-	18/6	✓
,, 141	48	4/-	9/-	3/-	1/-	17/-	✓
,, 136	30		34/6	6/6	1/9	45/9	✓
,, 140		16/-	10/-	3/-	1/-	30/-	✓
,, 137	20/7	6/-	40/-	3/-	1/6	50/6	✓
,, 142	50		5/6	13	6	6/10	✓
,, 139	60	2/-		6	1/-	3/6	
,, 138	50	3/-		6	1/-	4/6	
,, 143	36	5/6		1/6		7/-	✓
,, 144	22	4/6		6/6		11/-	✓
,, 145		6/-		4/3		10/-	✓ 2
,, 99	12		6/-	8	6	7/2	✓
,, 148	30	9/-	16/-	3	1/6	29/6	✓
,, 150	40	6/-	6/-	1/6	9	14/3	2/-
,, 151	50		6/-	10	1/-	6/10	
,, 152	120		1/3	10	6	2/4	✓
,, 146	30	6/-		3/6		9/6	✓
,, 66. 63/4 28		8/-	24/-	4/-	1/6	37/6	✓
,, 147 24		5/-	20/-	3/6	3/6	32/-	✓
,, 149		2/6	4/-	1/6	1/-	12/-	✓
,, 153			18/6	2/6	9	21/9	✓ 4
,, 154			12/6	1/3	6	14/3	
,, 155			5/6	1/3	6	7/3	
,, 156			4/6	8	4	5/6	✓

Number	Articles	Cost	Sale
W. 680	9" Guard Vase	Woodall £8.10.0	see Cos" on &c
K. 102	4½ Mottled Vase Carved & Gilt	Kritchman 15/- Facer 7/6 Barbe 6/6	80/-
F. 100	6½ 26" Vase Carved & Gilt	Facer 15/- Eng 2/6 Barbe 4/6. nash 1/6	63/-
F. 100½	7½ Vase " "	C/- 15/- B. 4/6 Eng 2/6 N. 1/6	60/-
F. 102	8½ Flat side Vase Carved & Gilt	C/- 18/- B. 4/6 Eng 45/- N. 2/-	
F. 102½	8½ " " "	C/- 20/-. B 15/-. Eng 45/- N 2/-	
F. 103	5½ Vase Carved & Gilt	C/- 3/- B 2/- Eng 9/- nash 6	£6. 40/- 4.10.0 with Case
W. 2420	4 Small Guard Vase	Woodall 20/-	
W. 2421	4 " "	" 24/6	
W. 2428	6½ Jade Flat Side Vase	Woodall 46/- Barbe 6. nash 1/-	£ 5.
F. 101	7" Vase Green on Burmese	C/- 10/- Barbe 2/6 Eng 20/- nash 9	£ 5. 5. 0
K. 103	" " "	C/- 12/- Eng 25/- nash 9	£ 6. 4.10.0
K. 100	5¾" Flat side Vase	Kritchman 84/- nash 1/6 Facer 30/-	
W. 2440	9" " " "	Woodall £6.15.0 nash 2/-	
W. 2342	6½ Vase Ruby or opal & on flint	Woodall 33/- n 1/6	£ 5. 0. 0
W. 2336	6" Vase opal on Flint	Woodall 37/6 n 1/6	£ 4.17.1
W. 2400	4" " White on Yellow	Woodall 12/-	33/- 3/-
W. 2413	Green on Burmese Ground 6" " Ruby Brown & 6	Woodall 40/- nash 6 Barbe 2/-	£ 6. 6. 0
W. 2415	6" " Do	Woodall 38/- nash 6 Barbe 2/-	
W. 7737	Paper Weight White Med & White on flint Solid Ruby Blue filled on Flint	W. 20/- nash 6 W 13/6	5/- 32/-

Number	Article	Costs	Sale
W. 2423	6 in. Vase Green on Burmese body Ruby & Brown	Woodall 45/- Nash 6 Barbe 2/-	
W. 2273	6½ Vase Burmese & Opal	9/6	28/-
W. 2381	6½ „ White on Yellow	6/3 · 45/- 25/-	
W. 2385	6½ „ White on Tricolore on Burmese	23/9	80/-
W. 2281	6 in Bowl perforated Green Pink & White		
W. 2442	3½ Bowl	W. 37/6 Nash 1/-	£4. 16-6
W. 2448	3½ Do	29/6 nº 9	70/-
W. 2444	2 Hd. Cup	W. 33/6 Nash 1/-	£3. 12. 6
W. 2430	5½ Jade Vase	23/- nº 9	50/-
W. 2441	5 in Flat side Vase	34/-	75/-
W. 2429	4¾ Jade Vase	W. 19/6 N. 6	46/-
W. 2402	16 in 2 Hd. Vase Figure &c	✳ £ 28. 0 - 0	£ 60.
W. 2403	„ 2 Hd „ the Fruit seller	£ 28. 10. 0	£ 60. £50
	8½ Vase Fleur on White Blue, White, Turquois. &c	W. 58/- Barbe 6/6 n. 1/6	
W. 2481	6 in Vase Coloured body	W. 72/-. P.T. 10. n. 2/-	£12.
W. 2459	9 in flat side Vase Jade	W £ 6. 2. 0. Robed 2/- Plain 10/	£ 14
W. 2477	6½ „ Vase Coloured Metal	W. 76/-. P.T.10. n. 2/-	£ 12
W. 2426	7½ Vase Carved Coloured Metal	W. 24/6. B 5/-. n 1/3.	70/-
W. 1810	6 in flat side Vase White on Red Carved & Gilt	W. 14/6 B. 10/	.
W 2282	Vase	Woodall 82/- Barbel 30/-	1.00 12.0.0

3

Number	Articles	Cost	Sale
W.2442	6 1/2 — Vase Jade	W. 42/- B.6. n.9	100/-
W.2445	6in Bowl Jade	W. 97/- n.4.	£10.
W. 2446	6in " "	W. 90/- n./6	£10.
W. 2493	4in Bowl Light Brown on opal on flint	W. 21/6 . P. 1/6	55/-
W 2467	5in Vase Curio	W. 24/- . n.6	60/-
W. 2472	6in Vase Curio carved & gilt	W. 42/- P.T.10 n2/6. B/6	£ 15.
W. 2489	8in Vase Curio Carved	W. 62/- P.T.10 n.2/-	£ 8. 8.03
W. 2482	5 1/2 in Curio Carved	W. 115/- P.T.10. n.9	£ 5. 5.0 with case
W. 2466	4in Vase " " & Gilt	W. 21/6 n. 9. P.T.14. B 2/6	75/-
W. 2487	4in " " " "	W. 12/6 . n.4-	32/-
R. 11.	6in Flat side Vase Jade	L. 84/- Facer 28/-	£ 10-10-0
W. 2478	5 1/2 Vase Curio carved	W. 63/- P.T. 14. n.6	£ 7-7.0
W. 2475.	5 1/2 " " "	W. 56/- P.T.14. n.8	£ 7. 7.0
W. 2480	6in Vase " "	W. 96/- P.T.10 n.6.	£ 12.
W. 2470	6 1/2 " " Carved & Gilt	W. 50/- B.5/6. n.1/6.	£ 8.
W. 2498	3 1/2 Bowl " "	W. 41/-	£ 4.
W 2471	7 1/2 Vase " " "	W. £ 5.15.0. B 3/-	£ 10-10-0
W. 2473	5 1/2 " " " "	W. 38/- B. 4/-	£ 7. 0.0
W. 2426	5 3/4 " " " "	W. 40/6 B. 5/- n.1/-	£ 4. 4.0

178

Number	Article		Sale
	7in Vase	T.W.&S.	£25.
	Curio Ca	Neo	sale £12.
W.2483.		0.×	„ £18. 7.
F.104	6in Vase Carved	0.0	„ £18. 35/-
K.105	3½ Vase Curio	£8.5.0	35/-
W.2486.	4½ „ „ Carved	W. 34/-	105/-
W.2491	„ „ „ „ Gilt	W.28/- Barbe 15/6	£9.
W.2497	6½ Vase „ Carved	W. 32/6	66/-
W.2496	5½ „ „ „ Gilt	W. 43/6. B 7/6	140/-
W.2485	4½ „ „ „	W. 36/6	105/-
W.2516.	9in „ „ „	W.12/6 ~~15/6~~ ~~Rd~~ Plain ~~13/6~~	34/-
W.2517.	„ „ „ „	W. 13/-	34/-
W.2518.	6in „ „ „	W. 14/6	35/-
W.2519.	6½ „ „ „	W. 13/6	33/-
W.2520	6½ „ „ „	W. 13/6	33/-
W.2521	5in „ „ „	W. 12/6	30/-
W.2522	6½ „ „ „ „	W. 8/-	21/-
W.2523	6½in „ „ „	W. 8/-	21/-
W.2524	6in „ „ „	W. 8/6	30/-
W.2525	6¼in „ „ „	W. 8/6	22/-
W.2526	6in „ „ „	W. 13/-	30/-
W.2513	„ Flower Girls	W. 16.10.0	£45.0.0
W.2514	„ Fairies Spring	W. 16.15.0	£42.0.0

Number	Articles	Costs	Sale
W. 2527	6 in Vase Curio Carved	W 13/-	30/-
F. 108.	6" " " "	F. 4/. Engd. 8/-	25/-
F. 109.	6½ " " " "	F. 3/. " 6/-	26/-
W. 2543. x	6" " " "	14/9-	34/-
F. 105.	8½ " " " Hills	F 20/- Engd. 25/. B.12/6 n/65	£ 10.
F. 106	4½ Bowl " " "	F 40/. Engd 2/6 B. 4/.	£ 6.
W. 2488	4¼ " " "	W. 59/6. n. 1/6.	£ 10.
W. 2490	5½ Vase " " "	W. 56/. B3/6.	£ 7.
W. 2496	5½ " " " "	W. 39/. B. 3/6	£ 5.5.0
W. 2492	6½ " " " "	W. 40/. B.16/6	£ 8.0.0 with care
W. 2494	5½ " " " "	W. 43/6. B7/6. n 1/9.	£ 7.0.0 9.0.0 with
W. 2500	3½ - Bowl " "	W. 25/.	60/-
W. 2533.	" " " "	W. 22/6. n 1/.	80/-
W. 2515	" " " "	W. 26/6 n 1/.	60/-
W. 2529.	" " " "	W. 28/6. n 1/-	60/
W. 2512	8 in Vase " "	W. 45/- n 1/.	120/-
W. 69	3 in " " " "	W. 16/. B. 6/6	40/-
F. 107	8½ in " " " "	F 10/. Engd 8/. B.8/-	100/-
F. 110	9 in " " " "	F. 25/-Engd 15/-B 2/.	100/-
W. 2481	Vase Curio		12.0.0

Number	Articles	Costs	Sale
W.1951	Sorbet Cup Curio	W. 1/9	5/-
"	Saucer Do	"	5/-
W.2566	6½ Oval Curio Carved (in case)	W. 144/- case 45/- Plain 20/-	£25.
W.2530	11 in Vase Curio Carved	W. £7-6-0 flaws, reduced to £10. Nash 2/6	£18. £10.
W.2531	11 in Vase " "	W. £5.10.0 n 2/6	£15. 12.10.0
W.2534	5 in Vase " Carved Hji	W. 42/- B 8/6	£5.
W.2510	2 Ft ⁴ Vase Carved	Cens recurring from Baccarus a restorative cup	£35. 27.10.0 £35.
W.2537	3¾ in Bowl Curio Carved	W. 25/-	63/.
W.2538	6 in Vase " "	W. 12/6.	33/-
W.2539	6 in " " " "	W. 12/6.	33/-
W.2540	6 in " " " "	W. 17/-	45/-
W.2541	6 in Bowl " "	W. 39/-	100/-
W.2542	3½ " " " "	W. 32/6	80/-
W.2543			
W.2544	5¾ in Vase		£7.
W.2545	6¼ in Vase Curio Carved	W. 36/-	£6.
W.2546	6 in Bowl " "	W. 5/2/-	120/-
W.2554	4 in " " " "	W. 32/-	70/-

Number	Article	Cost	Sale
ℱ 1114	5½ Vase Jade Carved	ℱ 12/. Eng⁹ 4/. Cut 2/-	£6.10.0
K 107	6 in flat side Vase Cameo		£6.15.0
W. 2551	Hd Cross Curio Carved	W. 28/-	£4.
"	Tumbler " "	W. 10/6	25/-
W. 2552	Hd Cross " "	W. 26/- "	70/-
"	Tumbler " "	W. 9/6	25/-
W. 2555	Claretein " "	W. 28/6	70/-
W. 2556	" " "	W. 58/-	120/-
W. 2568	" " "	W. 50/-	95/-
W. 2569	" " "	W. 44/-	95/-
W. 2584	Small Tube Cameo	W. 2/-	4/6
W. 2585	" " "	W. 2/3	5/-
W. 2586	" " "	W. 1/9	4/-
W. 2179	12 in Vase "	W. £6.10.6	
W. 2043	12 " " "	W. £7.	
W. 1776	12 " 2 Hd " "		
W. 2577	Paper Weight Curio	20/.	45/-
W. 2574	" " "	16/.	38/.
W. 2445	6 in Bowl Flus Carved	W. 82/-. N 3/. (plain 5/6)	£ 10.10.0

182

Number	Article	Cost	Sale
W. 823.	Hock, Cameo		70/.
W. 655	" "		84/.
W. 2322	" "	W. 36/.	70/-
W. 2321	" "	W. 40/-	76/-
W. 2575	9in Vase "	W. 58/-	£ 6.6.0
W. 2550	Globe Bowl Curio		£ 10.
W. 2571	6 1/2in Vase "	W. 42/-	£ 5.5.0
W. 2572	Puff Box "	W. 46/-	£ 5.5.0
W. 2573	6in flat side Vase "	W. 62/-	£ 10.10.0 ~~£ 8.8.0~~
W. 2578	8in Vase Cameo	W. £5.10.0	£ 12.10.0
W. 2579	8in " "	W. £5.10.0	£ 12.10.0
W. 2580	8in " "	W £ 6.	£ 12.10.0
W. 2581	8in " "	W. £ 5.5.0	£ 12.10.0
W. 2582	10in " "	N. £ 11.12.0	£ 25.
W. 2676	10in " "	W. £ 6.10.0	£ 15.
W. 2601	Honey "		
W. 2591	Basin "	W. 2/4	7/
N. 2590	" "	W 2/6	7/-
W. 2595	7in Vase Curio	W. 70/-. N 4/-.	£ 10.

Number	Article	Cost	Tra...
W. 2599	7ᵢₙ Vase Curio	Plain 15/. W 44/-	£ 6.10.0
W. 2447.a	9ᵢₙ " Cameo	W. 39/-	70/.
W 2447.B.	" "	W. 39/-	70/.
W 2447.C.	" "	W 32/.	70/.
W. 2593	4ᵢₙ Globe Curio Carved Bowl & Gilt	W. 19/6 B.H/.	63/-
W. 2549.	10½ₙ Vase Curio		£ 10-10.0
W. 2567	9½ₙ Vase & Cover Cameo	W. £29.	£ 80.
W. 2638	4ᵢₙ Globe Curio	W. 18/6 n/6	45/-
K. 109	5ᵢₙ Vase Jade	K. 23/ 7 7/6 n/.	70/.
W. 2604	6½ₙ Curio	W. 73/.	£ 10.
W. 2605	8½ₙ Vase Flat side Curio	W. 108. Cut 3/6 (Plain 30/.)	£ 14.14.0
W. 2617.	3½ₙ Globe Toilet Curio	W. 22/6. n/6⁵	45/.
W. 2618	" " " "	2½lbs W. 19/6 n/6⁵	45/.
K. 111	5ᵢₙ Bowl Curio	30/V. 7 15/ K 18/6 n 3/-	85/.
K. 110	6ᵢₙ Flat side Vase Jade.	K 42/. W 11/. n/6. 7 7/6	£ 7. 7.
W. 2602	9ᵢₙ Vase Cameo	W. 64/-	£ 8.8.0
W. 2610.	2ᵈ Doctᵣ Curio	W. 42/.	88/.
W. 2615	8ᵢₙ Vase " Gilt	3½lbs plain 30/. W 58/- B.3/6 n 4/6	£ 8. 8.6
W. 2616	8½ " Jade " "	W. 35/- B 16/6 n 3/6	£ 5.10.0

10

Number	Articles	Cost	Sale
W. 2626	9ᵘ Vase Cameo	W. 56/-	£ 9.9.
W. 2638	4ᵘ Globe Bowl Curio Gilt	W. 52/- B. 1/- N. 1/8	110/-
F 116	8ᵘ Vase Curio Gilt	F 25/- B. 8/-	100/-
F 113.	9ᵘ Vase Curio	F 15/- N/6 B. 5/6	55/-
F 111	6½ᵘ " Curio	F 35/- N 2/6 (Plain 15/-)	£ 4.10.
W. 2636	Scent Jar & Cover Curio		£ 2.2.
W 2637.	" " " "		33/-
W. 2643.	" " " "		45/-
W. 2644	" " " "		45/-
W. 2652	" " " "		18/-
W. 2656	" " " "		50/-
W 2654	" " " "		50/-
W. 2658	" " " "	W. 23/- (7/6 Plain) N /3 Lining 2/6	60/-
W 2609	15½ᵘ 2Hd Vase Cameo figure	W. £ 25. 3 P.T. (for cost 25/6)	£ 55 £ 66.
W. 2582	12ᵘ " " "	10 PT. W £ 11-15.0	£ 30
W 2341	Hock "	W. 34/6	70/-
W. 2340	" "	W. 27/6	55/-
F 115	7ᵘ Vase Curio Gilt	F 15/- Eng⁰ 15/- B 8/6 N 1/6	£ 5.0
112	11½ᵘ " " "	F 10/- Eng⁰ 24/- B 3/- N 2/6	90/-

185

Number	Articles	Cost	Sale
F. 114	7 in Bowl Curio Gilt	J 10/- B1/3 $^{pt}_{123}$	58
W. 2627	L/S Vase ~~Hover~~ part Cameo part End	2 1/2 lbs } W. } N. }	£ 13..10.0 }
"	" Cover "	1/4 } ov. } pd }	
"	" Stand for do "	2 lbs 19/6 5/-	£ 3.
"	S/S Bowl "	2 3/4 lb W } N }	£ 12.10.0
"	" Cover "	1/4 } un/. } pr/d }	}
"	" Stand for do "	1 3/4 17/6 - 3/6	£ 2.10.0
. 2588	12 in Vase Hover Cameo	W. £ 25. 5.0	£ 65.
2660	12 " " Curio Cameo figure	W. £ 28.10.0	£ 80.
2390	6 1/2 " Cameo	W. 25/.	80/.
2659	5 in " Curio	Plain 7/6 W. 12/6 n 2/6	40/.
2365	7 in " "	W. 18/6	42/.
2382	5 in " Cameo	W. 5/3	25/.
2690	Claretun Curio	W. 14/6	. 40/.
. 2684	" "	W. 20/6. n 2/6	50/. .
. 2682	" "	W. 28/6. n 2/.	63/.
2677	11 1/2 Vase Hover Cameo Figure	W. 25.10.0	£ 63.
2710	Oval for Brush Back Cameo	W. 22/-	60/.
2711	" " " " menno }	W. 21/-	60/.

186

12

Number	Articles	Costs	Sale
W. 2686	Vase & Flower Cameo	W. £32.70.0	£ 100.
W. 2715	Jet Deer Vine & Grape Flint	6 W. 50/ (colored)	£ 6-10.0
W. 2713	Vase Cameo	W £ 5.5.0 (colored)	£ 15. 16/-
F. 2/115	9ʺ Flat Side Vase Curio		£ 18.
W. 2712	6½ Vase & Cover Cameo	W. £ 5. (Estimate)	£ 15.15.0 14-12.0
W. 2682	Cut Deer Curio	W. 25/-	70/-
W. 24.69	3in Vase Curio Gilt	W. 8/6 B 1/3. 72 P.9.	21/.
W. 2714	9ʺ Vase Cameo Dancing Girl	W £6.0.0	£ 15.
W. 2716	7½ Flat side Vase Flower Gatherer	W £ 9.15.0	£ 30. £20 was
W. 2718	10ʺ Vase & Flower Diana & nymph	W £ 33.5.0	£ 105.
W. 2720	2 76ᵗʰ Vase White on Dark Brown	W £ 15.0.0	£ 45.
W. 2679	Toilet Flint Coloured Metal Cameo	W. 11/6	30/-
W. 2681	„ Flint „	W 10/6	22/6
W. 2721	10in Vase White on Brown Psyche	W £ 10-5.0	£ 31.10.0
W. 2722	10in Do. Phyllis at the Fountain	W £ 11-5.0	£ 31.10.0
W. 2723	„ Do. a maid of Athens	W £ 11.5.0	£ 31.10.0 21-0 was
W. 2724	12in Vase White on Brown Subject Inspiration	W £19.10.0	£55.0
W. 2726	7in Jar & Cover Subject a Priest nook	W £17.5.0	£50.0.0 42.10.0
W. 2710	15in Vase White over green Subject Hebe &c	W £ 20. plain 40/ nash 6/	£ 65.0.0

6, Church Grove

187

Number	Articles	Cost	Sale
W. 2635	S/S Scent Jar & Cover Dark Brown & White		63/-
W. 2651	Scent Jar & Cover Flint cameo	12/6	40/-
W. 2662	2 Hd Scent Jar & Cover Flint cameo	W. 10/6	30/-
W. 2728	White on Brown Natures Mirror	W. £ 15.5.0	£ 45.0.0
W. 2730	(Pandora) Vase, White 13½ in on Brown	W. £ 38.10.0	£ 100.
W. 2702	Tusk for Mt Ruby & Opal & Topaz on Flint	W. 29/- Nash 4/6	70/-
W. 2688	Claret Decr flat side all flint	W. 20/6 8 "	50/-
W. 2661	2 Hd Scent Jar & Cover Flint cameo	W. 19/6	45/-
W. 2725	15 in 2 Hdd Vase White on Blue, filled to foot	Nash and D.P. 5/- W. £22.10.0	£ 50 £ 75
W. 2731	13 in Vase, White on Brown (Feathered Favourets)	W. £ 20.10.0	£ 55.
W. 2552 D.	3½ Globe Bowl	W. 7/6	21/-
Z. 118	10 in Vase White on Blue	W. Estimate 75/-	£ 10.10.0
Z. 119	Jug White on Ruby	" " 8/- (Ivordale Estimate made 15/-)	42/-
Z. 120	10 in Vase White on Ruby (18)	" " 30/-	£ 5.10.0
Z. 121	10 in " White on "	" " 12/- diaper ex 5/6	55/- 45/-
Z. 122	6 in Vase " "	" " 6/-	26/-
Z. 123	5 in Vase " "	" " 5/6	18/-
Z. 124	2½ Violet " "	" " 7/6	20/-
Z. 125	5 in Vase " on Topaz	" " 3/6	12/6
W. 2693	Vase Cameo roughed for Mounting	£ 24.0.0	

14

Number	Articles	Cost	Sale
F. 126	5 in Vase White on Blue on Ruby	Wood & Co Estimate 6/-	21/-
F. 127	8½ in Vase, White on Ruby on Blue	" " 25/-	84/-
F. 128	" Vase White on Topaz ⑳	" " (with diaper 16/3)	58/3 50/-
F. 129	Toilet square White "	" " 12/-	30/-
F. 130	8 in Vase White on Blue on Flint	" diaper extra 6/- 16/ (with diaper 63/-)	50/-
F. 131	7½ Vase White on Ruby on Flint	" diaper 5/9 added 30/-	£4. 10. 0 90/-
F. 132	9 in Vase White on light Blue	" " 16/1	63/-
F. 133	7 in Vase White on Blue on Ruby	" (diaper 5/ 10/6)	50/. 42/-
W. 2729	Champer Brown on Green on Flint	W. 18/-	50/-
F. 134	3½ in Vase White on Pink on Topaz	W. estimate 1/6 diaper 1/6	6/- 8/6
F. 135	4½ Vase Red on Ivory	W. " 7/- diaper 3/3	20/- 26/
F. 136	4/- Vase White on Red on Ivory	W. " 7/-	20/-
F. 137	5/- " White on Ruby on Topaz	W. " 4/-	15/-
F. 138	6 in Vase White on Ruby on Topaz	W. " 5/.	18/-
F. 139	" " White on Blue	W. " 3/- diaper extra 2/9	12/6 18 with diaper
F. 140	8 in Vase White on Topaz	W. " 10/- diaper 5/3	32/- 40/-
F. 141	9½ " "	W. " 12/- diaper exc 7/9	44 55/ 35/
F. 142	10 in Vase "	W. " 14/-	42/-
F. 143	" " White on Blue	W. " 15/-	45/.

189

Number	Articles	Cost	Sale
W. 2335	6 in Vase White on Topaz	W. 11/6	35/-
W. 2468	5½ in 2 Hd Vase Curio Ivory on Ruby	W. 44/6	40/-
F. 144	9 in Vase White on Blue	W. Estimate 30/-	88/-
W. 2669	8¾ in Vase White on Blue	W. 16/6	Sale 63/-
F. 145	6 inch Flat sid Vase Ruby on Green on rich yellow opal inside	W. £4.0.0 Estimated at	£ 15/-/- £12 11
W. 2693	Vase for mounting Flint body brown on opal outside	W. 90/-	£14-14-0 }
F. 146	Ivory on Flint part carved + part Eng[d]	Fritsch Estimate 30/-	£24.0-0 £.4.0.0 }
W. 2733.	3¾ in Plaque "Floralia"	£37.0.0	£110.
W. 2734	Plaque "Cupid in Disgrace"	£40.0.0	£120
W. 2732	3¾ " "Aphrodite"	£42.00	£125. £125/-/-
W. 2533	7 in Bowl Ivory + flint	Cost 8/6	30/-
W. 2746	Menu 5 in x 3½ full White on Lght Brown		
2747	do		
2748	Do		
W. 2749	do		
W. 2756	Small Egg Scent Bottle Ruby on White on Topaz	W 3/-	7/-
W. 2759.	Plaque "Favourits"	W. £48.0.0.	£150.
W. 2760	Panel White on Brown Plaque "Flora"	£16.5.0	£35 guin
W. 2765	Vase "Penelope"	15 10	£42.-

16

Number	Articles	Cost	Sale
W 2767	13+10 "Panel" a nymph of the sea	£ 32.10.0 (Frame 10/-)	£63/-
W 2757	8 i Vase Cameo spray White on Ruby on Topaz	Estimate in all 17/9	45/-
T 147	Jade Vase flat side	" 24/-	63/-
W 2243	5 i Vase Cameo, colours W 3/6 purple body Barbe 6/-		30/-
W 2779	8 i Vase White on Blue Peacock Feather	Estimate 6/-	25/-
W 2778	9½ i Vase White on Blue	" 35/-	105/-
W 2777	12 i Vase White on Blue	" 25/-	90/-
W 1709	12½ " White on Topaz	"	75/-
W 2785	Panel White on Brown Floral	Cost £16.15.0	£45.0.0
W 2786	incl 17½ Plaque White on Brown "Diana & Endymion"	" £58.10.0	£180.0.0 £100 £150.0.0
W 2790	Panel White on Brown Sappho	£23.10.0	£52.10.0
W 2787	White on Brown 9 i Vase Jasmine	14/6	45/-
" do	White on pink on Brown Jasmine	14/6	50/-
W 2788	9 i Vase White on Brown (Begonia	17/6	50/-
W 2789	White on Ruby on Topaz 9 i apple Blossom	17/6	65/-
W 2793	in Plaque White on Brown 8¼ "Un jour d'été"	W/15.10.0 Frame 9/6	£38.0.0 £42
W 2792	Plaque Panel White on Claret Brown Psyche w Pandora	£13.6.0 Frame 7/6	£37.10/-
W 2692	12 i Vase Black on White Cut & Carved	W. 100/- Nash 25/-	£21.0.0
W 2796	3 i Vase White on Brown Cupid dancing	24/6	70/-

x reduced 8/8/01

191

Number	Articles	Cost	Sale
W 2795.	10 in Vase W on B Pomona	£ 23,10 0	£ 60.
W 2794	16½ in Plaque, W on B Intruders	£ 56 - 10 0	£ 160.
W. 2797	oval Plaque W on B 7½" x 5" Greek Girl	95/-	£15
W. 2801	Vase Corinna corinna	£ 22. 10. 0	£ 60.
W. 2802	Panel, Wandering Stars	£ 44. 10. 0	£ 120. Sold to Otto Müller Karlsruhe @ £95 nett
W. 2803	7½ in Vase, Clelie White on Brown	£ 5. 7. 6	£ 15. 15. 0
F 146	9 in Vase White on Blue	B orbe 4/6 Woodall Estimate 35/-	95/.
F 147.	8 in Vase Cameo Robe Etc White on Yellow	W. Estimate 10/- mob price diaper 5/6	40/-
F 148	4 in Vase White on Blue	W Est 4/- in all	40/.
W. 2377	6 in Vase White on Ruby		35/.
F. 149	Globe Toilet Jo. Ink & White on Ruby on Flint	Woodall W. Estimate 3/- diaper 2/6	16/6
F. 150	9 in Vase White on Ruby	Woodall Estimate 13/6 diaper 7/	50/.
F. 151	9 in light Blue on White on Ruby	" " 20/- in all extra 7/	50/.
F. 152	9½ Vase White on Yellow	diaper. 6/6	60/.
W. 2804	10 in Vase W on B Psyche	W £10 5 0	£ 28.
F. 153	9 in Vase White on Ruby flowers	W Estimate 13/6 diaper. 6/6	50/.
F. 154	9 in " White on Blue - flowers	diaper.	(old price 40/.) W.
F. 155	10 in Vase White on Topaz Jessom	W. Est 16/. diaper 5/6	50/. W
F. 156	6 in Vase White on Blue	W Est 18/6 in all	45/.

Number	Article	Costs	Sale
7.157	7" Vase White on Blue	W estimate in all 9/-	30/-
W. 2805	Oval Panel White on Brown 8 x 5½ (Water nymph)	W £ 7. 15 - 0 Finnigan 15.10. 15/11/5	£ 18. 15.10.0
W. 2806	9in Vase White on Brown (a Pompeian Girl)	W D 12. 6. 0	£ 30.
7.158.	4½ Vase White on Blue	diaper 2/6	14/6
7.159	6in Vase White on Topaz	" 3/3	30/-
7.160	7" Vase " " "	" 3/9	35/-
7.161	5" - White on Blue	" 2/9	36/-
7.162	7½" " " "	" 4/3	38/-
7.163 x	Claret (White & Ruby on Topaz)	diaper extra 3/6	old price 30/- } 38/-
7.164	9in Vase White on Topaz (Vine)	diaper extra 5/9	old price 40/- 50/- }
7.165	9in Vase White on Topaz	diaper extra 5/9	old price 40/- 50/- }
7.166	8in Vase White on Topaz	diaper extra 4/6	old price 30/- 38/-
7.167	8" Vase White on Topaz	diaper extra 5/-	old price 30/- 40/- }
7168	8in Vase White on Topaz	diaper extra 5/3	old price 30/- 45/- }
W2808	4½ Vase White on Flint	W 8/-	21/
W2809	6" " White on Lavender on Flint	W 1.16.6	75
W. 2811	8" " White on sea Green on Flint	W £ 4. 8. 0	£12·10/
W. 2812	5" " Light Brown on opal	W 7/9	20/
W.2816	5" " White on Sea Green	W. 14/6	35/

x 163½ Cut down As a Vase 38/- net)

Number	Articles	Costs	Sale
W. 2807	8 in Vase White on Brown Euterpe, Thalia etc ("Music")	W. £27.10.0	£65 £55. +
W. 2817	8 in Vase White on Brown " "Phyllis"	W£8-15-0	£22.0 22.0
W. 2810	7 in Vase White on sea Green Duck Etc	W. 28/6	£25 US 75/-
W. 2815	4 in Bowl White on Blue on Green	W. 35/6	90/-
W. 2818	Toilet Jar Mounting White on Ruby	W 8/-	20/-
W. 2822	10 in Vase White on Brown " "At the Portal"	W£18.15.0	£40. + £47.10/
W. 2358	2 Hd. Vases	W Cost £38.10.0	£100
W. 2824	Plaque 12 x 9½ in Velvet fram "music"	W £38.10.0	£110.
W. 2828	7½ in Vase on Brown "Dancing Girl"	1. £6.0.0	£17.10.0 £18.10/ +
W. 2831	7½ in Vase White on Brown "Psyche"	W £5.15.0	£17.10/
W. 2830 *april 1895*	9 in Vase White on Brown Vestal	W £12.10.0	£35/ 33.
W. 2827	9 in Vase White on Brown Hebe	W £10.10.0 £22.10/ Sold Finnigan 15/11/15	£27/-
W. 2834	Panel 12½ x 8½ White on Brown " "on the Terrace"	W £43.10.0	£180
W. 2840	13 full in Vase White on Brown "Aurora"	W £35.	£72.10.0 £90 X
W. 2842 *nov. 1895*	17 in Round Plaque W on Brown "Sunrise"	W. £87-10.0	£210. Nov/05
W. 2832	8 in Vase White on Brown "Euterpe	W £8.15.0	£25.
W. 2841	10 in Vase White on Brown "Harmony"	W £21-10.0	£55.
W. 2848	11 L Vase (on Cleopatra Egyptian Princess	W £35.0 Sold Finnigan £55. 15/11/15	£70. + £85. 26/11/06 11/3/01
W. 3930	17½ in Plaque White on Brown	£164	
W. 2843			£85. 75/ X reduced 8/3/01 (og

194

Number.	Articles	Cost.	Sale
W. 3111	2Hd Vase *Iris* Opal on Brown	W. 23.0.0	£60.
~	Vase *Narcissus* — (Sold to Buckley Hall) 2/7/07 £40/-. 23.0.0	£60.
W. 3128	7 Vase Yellow Green & opal, Cameo & Engraving	54/6	£7.
W. 3164	3 1/4 in Vase White on light Blue, Chrom	28/-	70/-
W. 3165	" ~ White on Yellow & White, flowers	18/-	50/-
W. 3151	4 1/2 Vase Ruby on rich Topaz flowers	3/9	12/6 30/-
W. 3160	11 in Vase White on Brown Spring Autumn	£ 30. £34.	£ 75. £85.
7 169	10 in Vase " " "		60/-
7 170	White on Pale Slate		
W 3170	12 in 2Hd Vase Light Blue & White	5.15.0	£17.10.0
W. 3167	Finger Green on Flint	7/-	16/- 10
"	Plate " ~	7/6	16/-
W 3168	Finger " "	9/6	20/-
W. 3173	6 in Bowl, Ivory & Painted by P.P. Woodall — in Colours	P.P. 10/ B. 4/6 12/6	£ 10.
7 171	6 in Bottle & Vase Flint with Green reed	P.J. Cut Base 30. 9 , 10/6	£ 4.
W 3195	8 in Vase Cane & reed cased White on Ruby Chrysanthemum	W. 68/-	£8.10.0
W. 2598	9 in Vase Ivory body Cased Ruby & Turquoise	W. cup 3/6 5/- 13 21/-	£4.10.0
W. 3189	6 in Vase White on Blue	W. 6/6	25/-
W. 3198	4 3/4 " " ~	Etched 12/6	35/-

May 1899

			Cost		Sale
W. 3200	7¾in Vase Green	6"2/.	W. 15/6		55/
W. 3194	" " Olive on Burmer	1/6	11/.		50/
W. 3203	8" " " "	1/6	16/6		~~80~~ 75/
W. 3201	" " " "	1/6	11/6		~~65~~ 70/
W. 3196	8 " " "	1/6	34/.		90/
W. 3202	12 2 Hd Vase White on Blue		95/.		£15
F. 172	Globe Toilet {White on Blue} {fo mtg}				18/.
F. 173	" " " "				18/.
F. 174	" " " W on Topaz				12/.
F. 175	Salad Bowl W on Blue				33/.
F. 176	" " W on Ruby				36/.
F. 177	" " W on Bu on Topaz				28/.
F. 178	Biscuit W on Topaz				18/6
F. 179	" W on Ruby				25/
F. 180.	6in Vase Curio {Green Bronze inside iridescent} {then faint outside} 2 Hd	Cutting in all 1/6	Eng 4/6 13 3/6		100/-
W. 3192	Vase White on 6in Purple flowers	W 4/.	B 3/-		30/
W. 3187	6 Vase, Topaz inside, Teal outside pale Purple between	W 5/9	B 5/6		40/
W. 3169	Plate, Olive on Flint, Spray from Centre	12/-			25/
W. 1721 a	9 Vase White on Ruby Chinese Yellow body	W. 16/6			55/

No.	Description		Cost W	B	
W.3206.	7in Vase Br on F. Blackberry	X	10/6	2/6	45/.
W.3190	Opale on Earthenware Parrot & flower		15/6	2/6	100/.
W.3188.	6 Vase Curzon Red on Won Jet		12/.	6/6	55/.
W.3211	3in Vase Vase Won J Spray		7/.		18/
W.3212	3 " " No B Berries		8/6		21/
W.3213	" " White on Blue Lillies		8/.		20/
W.3214	2" " " Won Spray		8/6		21/
W.3215	" " " Hot deep Jall		12/.		30/
W.3125	3½ Toilet Flint Cameo		12/6		30/.
G.W.1	Cameo Ware Poetry.		£ 45.0.0		£130
G.W.2	Vase Autumn.		£ 30.10.0		£85
G.W.3	Vase Night		£ 45.0.0		£120.
G.W.4	Small Panel 1 as Cleopatra		£ 2 15.0		£6.10.0
" "	Vase see 2848 painting Cleopatra				
" 5	" Morning		£ 45.0.0		£120
W.3185	Plaque "Toilet of Venus	Frame £ 6.x.x.	Total Cost £ 214.10.0		£500
W.3139	" "Moorish Bathers"		Total Cost £ 222.		£ 500.
W.3172	18in Plaque "Pompian" JP Italian panorama with figures		Total Cost £ 190		£350
W.3058	18in Plaque "Anthony & Cleopatra"		Total Cost £ 195		£450

Oct - 99

Nov 79

Sene 1901

1897

W. 3207	4" Bowl White on Brown, flowers & border		12/6		35/-
W 3224	8" Vase W on Blue, Passion flower		50/-		
W. 3218	8" Vase Green, Brown, & Burmese on Flint "green strap outside" sea weed, sea nymph, & fishes	cup 1/6	35/-		90/-
" 3222	6" Vase		25/6		65/-
" 3222½					65/-
" 3225	7" "		15/-		42/-
" 3226	10" " Birds & Sunset aqua on White on ruby on flint, flower ground		82/- P 2/-		£2.10.0
" 3209	7" " Vase Olive on Burmese		13/6 1/3		50/-
" 3210	8" Vase Burmese not burned on Lemon, swan &c thistle	Brushwk 1/3	W 14/6 Barke 6/-		52/6
" 3214	7½" Vase Green shaded on aqua, Passion flower	1/6	8/- " 3/-		35/-
	12" Vase Ivory inside Blue & buff outside (Cupid)	Woodall 7/6	Barke 21/-		£4.0.5
G.W.6	Vase flat side White on Brown	£27.10.6		£63	
W 3186	6½" Vase opal Ruby topal sea foam Mice & Trellis work	W.17/6 7/6		£4.10.0	
W. 3219	Vase Fish sea weed shell &c Burmese on Eau du nil	W. 85/-		£11.0.0	
W. 3255	Vase mermaid & sea weed green on Burmese & green	£6.17.0		£15.15.0	
W. 3254	3" Vase White on Amber, jasmine	W 11/6		27/1	
	8½" Vase Pink on Lemon	B 35/- W 4/-		about £7	
W 7118	Vase White on Ruby arum lily	W 3.15.0 16/- panels		10.10.0	

24

			Cost	£95
G.W. 7	11 in Vase White on Brown "Pharoh's Daughter"		£40.0.0	£XXX
G.W. 10	7 in Vase White on brown on Hint "Flora"		£5.10.0	£14.
G.W. 11	7 in " " " on flat "Pluvia"		£5.10.0	£14.
W.3259	7½ in Vase Olive on Burmese	28/-	1/6	75/
W.3260	7½ " " " "	42/-	1/6	110/
W.3261	7½ " " " "	30/-	1/6	85/
GW 13 - 6¾ Vase White on Brown "Physche"		£6.10.0	£13.16/
see GW 13a on folio 25			
G.W. 8	9 in Vase "Luna"		£7.5.0	
G.W. 9	7 in " "Aurora"		£8.0.0	
G.W. 12 - 7½ in Vase flat side "Penelope" Feb. 1901.		£6.10.0	£16
G.W. 14 - 7 in Vase "The Message"		£6.15.0	£16
G.W. 15 x 6½ Vases White on Brown "Chase"		£7.0.0	£17.
G.W. 16 x } Sold to Buckley July 3/07 @ £12/- "Caught"		£7.0.0	£17.
G.W. 17	7½ " " "Terpsichore"	£8.0.0	£18.
G.W. 18	8 in " " "Juno"	£8.0.0	£18.
W 3220	11 in Vase (amber shaded Ruby Cased marine green) Curio	W. 72/-	Brush work 3/-	£10.
G.W. 19	7½ Vase W on B "Serpentina"	8.5.0	18.10.0
G.W. 20	7 in " " "Dawn"	8.10.0	18.10.0
G.W. 21	6½ in " 7.5 W on B "Ceramia"	8.0.0	18.0.0

					Cost	Sale
G.W.	24	8½ Vase Won B	"Morning"		£ 8. 5. 0	18.10.0
"	23	" " "	"Night"		£ 8. 5. 0	18.10.0
→	22	9 " "	"Painting"		£ 13.10.0	35.0.0
"	25	8½ " "	"Sirene"		£ 11.10.0	30.0.0
"	26	7 " "	"Diana"		£ 8. 5. 0	18.10.0
"	27	7½ " "	"Hebe"		£ 8. 0. 0	18.0.0
"	26a	7¼ " "	"Diana"		£ 8. 5. 0	21.0.0
	13a.	7½ " "	"Psyche"		£ 7.10.0	18.0.0
G.W.	28	17½ Plaque "	"Diana & Endymion"		£ 73 10.0	175.0.0
	or W 2786					
"	29	7 " Vase	Pomina		£ 8 10 0	18.10.0
"	30	Plaque " ..	"The Dance" (figures)			
		" ..	Kermi	Estimate July/02 £75	£180.

			note		
W. 3216	3¼ " Vase White on Light Blue		W 9/.		25/.
F 181	14 " Vase White on China Yellow	(one of Stocks)	G.W. Estimated £ 20. in all	}	£ 45.
	Figure playing Tambourin & 2 Children with flowers }	1803			
W 3246	8½ Vase White & Ruby on Ean-d-vul, flowers		W. 17/6		42/-
W 3265	13 " Vase White on dark Brown		W. 78/.		10 guine

26

		Woodall's Cost	Sale
G.W. 30	20ᵘ Plaque "The Dance"	£ 175	£ 450 / 350 with frame
G.W. 31	Panel "an Undine"	£ 35	£ 90
G.W. 32 oct. 1902	" "Calypso"	£ 35	£ 90 £ 60/
G.W. 33	" "Andromache"	£ 35	£ 90
113	Plaque on aphrodite	63/-	7.7.-
GW 114	"Sirene"	63/-	7.7.-
GW 115	Sirene. L Warehouse	63/-	7.10.- on green marble vase
GW 116	Flora	63/-	7.10.-
Ovals for Brooches not	"Greek Slave	2/- perish 1/	2.5.
	Natures Mirror	2/- 1/	2.5p-
	Plaque Toilet of Venus	Nich	£380 £350 with frame

Feb 23. 3 more ovals for Brooches @ 2/- — 2.5. ea
The Dove. Sea Nymph
1 " @ 2/- — 2.5. -
March. 3 " " The Dance, Gathering Pearls, Venus rising from the sea @ 2/- 2.5.-
" 30ᵗʰ 3 " Sappho Penelope - A Syren. @ 2/- ea. 2.5. "
May 2ⁿᵈ 7. More. Diana, Pandora, Bacchante, Natures Mirror @ 2/- ea 2.5.-
Girl in the Clouds. Venus rising from the Sea
B - G.W. 13ᵘ Rᵈ Plaque "Wild Waves" £40 (180/) £120 ✓ 45/08
May 9ᵗʰ 08 GW "The Polar Vase" £3 Van Clifton 40/ £10.10.- GW £35 B 50gm
May 9ᵗʰ 08. GWᵐ 18ᵘ Plaque "At Cupids Shrine" £110 GW £300/ £450/
Sold to Finnigan Feb 14. 1917 £250/
Feb, '91

201

Sold. price

GW 131
Feathered
favored

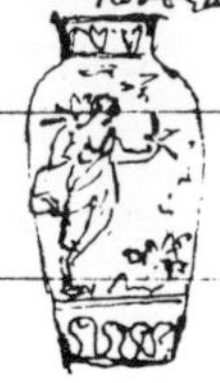

GW 130
a Message

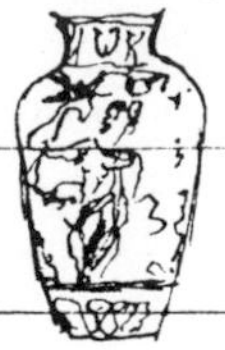

16/16/-
16/16/-
18/10/-
18/10/-
L.W.H.
L.W.H.
L.W.H.
L.W.H.

GW 140   GW 139
night   Morning

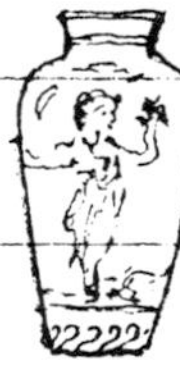

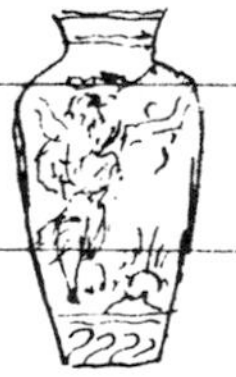

Sept 29, 1910

202

				Cost		Worth Price Sale
G.W.	130	7" Vase	"A Message"	✓ 4/10/.	13/-	£ 12/-
G.W.	131	7" "	"Feathered Favourits"	✓ 4/10.		£ 12/-
G.W.	132	73/4"	"Ocean Gems"	✓ 4/10/.		£ 14/-
G.W.	133	7/34 "	"Seawed "	✓ 4/10/.		£ 14/-
G.W.	134	7" "	"Soppa"	✓ 4/10/.		£ 12/-
G.W.	135	7 "	"Tambourina"	✓ 4/10/.		£ 12/-
G.W.	136	6" "	Nautilus	✓ 4/10/.		£ 12/-
G.W.	137	6" "	Dolphin	✓ 4/10/.		£ 12/-
		Vase, white inside brown - flint with colored peaks roughly carved		2/10/-	sent to Erskine 1909	

203

GW 139	1¾ Vase	"Morning 7in	G.W. 100/-	£15/-/-	(aug)/09
GW 140	1 Do.	"Night 7in	100/-	£15/-/-	
GW 141		"The Antarctic"		£42. -.	£63/-/- eschibte
G.W.	9in Plaque	Edin	40/-/-	£90/-/- works new	£136/-/- too
G.W.	8in Vase	Flora Capture	10/-/-	£23/-/- WP	£35/-/-
G.W.	" "	Flora Surprise	10/-/-	£23/-/- WP	£35/-/- too
				Sale	Brann EX
GW 145.	11in Plaque "Origin of Painting"	"/30	Woodall £80.	£120	

204

Dear 1911

				Date

GW.146 in Plaque "Aphrodite"   G.W. presentation price £0x/.   £ PRX/-/.
orders price £VX/-/.   works price £ PRX/-/.
Turin Exhibition PN X/-/.

GW. 147 5in Rd Slab "Sea Shells"   90/.   works price PR/-/.
Turin Exhibition £ PN/.

GW. 148 5in Rd Slab "Idle Moments"   90/.   works price PR/-/.
Turin Exhibition £ PN/.

GW. 149 4in Rd Slab "Seaweeds"   60/.   works price Turin Exhibition C/-/.
£ PO/H/

GW. 150 4in Rd Slab "Nautilus"   60/.   works price C/-/.
Turin Exhibition £ PO/H/.

GW. 151 7in Vase "Stringtime"   £6/-/.   works price Pi/-/.
Turin Exhibition £ RA/H/.

205

As sent to Leipzig Feby 1913.

A.	1	soapbody	Cameo	White on Blue	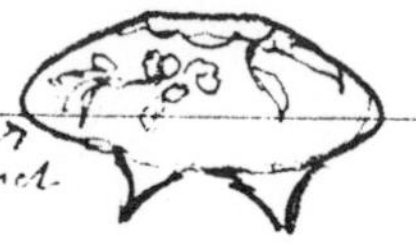	Apple Blossom	33/
B.	1	" "	"	White & Ruby on Topaz		Coloseandro & Butter fly	33/
C.	1	" "	"	" " "		Hawthorn	33
D.	1	" "	"	" " " 5½			33

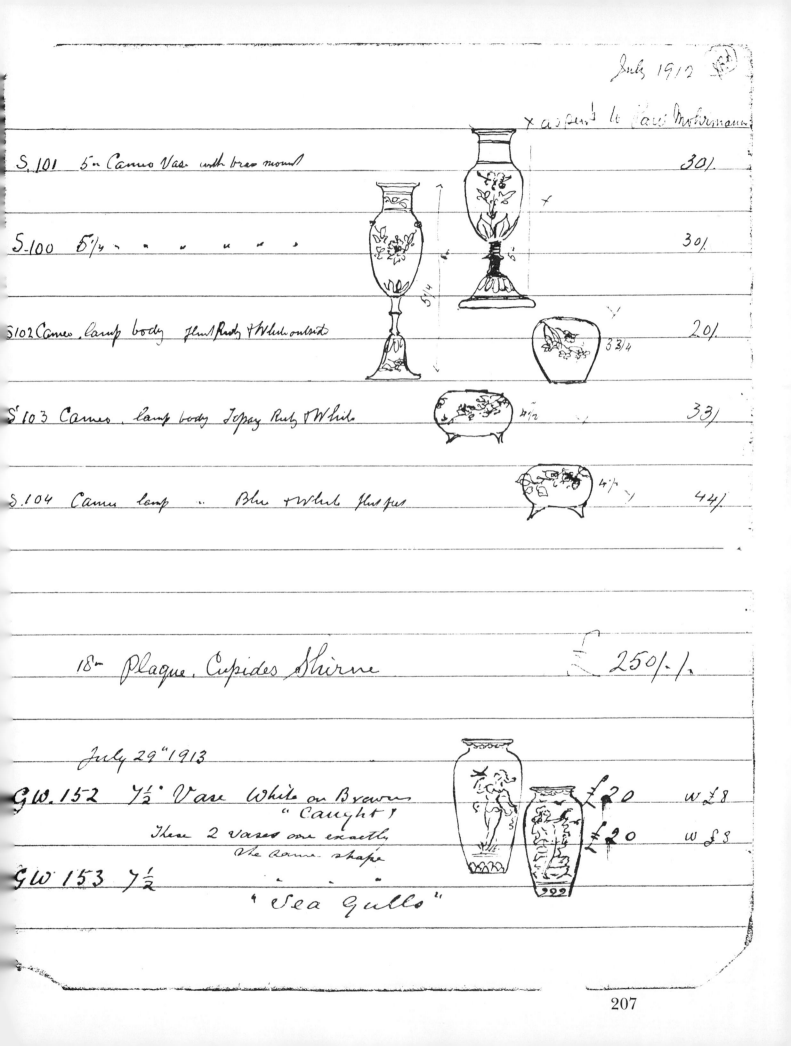

× as pent to Paul Mohrmann

S.101   5" Cameo Vase with brass mount   30/.

S.100   5¼" " " " " " " "   30/.

S.102 Cameo, lamp body   flint Ruby & White outside   20/.   3¾

S.103 Cameo, lamp body   Topaz Ruby & White   4½   33/.

S.104 Cameo lamp   "   Blue & White flus flus   4½   44/.

18" Plaque. Cupides Shrine   £ 250/-/.

July 29" 1913

GW.152   7½° Vase White on Brown   £20   w £8
              " Caught !
          These 2 vases are exactly
              the same shape
GW 153   7½   " " " "   £20   w £8
              ' Sea Gulls "

207

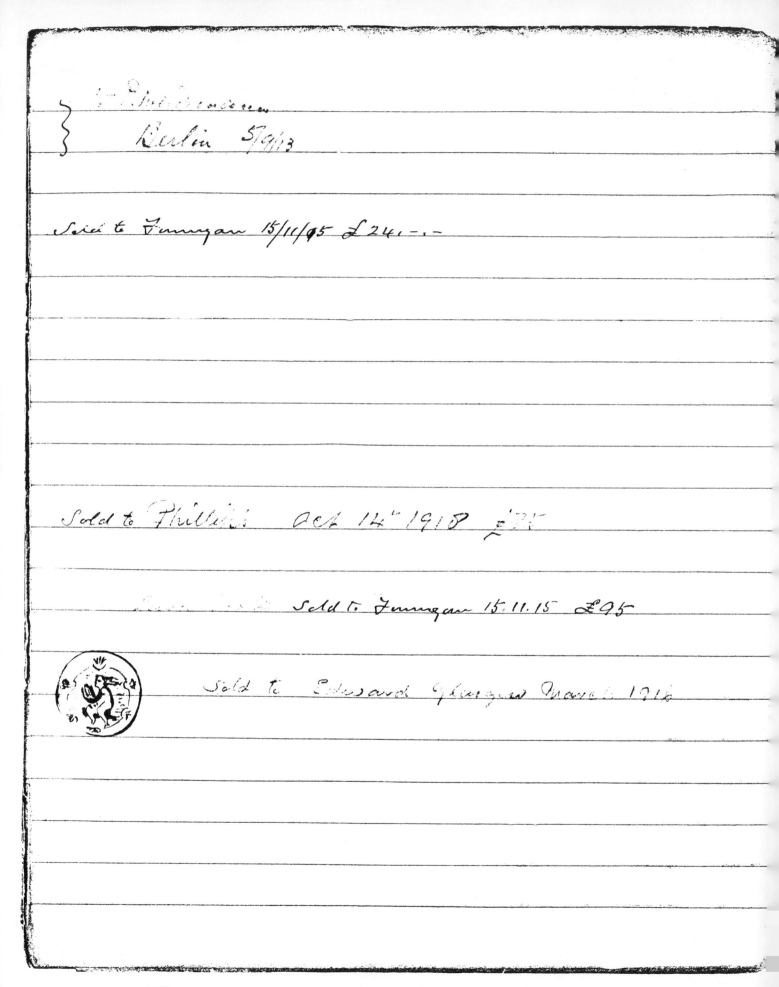

Studemann

Berlin 5/9/13

Sold to Finnegan 15/11/95 £241 -.-

Sold to Phillips Oct 14" 1918 £75

Sold to Finnegan 15.11.15 £95

Sold to Edward Glasgow March 1916

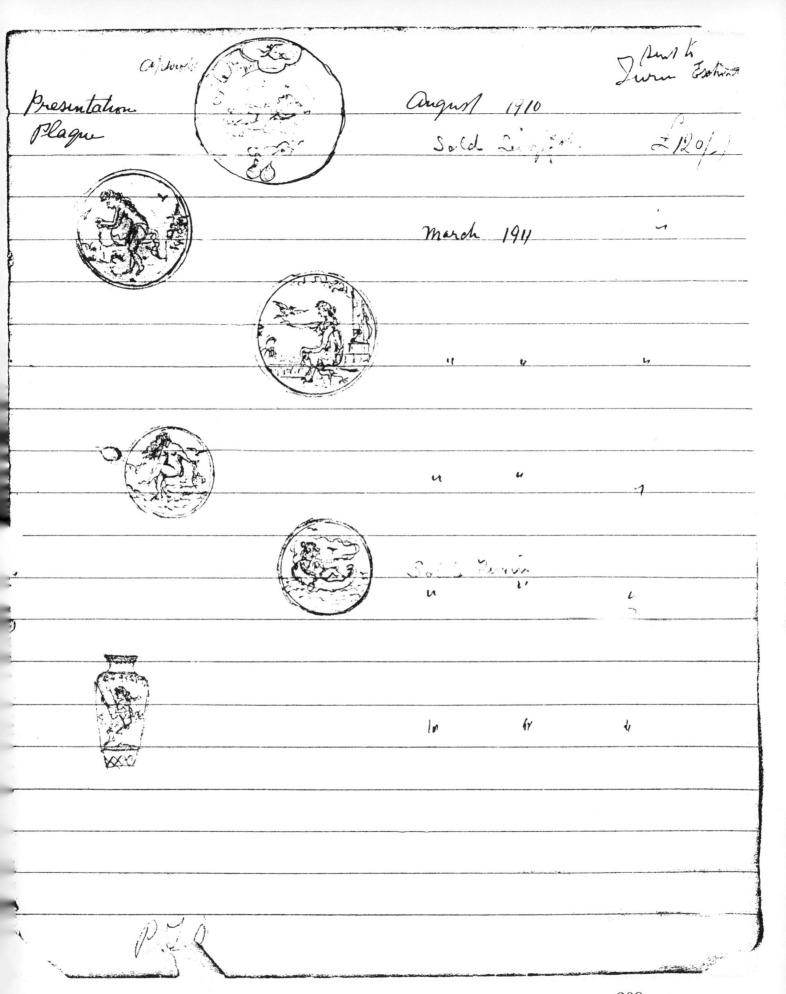

Presentation
Plaque

August 1910

Sold ~~~~~~ £120/-

March 1911

Sale

7/2/18

G.W. 163 Vase 7" oval. body 5½ × 4½

      The Origin of the Harp

28. 5.1918

Philiponett 40. -. -

         Cost 12. 10. - £40. net

Feb 1918 "Antarctic Vase" (2nd)

Philips' High   Wide 5/-. Etching 100/-. Fereday £5 £50.
£45.

210

mouth 3 7/8 × 3 1/8

THE ORIGIN OF THE HARP.

"Tis believed that this Harp, which I wake now for thee,
Was a siren of old who sung under the sea;
And who often at eve through the bright billow roved,
To meet, on the green shore, a youth whom she loved.

"But she loved him in vain, for he left her to weep,
And in tears all the night, her gold ringlets to steep,
Till heaven looked with pity on true love so warm,
And changed to this soft Harp the sea-maiden's form.

"Still her bosom rose fair-still her cheeks smiled the same,
While her sea-beauties gracefully curled round the frame;
And her hair shedding tear-drops from all its bright rings,
Fell over her white arms to make the gold strings. "

Moore's Irish Melodies.

No.	Articles	W or L. No.	Making per three	Engraving	Brushing	Cameo	Barbe Painting	Sale
J. 1	6 in Flat Sided Vase	W. 1849						65/-
" 2	Small Jug	L 632						36/-
" 3	4 in Vase	W 1833						22/6
" 4	4 1/2 "	W 1893	60					10/6
" 5	" "	W 1894	"					11/6
" 6	5 in "	L 637	50					18/-
" 7	5 1/2 " "	L 636	36					21/-
" 8	5 in "	W 1906						12/-
" 9	" "		50	Eng 7/6	1/3		1/6	16/6
" 10	" "		50	6/-	1/3		1/6	
" 11	4 in Bowl	W 1908	72		1/4	17/6	3/-	
" 12	3 3/4 Vase	L 638	65		1/3			14/-
13	" "		65	7/-	1/3		1/-	15/-
14	3 1/2 Hd Vase	W 1868						32/-
" 15	3 1/2 Hd Vase	W 1900				4/3	1/6	12/6
" 16	4 in Bowl	W 1925	60		1/3	12/6	1/6	
" 17	5 in Vase			4/-	1/3		1/6	
" 18	Hexagon 5 in Vase	L 620						80/-
" 19	8 in Vase	L 633	30					60/-

212

No.	Articles	World No.	M	C	B	G	P	Sale
J. 20	6½" Vase	L635	not turned	18/-		18/-	4½	70/-
" 21	5" "	W1891						32/-
" 22	6½ Vase		50	5/-	1/6	51/2/-	2/6	~~26/6~~
" 23	8" "	W1911	30		2/-	24/6	2.	64/-
" 24	6" Ha Vase	W1915	20		1/6	19/6	3/6	
" 25	5½ "	W1910	36		1/3	11/6	1/6	
" 26	8½ Bowl	W1923	30		2/-	35/6	6/6	
" 27	5" "	W1924	72		1/6	23/-	3/6	
" 28	13½ Vase		28	24/-	3/-	37/6	7/6	
" 29	6½ "	W1846	70		1/4	7/6	2/-	
" 30	8" "		40	12/-	1/4		3/6	
31	10" "	W1902	50		1/6	17/6	3/6	
" 32	9" "	W1917	30		1/6	17/-	4/-	
" 33	6" Jar & Cover	L	18 2 pieces	35/6	3/-	25/-	6/-	
" 34	8" Bowl	W1912	28		2/-	25/-	5/-	
" 35	Triangular top Bowl	W1903	18		1/6	17/-	3/6	45/-
" 36	" "	" "	"		1/6	"	"	45/-
" 37	" "	W1905	"		1/6	13/6		
" 38	Small Jug	W1904	45		1/6	6/-	2/-	

213

Nº	Articles	Wor Lnº	Making	Engª	Brusting	Carnes	B. Painting	Sale
I.39	9½ Vase		per turnt .30	9/-	2/-	4/-	4/0	4/-
" 40	6in "		40	15/-	1/6		2/-	3/-
" 41	9in Jusk		24		Cup 3/6+3/-	28/-	6/-	85
" 42	8in Vase		50	2/6	1/6	15/ 18/-	3/6	42/
" 43	9½ "		30	8/-	2/-	3/6	4/6	40/
" 44	8in 2 Hdd Vase	W1875	20		1/6	23/6	5/-	109/4 63/
" 45 in Now 6/14 ×	4½ Vase	" W1907	24 60		1/3 1/2	18/6 4/-	4/4 1/6	50/ 14/
" 46	5 Vase	W1916	.40	✗	1/6	15/6	2/-	36/
" 47	4½ Vase		60	2/6	1/2		1/-	9/
" 48	8in 2 Hdd Bowl	W1913	14		2/6	25/6	5/-	40/
" 49	8 2 Hdd Vase		20		1/6	38/-	5/6	85/
" 50	4 " "		15		6	1/3	1/-	6/
" 51	Flat side 14dd Vase		24					
" 52	Small Vase	1322				6/-	3/6	10/6
" 53	7in Vase		40	10/-	1/6	8/-	3/6	42/
" 54	2½ Lent Bowl	W1862				5/3	4/-	13/
" 55	3in " "	" 1863	130			5/6	4/6	21/
" 56	" " "	L618		1/-				
" 57	3½ " "	W1834	100			11/6	4/-	25/
× 44	10in	W1875 — 18		—	2/- — 38/- —			78/-

214

No.	Articles	Wor.No.	M.	E.	B.	C.	B.P.	Sale
J 58	6½ Vase		60		9	3/6	9	10/-
J 59	6½ Vase	W.1928	70		1/6	11/6	3/6	32/-
J 60	" "	"	70			"	"	3⁰ --
" 61	3 Sent Bottle	"					1/-	3/-
" 62	5½ Vase	W 1929	40		1/6	20/-	3/6	50/-
" 63	6" H. Vase		20	2/6	1/6	20/-	3/6	46/-
" 64	Small Vase		65	6/-	1/3		1/-	15/-
" 65	6" Vase		50	7/-	1/6	9/-	3/6	40/-
" 66	5½ "		36	13/-		9/-	3/6	50/-
	6¾ "		28	24/-	1/6	Etching 8/-		70/-
" 67	10" Vase		30	13/-	2/-	26/-	6/6	84/-
" 68	9" "	W 1927	30		2/-		7/-	130/-
" 69	8½ Vase	W 1933	30		1/6	22/6	5/-	57/6
" 70	8" Task	W 1890	24		1/6	36/6	6/6	100/-
" 71	5" Vase	W 1925	45		1/4	12/6	3/6	36/-
" 72	4" Vase	W 1932				16/6	3/6	45/-
" 73	4" Vase	W 1941	80		1/6	8/-	3/6	24/-
" 74	4" Vase	W 1942	80		1/6	7/-	3/6	22/6
" 75	8" Bowl	W 1926	30		2/3	26/6	7/-	80/-
" 76	6¼ H'd Vase	W 1956			1/3	68/-	6/6	147/-

No.	Articles	W or L No.	Making	Engd	Brushing	Cameo	B. Painting	Sale
I 77	4in Vase	W 1943	60 –	5	1/4	3/6	1/–	12/
" 78	5¼ Vase	W 1939	30		1/6	30/	4/6	68/
" 79	8in Fld oval Vase	" 1934	24		2/–	21/6	5/6	60/
" 80	5 – Vase		40	14/6	1/4	14/	3/6	65/
" 81	4 " "	Guest	50	[illegible]	1/3	8	1/–	6/6
" 82	8½in Rd Fld Vase	W 1935	24		2/–	22/6	5/6	60/
" 83	5½in Bottle	W 1254			1/	1/4	1/6	16/6
" 84	6in Fld side Vase	W 1957	80		1/6	31/6	4/6	84/–
" 85	" "	W [illegible]	Owned by [illegible], Dallas, Texas apple blossoms in rose cut cameo					90/–
" 86	3¾in Vase	L 624	80					1[illegible]/
" 87	" "	" 625	80					16/6
88	6½ "	" 621						14/–
89	4 " "	" 626						nc/d
90	6in Fld side Vase	W 1958		60	1/6	27/6	4/6	80/–
91	" "		60	40/–	1/6	20/–	4/6	126/–
92	5½ Vase	W 1945	72		1/3	9/6	2/–	21/–
93	4½ "	W 1944	60		1/2	10/–	1/–	22/6
94	5¼ "		50		1/3	5/6	1/9	17/6
95	" "	W 1936	50		1/3	5/6	1/9	17/6

Mo.	Articles	W or L	Making	Engᵍ	Brushing	Cameo	B. Painting	Sale
9 96	8 Vase	L 622	50					40/-
" 97	S. Bottle	W 1960			4	d/-	6	12/-
" 98	S "	W 1959	100		3	1/10	6	5/-
" 99			72	6/-	6		8	14/-
9 100	7. Rd Bowl	520		7/-		14/-	4/6	45/-
100½	" "			7/- 2/3		10/- 60/-	4/6 4/-	40/- 140/-
" 101	8 " Bowl	W 1937	30		2/3			
" 102	10 " Bow	W 1940	22		3/-	5-0	10/6	130/-
" 103	10 " Vase	W 1961	18		2/3	49/-	7/6	168/- 147/-
" 104	12 " Vase	L 619						
" 105	8 " Bowl	W 1938	36		1/6	36/6	5/6	84/-
" 106	2¼ Rd Bottle	W 1897			6	1/-	8	5/6
" 107	2½ "	W 1966				2/9	10	8/6
" 108	" "	"				2/9	10	8/6
" 109	8 " Vase		48	9/-	2/-	27/-	3/6	70/-
" 110	5 " "	50	50	4/- 6/6	1/3	8/6 8/6	1/9 1/9	32/- 32/-
110½	" " "	50	50					
" 111	8 " "	26	26	9/- 12/-	2/- 2/-	4/- 4/-		36/- 36/-
111½								
" 112	6 " "		40	20/-	2/-	24/-	3/6	100/-
113	5 " "	W 1931	40		1/6	20/-	3/6	50/-
" 114	4½ "	W 1930	80		1/6	15/6	2/6	36/-

No	Article	Work No	Making	Eng'd	Brushing	Cameo	B. Painting	Sale
J 115	7/4in Vase	W1918	30		1/6	24/6	3/-	56/-
J 116	" "	W1967	30		1/6	20/6	3/-	50/-
" 117	8in Task		30	28/-	1/9	20/-	6/6	120/-
" 118	6in Vase	Guest	50		Guest 1/-		2/-	10/-
" 119	8in Vase		35	10/-	1/9	12/-	3/6	50/-
" 120	7in Bowl		36	9/6	1/6		2/6	21/-
" 121	Small Jug		30	12/-	1/6	3/6	3/6	42/-
" X122	4in Bowl (no jewels sale 55/-)		60	12/6	1/4	7/-	2/-	65/-
" 123	5in "		45		1/4	5/6	1/6	16/6
" 124	7in "	Guest	36		1/6	1/6	3/6	17/6
" 125	8in Vase	Guest	30		1/4	1/-	1/-	12/-
" 126	4in Bottle		120	1/8		9	1/6	9/-
"	3 1/2 "		120	1/3		6	1/-	7/-
J 127	12in Vase		30			6/-	4/-	28/-
J. 128	13 1/2 "	W1962	16		2/6	89/-	10/-	10 guns
" 129	10in Hd Vase	W1973	18		2/3	43/6	7/6	£8
" 130	" "	W1972	18		2/3	40/-	7/6	6 guns
" 131	Small Tankard Jug	W1962	45			32/-	2/-	£3
132	5 3/4 Vase		50	3/-	1/-	1/3	1/6	14/-

+ ...

No	Article	W or S No	Making	Engᵈ	Brushg	Etching Pairs	Paintg	Sale
J. 133	4in Rd Tray				1/-	6 11/-	1/-	25/-
" 134	9in Vase		30	10/6	2/-	3/-	3/-	37/-
" 135	" "		30	10/6	2/-	2/6	3/-	37/6
" 136	8in Tusk		30		1/9	37/6	6/6	110/- pit
" 137	8in Tea Vase		20	40/-	1/6	6/-	3/-	100/-
" 138	6¾ Vase		50		1/-	3/-	6	10/6
" 139	6¾ "		60		1/-	2/-	6	8/6
" 140	7in Vase		60	10/-	1/-	16/-	3/-	56/-
" 141	8in Vase		48	9/-	1/-	4/-	3/-	32/-
" 142	3¾ "		55	5/6	6	/	10	14/-
" 143	5¼ "		36			5/6	1/6	15/-
" 144	10 Rd Bowl		22			4/6	6/6	32/-
" 145	12in Vase		30			6/-	4/-	28/-
" 146	9in Vase		30			6/-	3/6	28/-
" 147	8in Vase		24	20/-	Cutting Etc 3/6	5/-	3/6	63/-
" 148	7½ "		30	16/-	1/6	9/-	3/-	60/-
" 149	6in "		50	7/-	1/-	2/6	1/6	22/6
" 150	5in Vase		40	6/-	9	6/-	1/6	28/-
" 151	4in Vase		55	5/-	4/-		10	14/-

No.	Articles	Work No.	Making	Eng'g	Brushing	Cameo	Barto Paintg	Sale
J. 152	4in Vase		120		6	1/3	10	5/6
" 153	Gin Hot Bottle			18/6	9		2/6	42/-
" 154	6½in " "			12/6	6		1/3	26/6
" 155	6½ "			5/6	6		1/3	15/-
" 156	3½			4/6	4		8	10/6
" 157	12in Hd Vase		15		4/-	44/-	10/6	200/-
15/7½ " 158	10in " "		18		3/-	72/- 138/-	16/6	£ s p 18-18-0
" 159	3in Square Bowl		80		3/-	19/6	3/-	28.0.0 50/-
" 160	12in Jusk	W.1995	18		2/6	77/-	10/6	180/-
" 161	4in Vase		120		6		10	
" 162	" "		65		1/-	1/-	10	6/6
" 163	3½ "		120	2/6	8 X	8	10	10/-
" 164	3½ Vase		120	3/4	8 X		10	10/-
" 165	3½ Vase	Guest	120	1		6	10	3/6
" 166	6½ Vase	W 1997	40		1/-	2/6	7/6 1/3	12/-
166.a in Sketch Book								
" 167	7in Vase		60		10 7/3	2/6	1/3	10/6
" 168	6½ Vase	W 1997	40		1/8	2/6	7/6 1/3	not polished 12/- 10/
" 169	7in Vase		40	8/-	1/6	4/-	2/6	30/-
" 170	12 Vase	W 2010	18		3/6	78/-	20/-	£ 12.10/

X as 152   ※ 1

No.	Articles	Work No.	Making	Engg.	Brushing	Etching or Cameo	Bark Painting	Sale
J. 171	3 Toilet		130 140			6/4	8/6	3/3 2/6
" 172	2½ " 4" Vase		80		8/-	2/-	1/-	9/-
" 173	6¾ Vase		50		10 1/3	2/6	1/3	11/6
" 174	5½ Vase		50	5/6	8 4/-	1/9	1/3	18/6
" 175	4" Vase		72		8 4/-	1/9	10	7/6
" 176	4" Vase		72		6 4/-	1/6	10	7/6
" 177	4 Vase		72		4/-	1/6	1/-	8/6
" 178	4" Vase		72		4/-	2/-	1/-	10/-
" 179	6" Vase		50		1/3	2/6	1/3	11/6
" 180	6½ Vase	W 2000	40		1/6	2/10	1/3	12/6
" 181	" "	W 2000	40		1/6	2/10	1/3 10/6	12/6
" 182	" "		40		1/6	2/8	1/3 10/6	12/6
" 183	" Vase	W 2019	28		1/-	18/6	2/-	42/-
" 184	6" Hd Vase	Guest —	24			2/6	1/6	14/-
"	10 " "	" —	18			4/- 3/6		2/4
"	8 " "	" —	20			3/- 1/6		17/-
"	12 " "	" —	15			5/-	5/-	3/-
" 185	5½ Vase	W 2002	40		1/6 3/6	3/6	1/6	20/-
" 186	6" Vase	W. 2001	48		1/6	4/-	2/-	24/-
" 187	" Vase		40	22/-	1/4	6/-	3/-	63/-
" 188	5½ Vase	W 1987	72		1/4	16/-	3/-	40/-

221

Number	Articles	Word No	Making	Engg	Brushing	Etching or Cameo	Barke Painting	Sale
I 189	4" Vase	Guest	50		#	4	10	4/4
" 190	5" Vase	Guest	50			8	Po	5/6
" 191	6" Vase	W2003	40		1/3	4/6	1/6	15/-
192	5¾ Vase		30	16/-	1/6	9/-	1/6	75/-
" 193	4" Bowl	W1986	60		9	8/-	2/-	21/
" 194	5" Bowl	W1984	45		1/-	11/6	3/-	30/
" 195	" "	W1992	45		1/-	14/-	3/-	34/
" 196	" "	W1993	45		1/-	9/6	3/-	27/6
" 197	14" Vase	W1914	30		1/6	19/-	5/-	50/
" 198	8" Hd Vase	W2014	20		1/-	13/6	4/-	44/
" 199	" "	W2013	20		1/-	17/-	4/-	48/
" 200	10 Vase	W2017	20		2/-	43/6	5/6	86/
" 201	8" Bowl	W2005	24		1/6	7/	3/6	26/
" 202	6½ Vase		60	5/6	1/-	1/8	1/6	70/
" 203	8" Bowl	W2006	30		1/6	8/6	4/6	28/
" 204	Jug	W2016	35		1/4	24/-	3/6	56/
" 205	9½ Vase		30	4/6	1/-	3/-	3/-	25/-
" 206	10½ Vase		50		1/-	4/6	3/-	17/6
" 207	8/4 Vase		36	15/6	1/3	15/-	4/6	70/

No.	Articles	Work No.	Making	Engg	Brushing &c	Etching Cameo	Barbe Painting	Sale
J. 208	8½ Vase		35	7/6	1/-	12/6	3/6	45/
„ 209	6" Vase	W 1982	40 / 60	8/-	1/7	6/6 / 20/	3/6 / 4/	3.5/
„ 210	8- Vase		30	9/	1/3	16/-	4/-	60/
„ 211	7½ Vase	W 1982	60	8/	1/-	20/-	4/-	60/
„ 212 212.B	8¾ Vase 8¾		28 28	20/- 20/-	1/3	8/- 8/-	8/6 3/6	75/ 43/
x 212.a.	„				8	2/4	4/ 24/ 1/3	45/
„ 213	6" Vase		70	-		2/4	1/3	9/6
„ x 214	6" Vase		70		9	2/4	1/3	9/6
„ 215	6½ Vase		30	21/	1/	12/-	3/6	72/
„ 216	5½ Vase		30	21/	1/	12/-	3/6	72/
„ 217	8" Vase		48	6/-	9	1/9	1/6	20/
„ 218	5½ Vase		40	17/-	1/	11/-	3/6	63/
„ 219	3¾ Vase	W 2028	50			2/8	1/3	10/-
„ 220	8- Bowl	Guest	20			5/6	5/6	28/-
„ 221	4- Vase	Guest	30			1/6	1/6	10/-
„ 222	6½ Vase		70	8/-	8	4/-	2/-	27/6
„ 223	„ „	W 2026	70		9	3/6	1/6	12/6
„ 224	„ „	W 2025	70		9	3/3	1/6	12/6
„ 225	6½ Vase		50	#	9	1/-	1/3	8/6
„ 226	4" Bowl	W 2024	84		8	2/2	10	8/-

x 212 13" Vase   3/   100/-   42/-   £12.10
   x 214 decorated forget me not - sale price   1/3   4/-

No	Articles	Worc'r No	Making	Eng'g	Brushing	Etching &c	Borde Painting	Sale
227	3½ Vase		80		6	9	10	5/6
228	5½ Vase		50	4/-	8	9	1/-	14/-
229	4¼ Vase		120		6	1/-	10	57-
230	" "		120		6	1/-	10	57-
231	3¾ Vase	W 2022	65/120		6	3/6	10	10/-
232	6½ Vase		70			1/-	1/3	6/6
233	Small Jug		3/6		8	1/6	1/-	8/6
234	4½ Vase	W 2027	120		6	3/-	10	8/-
235	8" Vase		40	65/-	1/6	20/-	5/-	180/-
236	" "		40	5/6	10	2/-	2/6	25/-
237	7¼ Vase		30	8/3/-	8	4/6	3/-	33/-
238	5" Vase			7/6 3/-	6	3/-	2/-	25/-
239	8" Vase		30	9/-	1/-	5/6	3/6	37/6
240	5½ Vase	W 2020	40		8	6/-	2/-	16/-
241	5¾ "	W 2031			8	16/-	1/6	37/6
242	12" Vase		30	8/-	1/6	3/-	3/6	30/-
243	8½ "		50	3/6	1/-	2/6	2/3	18/-
244	7"		70	2/9	8	2/-	1/-	12/6
245	4½ Vase		50	6/6	9	7/-	2/-	30/-

No	Articles	WoS No	Making	Engg	Brushing	Etching &c	Barb Painting	Sale
J 246	5½ Vase		40	6/6	To	7/-	2/6	35/-
" 247	" "		"	6/6	To	3/6	2/6	30/-
" 248	3½ Vase	W 2004	50		8	9/-	1/6	22/6
" 249	5¼ Vase		50	7/-	8	2/-	2/-	22/-
" 250	9" Vase	W2038	30		1/3	27/6	4/6	60/-
" 251	4½ Vase	(6 quels 4¼)	60	14/6	1/3	6/-	3/-	60/-
" 252	14½ Vase	Quest	30			4/-	5/-	22/6
" 253	10½" Jug	"	35			3/6	3/6	21/-
" 254	7¼ Vase	W 2035	30		1/3	18/6	4/-	50/-
" 255	6¼ Vases	W 2036	24		1/3	8/6	4/-	32/-
" 256	8½ Vase		50	3/6		2/6	2/3	18/-
" 257	8" Bowl	W 2018	30		1/6	6/-	4/6	30/-
" 258	7" Vase		70	2/9	8	2/-	1/-	12/6
" 259	5" Bowl	W 2049	72	1/3		10/-	2/6	27/6
" 260	8½ Vase		50		4/-	3/6	2/3	13/6
" 261	9¼ Vase	W 2023	50		4/-	7/6	2/6	23/6
" 262	8¼ Plate	Quest				3/6	4/6	17/6
" 263	7½ Vase		30	10/-	1/3	24/-	3/6	70/-

No.	Articles	No.	Make per turn	Eng	Brushing	Etching	Bart. Painting	Sale
J. 264	8" Vase		30	5/-	1/3	2/6	1/6	25/-
265	6" Vase {flat side}		60	66/-			3/6	12/-
266	6 Tube		72	3/6	~~8~~	1/6	9	10/6
267	S/S Globe		130			8	3	2/-
"	M/S "		120			8	4	2/6
"	L/S "		110			10	6	3/-
268	10¾ Vase	W2059	50			3/6	2/6	13/6
269	12" Vase		30	8/-		3/-	3/6	30/-
270	8½ Vase		50	3/6		2/6	2/3	18/-
271	" "		"	3/6		2/6	2/3	18/-
272	7" "		70	2/9		2/-	1/-	12/6
273	" "		"			3/-	1/-	9/-
274	" "		"	2/9		2/-	1/-	12/6
275	6" Vase Dronkler	W2068	40			2/4	1/-	8/6
276	6" Vase	W2039	40			8/6	1/6	20/-
277	5½ Vase	Quest	55			9	8	4/6
278	9½ Vase		30	20/-	1/6	1.6/-	4/6	85/-
279	" "		30	15/-		8/-	4/6	52/-
280	8" Vase		30	24/-		18/-	3/6	84/-
× 277 m/S			50			1/6		
" L/S			45			1/-	1/-	8/-

226

No.	Articles	No	Make per turn	Eng	Brushing Ht	Etching Ht	Barh Painting	Sale
I. 281	8- Vase		30	8/-		8/-	3/6	40/-
„ 282	6½ Vase		40	13/-		7/6	2/6	50/-
„ 283	6- Vase		50	2/6		8	1/3	10/-
„ 284	8½ Vase		28	10/-		8/-	1/-	40/-
„ 285	5" Sprinkler	W2079	60			2/-	To	7/-
„ 286	2¾ "	2080	72			1/3	7¼	3/9
„ 287	" "	"	72			1/3	7¼	3/9
„ 288	8" Vase		40	6/6	1/-	2/9	2/6	21/-
„ 289	" "		40	6/6	1/-	2/9	2/6	21/-
„ 290	7½ Tusk	W2047	16			18/6	3/6	50/-
„ 291	12" Vase with Cover		18	33/-	2/-	26/-	5/-	7 Guis
„ 292	" " "	"		30/-	2/6	24/-	5/-	7 Guis
„ 293	6" Sprinkler	W2068	40			2/4	1/-	8/6
„ 294	" "		40			2/4	1/-	8/6
„ 295	8" Candlestick	W2057	25			10/6	2/-	25/-
„ 296	8" Candlestick	W2058	25			11/6	2/-	28/-
„ 297	9" Candlestick	W2056	25			13/6	2/-	30/-
„ 298	10" Candlestick	W2040	30		1/6	20/6	3/-	
„ "	8" Do		35		1/-	16/6	2/-	

No.	Articles	No	make per turn	Eng	Brushing H	Etching H	Barh Painting	Sale
I 299	5 Sprinkler	W2054	60			3/6	1/6	12/-
" 300	8½ Vase	Guest	60			1/6	2/6	10/6
" 301	6½ Vase	"	50			1/-	1/6	4/6
" "	8½ "		40			2/-	2/6	10/6
" 302	5" Sprink"	W2079	60			2/-	10	7/-
" 303	4¾ "	W2078	60			1/3	8	5/-
" 304	" "	"	60			1/3	8	5/-
" 305	" "	"	60			1/3	8	5/-
" 306	9" Vase	W2050	30		1/9	19/6	4/6	50/-
" 307	" "	W2051	"		1/9	17/-	4/6	48/-
" 308	5¾ Bowl		60	15/-		18/-	5/6	70/-
" 309	8" 2Hd Vase	W2042	20		1/-	15/6	4/6	42/-
" 310	"	W2045	"		1/-	16/-	4/6	42/-
" 311	6½ Vase	W2061	50			2/10	1/6	10/6
" 312	6¾ Vase	W2082	50			4/-	1/6	12/-
" 313	8¼ Vase		35	20/-		12/-	3/6	65/-
" 314	6¼ Vase	W2083	50			5/3	1/6	13/6
" 315	4" Vase		120			9	10	3/3
" 316	4" Bowl		60	5/-		2/3	1/9	17/6
× 300	7"		70			1/-	1/6	7/6

228

No.	Articles	No	Pattern	Eng	Brushing	Clothing	Barbs Painting	Sale
J. 317	8in Vase		30	6/-		6/6	3/6	32/-
" 318	6¾ Vase W2032	W2030	30		1/2	24/6	4/-	60/-
" 319	6½ Vase	W2060	50			3/-	1/6	10/6
" 320	6¼ Vase	W2037	24		9	8/6	3/-	30/-
" 321	6½ Vase		30	13/-		20/-	3/-	70/-
" 322	9in Vase	W2092	30			7/9	2/-	22/-
" 323	" "	"	36			7/9	2/-	22/-
" 324	7in Vase	W2102	70			5/9	1/-	13/6
" 325	6¼ Vase	W2094	50			4/2	1/6	12/-
" 326	4in Bowl		72			8	1/-	5/-
" 327	4in Bowl	W2112	80			9	1/-	4/6
" 328	11in Vase		50			4/6	2/-	15/-
" 329	9in Vase	W2071	30			7/6	2/-	22/-
" 330	9in Vase	W2070	30			6/-	2/-	22/-
" 331	8½ Vase	W2069	40			4/-	2/-	15/-
" 332	7½ Vase		30	2/6		1/-	1/3	17/-
" 333	6in Vase	W2085	70			10/-	5/-	26/-
" 334	m/s Violet	W2113	120			4/2	3	1/10
" "	2/s "	"	110			6	4	2/3
" "	4 "					10/-	6	4/6

No.	Articles	no	Make nurturn	Eng	Brushw	Etching	Barbi Painty	Sale
I. 335	8" Vase	W2084	45			5/9	1/-	15/-
" 336	2 inch Watch Bottle	W2075	100			1/- Colour 1/3		3/6 coloured
" 337	5½ Vase	W2065	50			10 Colour 1/4		4/-
" 338	5½ Vase	W2111	72			10	1/-	5/-
" 339	5" Vase	W2106	40			4/3	1/6	12/6
" 340	Flat side 5½ Vase	W2100	60			13/-	4/6	32/-
" 341	8" Vase		30	5/-		2/6	2/7/6	21/- ✓
" 342	" "	W2092	30			7/9	1/6	21/-
" 343	" "	"	"			7/9	1/6	21/-
" 344	7 ..		"	5/-		2/6	1/6	21/-
" 345	3½ Vase	W2066	72			1/6	2/-	4/6
" 346	2¾ Vase	W2064	72			8	4	3/-
" 347	3" Vase		120	4		4	6 Colour 10	3/6
" 348	6" oval Bowl	W2103	60		c.1/-	5/-	2/1/3	16/6
" 349	4½ Vase		60			8	10	4/6
" 350	8½ Vase		50	3/6	1/-	2/3	2/6	18/-
" 351	" "	W2087	50			7/4	2/6	20/-
" 352	Flat side 5½ Vase	W2104	72			13/6	4/-	33/-
" 353	6½ Vase	W1997	40		1/-	2/6	1/3	not coloured 10/6 12/6

Number	Articles	No	Make per turn	Eng?	Brushing	Etching	Bark painting	Sale
I. 354	6½ Vase	W2150	40		1/-	2/10	1/3	not polished 10/d 12/6
" 355	13" Vase	Guest	16			8/6	5/6	45/-
" 356	8" Vase		30			7/9	1/6	21/-
" 357	7½ Vase		30	2/6	1/-	1/3		12/-
" 358	8½ Vase		50	3/6		2/3	2/6	18/-
" 359	8½ Vase	W2086	50			6/3	2/6	18/-
" 360	7" Vase	W2102	70			5/9	1/6	14/-
" 361	3½ Vase	Guest	72			8	6	3/3
" 362	4" Bowl	"	72			8	8	4/6
" 363	8" Bamboo	W2110	80			9/-	2/6	21/-
" 364	9 "	W2131	80			5/3	2/-	14/6
" 365	9 "	W2132	80			6/3	2/-	16/6
" 366	7" Vase	W2109	80			7/3	2/-	18/6
" 367	6½ Vase		28	20/-	1/-	12/-	2/6	65/-
" 368	7" Vase	W2108	72		1/3	13/-	3/6	34/-
" 369	7" Hd Bowl	W2088	20			8/6	4/6	30/-
" 370	7 " "	W2089	20			10/-	4/6	33/-
" 371	S/S Globe	G	130			4	3	1/6
" "	M/S "		120			4	3	1/9
" "	L/S "		110			4	4	2/2

363
X 364   deco. forget me not   Job B. 1/6 _____ 6/-
363   "   "   "   1/3 _____
358   "   "   "   2/6 _____ 7/6

231

Number	Articles	No	Make per turn	Eng	Brushing &c	Etching &c	Painting	Sale
S. 372	3" Candle niic	W 2114	72			1/8	4	4/-
„ 373	1½ „ „	„ „	130			1/8	4	4/-
„ 374	2½ „ „	„ „	120			1/8	4	4/-
„ 375	12½ Vase	W 2098	24		1/6	10/-	5/-	40/-
„ 376	12½ Vase	W 2096	24		1/6	19/6	5/-	50/-
„ 377	15½ Vase	W 1994	14		3/-	70/-	14/-	8 gns
„ 378	3½ Violet			8		4	8	4/-
„ 379	12½ Hd Vase	W 2033	15		3/-	78/-	10/-	£10.
„ 380	„ „		15	32/-		18/-	8/-	115/-
„ 381	12" Vase	W 2101	„		1/6	11/-	3/6	32/-
„ 382	6½ Vase	Guest	20			3/6	2/-	16/6
„ 383	Honey		50		8	1/6	1/-	
„ „	Butter		45		1/-	2/-	1/-	
„ „	Biscuit		28		1/6	3/-	1/6	
„ „	Salad		15 20		2/-	6/-	3/-	
„ 384	Honey		60		9	1/6	1/-	7/-
„ „	Biscuit		35		1/-	3/-	1/6	14/-
„ „	Salad Bowl Helpers		20		1/6	6/-	3/-	26/3
„ „	Butter		55		9	2/-	1/-	4/3 10/-

232

Number	Article	W No	per turn	Eng	Brushing	Etching	Painting	Sale
J 385	Beaker	~~5~~	55				1/6	1/-
" 386	Tusk Jug	~~30~~	30			5/-	2/6	21/-
" 387	5" Hd Vase	W 2142	30		1/6	7/6	2/6	30/-
" 388	10" Hd Vase	G	20			5/-	3/-	25/-
" 389	6½ Hd Vase		24	3/-		2/-	2/6	20/-
"	8" "		20	5/-	1/-	3/-	2/6	25/-
" 390	" "		24			8/-	2/6	22/6
" 391	L/S Bottle	W 2054				3/6	1/6	11/-
"	" M/S		"			3/6	1/-	
" 392	S/S Globe	G	130			4	3	1/6
"	" M/S "	"	120			4	3	1/9
"	" L/S "	"	110			4	4	2/2
" 393	12" Vase		30	8/-		3/-	3/6	30/-
" 394	12 Vase	G	30			4/-	3/6	20/-
" 395	6½" Vase	G	40			1/-	1/3	7/6
"	8½ "	"	35			2/-	2/3	
" 396	7" Vase	W 2143	60			6/3	1/3	16/-
" 397	" "	G	60			1/6	1/3	8/6
" 398	Tusk Jug	W 2099	30		2/-	9/6	2/6	28/-
" 399	7" Triangle Bowl	W 2143				9/6	3/-	32/-

233

Number	Articles	W. No	Return	Eng	Brushing	Etching	Painting	Sale
J 400	6" Vase	G	40			1/-	1/3	£ 7/6
" 401	2" Watch Bottle	W2163	100			10	5¾	3/6
" 402	3" Fig shape Bottle	W2160				9	5¾	3/3
" 403	2" Watch Bottle	W2162	100			1/2	5	4/-
" 404	3" Fig shape Bottle	W2160				9	5 "	3/3
" 405	" "	W2161				8	5 "	4/-
" "	2" Watch Bottle		100			8	5 "	4/-
" 406	" "	W2161	100			8	5 "	3/3
" "	3" Fig Bottle	"				7	5 "	
" 407	7 Vase		30			1/6	1/6	9/6
" 408	5½" Globe	2048			1/4	16/6	3/6	40/-
" 409	5½ Hd Hl Vase	W2138				14/-	2/6	35/-
" 410	7 Vase			45/- (40/2 doz)	1/6	12/-	4/6	130/-
" 411	" "			45/-	1/6	12/-	4/6	149/-
" 412	8" Bowl	W2144				8/3	3/-	32/-
" 413	Tush Jug	W2136	30	6		3/3	1/6	14/-
" 414	Ink	W2152		6		3/3	1/3	12/-
" 415	4½ Bowl	W2029	60	6		7/6	1/6	18/6
" 416	8½ Vase	W2124	50		1/-	7/4	2/6	20/-

Number	Article	W. No	Perform	Eng	Brushing	Etching	Painting	Sale
J. 417	4½ Bowl	W2125	60		1/-	5/-	1/3	14/-
" 418	11½ Vase		25			16/-	3/6	35/-
" 419	8½ Vase		40			8/-	2/-	18/6
" 420	10.. Vase	W2094	30		1/3	8/6	3/-	26/-
" 421	12 Vase	W2097	24		1/6	10/6	5/-	40/-
" 422	2/5 Bottle	W2155	50			4/8	1/6	13/-
" 423	m/s ..	W2154	60		6	4/-	1/3	14/-
" 424	9½ Vase	W.2115	30		1/6	6/-	3/-	25/-
" 425	15½ Vase	W2034	14		2/3	36/-	8/6	105/-
" 426	9.. Vase	W 2053	30			43/-	4/6	5 guin
" 427	8.. Vase		30	15/-	1/3	25/-	3/6	80/-
" 428	10.. Vase	W2052	18		2/-	20/6	5/-	50/-
" 429	1½ Jug	W2090	35			7/6	1/6	20/-
" 430	1½ Jug	W2091	35			7/6	1/6	20/-
" 431	Rose Jar	W2130	18 2 pieces			19/6	5/-	50/-
" 432	Rose Jar (Covers)	" "				4/6	3/6	24/-
" 433	Rose Jar	W2129	" "			10/6	3/6	30/-
" 434	Rose Jar	W2127	" "			8/6	3/6	30/-
" 435	Rose Jar	W2191	" "			6/6	3/6	24/-

Number	Articles	W. No	Per turn	Eng	Brushing	Etching	Painting	Sale
I. 436	11" Vase	Guest	24	6		3/6	4/-	22/6
" "	8½ "	"		'/-		3/-	2/6	16/-
" 437	13½ Vase	"	28	1/-		4/6	5/-	25/-
" 438	10½ Vase	"	35	3		4/6	3/6	20/-
" 439	7½ Vase	"	35			3/-	2/-	14/-
" 440	6½ Vase	"	40			3/6	1/6	12/-
" 441	5" Vase	"	40			1/-	1/-	8/-
" 442	8½ Vase	"	30	6		4/6	2/6	18/-
" 443	10" Vase	"	30	6		3/6	2/6	17/-
" 444	8½ Vase	"	50	2		4/-	2/3	14/-
" 445	8" Vase	"	40	6		3/6	2/-	14/-
" 446	8" Vase	"	36	7		3/6	2/-	15/-
" 447	5" Vase	"	50	6		1/-	9	6/-
" 448	6¾ Vase	"	30	2		1/6	1/3	10/-
" 449	9" Vase	"	30	2		3/6	2/6	16/-
" 450	8¼ Vase	"	20			3/6	3/6	21/-
" 451	7" Vase	W 2107	72		1/3	13/6	2/3	28/-
" 452	10" 8½ Vase	W 2095a	30		1/3	6/3	3/-	22/-
" 453	10" "	W 2095	30		1/3	6/3	3/-	22/-

236

Number	Articles	W. No	Per Turne	Eng	Brushing &c	Etching	Painting	Sale
J.+ 454	8½ Vase	35	35	5/-	1/-	2/6	2/-	18/6
" 455	7- Vase		70	2/-	8	1/6	1/3	10/-
" 456	5½ Vase		40			1/-	1/-	7/-
" 457	4in Vase	W 2073			8	5/6	9	14/-
" 458	8½ Vase	W 1876	35		1/3	29/-	3/6	70/-
" 459	6½ Vase		40		1/-	2/6	1/3	12/-
" 460	" "		"		1/-	2/6	1/3	12/-
" 461	" "		"		1/-	2/6	1/3	12/-
" 462	6¾ Vase		50	1/8	9/-	10	1/3	9/-
" 463	8½ Vase		30			2/6	2/-	12/-
" 464	9 Salad Bowl	W 2063	20			5/6	3/-	
" 465	8- Vase		20	5/-	1/-	3/-	2/6	25/-
" 466	7in Vase	W 2041	35		"	24/6	2/-	45/-
" 467	6½ Vase	Guest				3/6	1/6	12
" 468	4½ Vase	W 1861	30			29/6	3/6	63/-
" 469	6- Vase	W 1848				19/-	2/6	45/-
" 470	6- Vase		72		2/-	8/-	1/6	20/-
" 471	3½ Vase		72		1/-	7/-	1/-	20/-
" 472	4½ Vase	W 2139				1/9	1/-	8/6

x   454 dec forget no not   lot price   3/-   8/6

237

Number	Articles	W No	Per turn	Eng	Brush &c	Clothing	Painting	Sale
J. 473	3¾ Vase	W 2141	80			1/9	1/-	10/6
" 474	4½ Vase	W 2126				1/3	10	5/-
" 475	2½" Bottle	W 2159				1/7	5	4/-
" "	3"	"	130			1/10	6	5/-
" 476	3" "	"	"	3/6			10	8/4
" 477	3" "	W 2192ᵃ				2/6	6	4/12
" 478	S/S Inks	W. 2157	60		1/-	2/-	8	6/-
" "	L/S "	W. 2153	65		1/-	2/10	10	9/4
" 479	S/S Ink	W 2156	60		1/-	2/2	8	6/-
" "	L/S	W 2157	65		1/-	2/6	10	9/4
" 480	8" Hd Bowl	Guest	24			5/6	3/-	25/-
" 481	S/S Globe (viol)		110	7½		2½	6	3/3
" "	M/S "		120	5		2	4	2/3
" "	S/S "		130	4		2	3	2/-
" 482	L/S "		110	7½		2½	6	
" "	M/S "		120	5		2	4	
" "	S/S "		130	4		2	3	
" 483	L/S "		110	7½		2½	6	3/3
" "	M/S "		120	5½		2½	4	2/3
" "	S/S "		130	4		2	3	2/-

238

Number	Articles	W. No.	Per turn	Engd	Brushing &c	Etching &c	Painting	Sale
J. 484	7in Vase		70			3/6	1/3	9/-
" 485	5in Vase	W 1888		2/-		17/6	3/-	50/-
" 486	6in Vase		65			1/6	1/6	4/6
" 487	6½ Vase		70			1/6	1/6	8/6
" 488	8in Vase		50			2/-	2/-	10/-
" 489	10½ Vase		50			2/6	2/3	13/-
" 490	10in Vase		30			3/6	3/-	18/6
" 491	Ink	W 2158				2/9	1/3	9/-
" 492	3½ Globe Toilet	W 1898				2/4	1/-	
" 493	Large Tusk Jug		30			6/6	5/-	30/-
" 494	8in Hd Bowl					3/6	4/6	20/-
" 495	9in Vase	W 2182	30	1/9		9/9	4/-	35/-
" 496	7in Bowl					2/-	2/6	12/-
" 497	9½ Vase	Guest				4/6	4/-	25/-
" 498	8in Vase		45			2/6	1/6	9/-
" 499	12in Candleabrum Pedestal	W 2151		1/6		24/6	5/-	40/-
	"							
	"							
	"							

Number	Articles	W. No	Pattern turn	Eng	Brushs +6	Etching +6	Painting	Sale
J. 500	15"	(D.P. 1340) W 2093	18		2/6	27/-	5/6	84/
" 501	13" Vase		24	√2/-	2/-	24/-	4/6	4 gns
" 502	12" Vase		24		1/6	12/6	5/-	
" 503	10½ Vase	Guest	50			2/-	1/6	8/6
" 504	8" Vase	"	50			2/-	2/-	8/6
" 505	6" Vase	"	65			2/-	1/6	8/-
" 506	4¾ Vase	"	10			/6	9	3/6
" 507	6" Vase			3/-	9	1/3	1/-	12/-
" 508	5½ Vase		50	3/6		1/3	1/-	11/-
" 509	4¼" Vase			2/9		1/9	1/-	9/-
" 510	" "			2/9		1/3	1/-	9/-
" 511	" "			2/9		1/-	1/-	8/6
" 512	4" Bowl			2/-		1/6	1/-	7/-
" 513	4" "			3/-		2/3	1/-	12/6
" 514								
" 515	10" Vase		30	6/-	1/6	2/6	2/-	22/-
" 516	8½ Vase		30					15/- 22/-
516½								
" 517	8" Vase	W 2195			1/6	5/3	2/-	18/6
" 518	8½ Vase					3/-	2/-	12/
518½							3/6 extra painting	18/

240

Number	Articles	W. No	Per Turn	Eng.	Brush	Etching	Painting	Sale
	card Tray							
9 519	9 in Plate	W 2072	40		1/6	15/-	3/-	36/-
" 520	7 in Plate	W 2015	50			10/6 8/6	1/6	
" 521	7½ "	W 2187	70		1/-	6/6	1/6	20/-
" 522	11½ Vase		25			18/-	3/6	38/-
" 523	10 in Hd Vase		16	35/-	2/-	2/4	4/-	150/-
" 524	7 in Vase	W 2196	35		1/3	4/2	1/6	14/-
" 525	9½ Vase	W 2198	30			6/3	4/6	22/6
" 526	6 Hd Vase	W 2192	24	1	1/3	3/3	2/-	15/-
" 8	"	W 2192	20		1/6	5/-	2/6	21/-
" 12	"	W 2192			2/-	8/-	3/6	35/-
" 527	6 "	"	24/-	9/-	1/9	9/-	4/6	45/-
" 528	6 "	"					5/6	3/-
" 529	2/s Black Jugs		30	6/-	1/9	2/-	2/6	24/-
"	4/s "		40	4/-	5	1/-	10	12/-
"	5/s "		40	2/-	6	9	8	8/-
" 530	8 in Hd Vase		20		1/6	4/8	2/-	21/-
" 531	6 " "		24		1/3	3/-	1/6 2/6	15/-
" 532	8 in Vase		4	4/6		1/9	1/6	12/6

Number	Articles	W. No.	Per turn	Eng	Brush & Etching	Painting	Sale
I. 533	8" Vase	W 2206	45		9⁰	3/-	1/6	10/6
" "	7" "				7⁰	2/6	1/-	8/-
" "	5½ "		55		5⁰	1/8	8	5/3
" 534	8" "	W 2205	45		9⁰	1/8	1/6	8/6
" "	7" "				7	1/2	1/-	6/-
" "	5½ "		55		5¹⁰	10	8	4/-
" 535	6½ Vase					1/9	1/6	7/-
" 536	7" Vase					3/-	1/6	10/- 10/.
" 536½	" (Candle)							
" 537	5½" Stick	W 2212			4	1/10	1/-	7/6
" 538	" "	"	.		4	1/10	1/-	7/-
" 539	5½" Candle Stick	W 2213			5	2/4	1/-	8/6 —
" 540	7" "	W 2221			6	2/3	1/-	8/6
" 541	" "	W 2214			6	2/2	1/-	8/6
" 542	5½" "	W 2218			5	2/2	1/-	8/-
" 543	" "	W 2217			5	1/2	1/-	7/-
" 544	7" "	W 2215			6	1/10	1/- gilt 1/-	8/-
" "	" "	"						
" 545	6½" "	W 2222			6	2/10	4/- gilt 15/-	
" 546	5½" "	W 2216			5	2/4	1/- gilt 12/6 &	8/6

No	Articles	W. No	Per turn	Eng	Brushing	Etching	Painting	Sale
547	Candle 5/4 Stick	W 2216			5	2/4	1/-	8/6
" 548	H'd Candle 5/4 Stick	W 2218			7	2/2	1/-	8/6
" 549	5/2 " "	W 2219			7	1/7	1/-	8/-
" 550	5/4 " "	W 2220			7	2/7	1/- Gilt 13/6	10/-
" 551	3" Vase					1/6	1/-	
" 552	8" Vase	R		5/147-	9	4/-	1/-	37/6
" 553	10/2 Vase		50	5/-	1/3	2/6	2/3	21/-
" 554	Globe 3/2 Toilet			3/-		2/6	6	12/-
" 555	" "			3/6		2/-	6	12/-
" 556	" "			3/6		2/-	6	12/-
" 557	3in "			6/-			6	14/-
" 558	9 inch Salad Bowl					4/6 6	3/6 6	
" 559	Handle 5/2 Vase		30	8/-	1/-	12/-		
" 560	8/2 "							
" 561	3 N Tankard for mounts	W		1/6		6/-	2/3	20/-
" "	Gobld Bowl	W		6		2/6	10	7/6
" 562	3 N Tankard for mounts	4				4/6	2/6	17/6
" "	Gobld Bowl	-				1/6	10	6/-
" 563	3 N Tankard for mounts	4				3/-	2/3	16/-
" "	Gobld Bowl	"				1/-	10	5/6

243

Number	Articles	W N°	Per turn	Eng	Brushig &c	Clothg	Painting	Sale
J 564	10 Vase			55/		9/-	47/	
" 565	Biscuit							
" 566	"							
" 567	3/4 " Vase						decoⁿ 9/6	26/4
" 568	12ᵐ Vase						decoⁿ 95/	
" 569	6½ Vase						decoⁿ 30/-	
" 570	8½ Vase			15/	1/-	18/-	decoⁿ 26/-	126/
" 571	6½ Vase						Enameled 6½ 72/- 9½ 105/	Reves 6.10. 9.10.0 with Eliz
" 572	4ᵐ Flᵈ Bowl						Enameled 58/-	80/
" 573	6½ Vase						Enameled 76/-	
" 574	8ᵐ Vase						55/	
" 575	" "	"	Woodall 22/		Barber 5/6			x
" 576	7" "							£10.
" 577	8" "							
" 578	" "							
" 579	8½ Bowl							
" 580	7½ Vase							
" 581								
" 582	9½ Vase							

No	Articles	W. No	Per Turn	Eng.	Brush 46	Etchs. 46	Pansly	Sale
9.583	11ın Vate							£10/10
„ 584	10 „			35/-	1/1	26/-	31/6	£9.
„ 585	9½ „						6/-	
„ 586	8½ „			2/1		5/		
„ 587	13½ Ha Vate							£26
„ 588	11½ Vate							
„ 589	15 „ „			24/-		16/-	32/-	£7.
„ 590	12 „ „ „							£10.
„ 591	11 „ „							
+ 592	12½ „	9. 2233	24			35/-		
„ 593	8 „ „		50				2/6	7/-
„ 594	4½ „ „	W 2273	(decorated For set now not full price) Cost 16/5					32/-
„ 595	„ „							
„ 596	9 „ „							
„ 597	5½ „							
„ 598	3½ „ —							
„ 599	„ „							
„ 650	6½ „							
„ 601	8½ „		70					£4
+ 592	8½	9. 2233	40			23/-	3/6	£3/1.
„	6½	„	50			11/-	2/-	-30/-

Number	Article	W. Number	Plain Turn.	Brushes +6	Eng	Etchg	Paints	Sale
J 602	8in Vase							
" 603	" "							
" 604 9	" W.2312			2/6		95/-	55/-	
" 604½	"			2/6		95/-	4/6	£12/-
" 605 10 Bowl	2316	14		3/6		£7.3.0	£5.5.0	£26/10/-
" 606 6½ Vase	W 2327	40				34/-	15/-	£5.15/
" 607 4in "	W22			6		5/6	2/6	20/-
" 608 9in Flat side Vase	W2330	4		3/6		£6-4-0	5/- pair	£8.0.0 £8.8.0
" 609 Large Vase & Cov	W2318 .8			5/6		£11-13-0	£6-10-0	£42.0.0
" 610 4½ Bowl	W 2356		(F. 1/-)			41/-		£6
" 611 4 "	W2456					40/-		£7.10
" 612 16in Vase	W2317	12	4/6			8.14.0	70/-	£26.0.0
" 613 9 "	R	24				75/-		£9.17.6
" 614 6½ H.d Vase		24	42 Jernals 10/6	30/-		14/-	5/-	£5/0/0
" 615 8½ Vase	R	24				70/-		£8.8/
" 616 " "		"				80/-		£9.9/
" 617 9 Vase		28				60/-		£6.15/
" 618 7½ "		24				75/-		£7.7/
" 619 " "		24				55/-		£6.6/
" 620 " "		30				65/-	25/-	£12
604a		W2312a		2/6		92/-	23/6	£12

Number	Article	W number	Per Turn	Brush 4/6	Eng	Clds	Paints	Sale
S. 621	4½ Vase		40		35/-		1	80/-
" 622	5" Vase	K	50	Jewel 1½	12/6	3/6		45/-
" 623	4½ "	"			15/-	2/-		35/ 42/-
" 624	7½ Vase	W 2331	30		31/-	2/-		£4.10/-
" 625	8" "	W 2347	30	2/-	50/-	3/-		£6.6/-
" 626	6½ "	W 2346	30	1/6	32/-	1/10		£4.10/-
" 627	7" "	W 2328	30	1/6	30/-	1/6		£4.5/-
" 628	6½ "	W 2349	40	48 Jewel 3 cols 1/-	9/-	8/-	4/6	42/-
" 629	5½ "	W 2345	30	1/-	36/-	1/10		£4.4/-
" 630	6½ "	W 2325	35		34/-	3/-		£4.4/-
" 631	6" "	W 2332	40	1/-	34/-	3/-		£4.4/-
" 632	6½ Ha Bowl	W 2323	60	2/-	82/-	4/6		£10.10
" 633	6½ Vase	W 2352		8	20/-	1/6		50/- 7.10.0
" 634	7½ Ha Vase	K		(28 Jewel 10)	24/-	7/-		£3.12/-
" 635	8½ Vase	K	24		£6.0.0			£12.10/- £15
" 636	8½ Bottle	W 2387		1/6	18/6	2/-		40/-
" 637	6" "	W 2388		1/-	10/-	1/-		22/6
" 638	3½ "	W 2386		9	7/-	6		16/-
" 639	2" "	W 2113a			4½	3		

Number	Articles	W No	Per Turn	Bruts	Eng	Etchs	Pands	Sale
J. 640	7" Vase	K.		bundle 1/	6/-	9/-	2/6	45/ 60/ with edge
" 641	6" "	2404 w		1/-		25/6	2/6	65/-
" 642	8½ "	K.	24		126/-			£ s d 12.12.0
" 643	5½ "	W 2413ʰ		6		17/-		4.2/
" 644	" "	W 2412ᵃ		6		17/-		45/ 60/
" 645	7 "	W 2412				27/-	2/6	80/- with fans
" 646	6½ "	. .			36/-			8/-
" 647	6½ "		(31 bundle 9)	1/-	15/-	16/-	4/6	75/ 70/ with fans
" 648	5½ "		bundle 1/-	1/-	18/-	20/-	4/6	90/-
" 649	5½ "	W 2324		1/-		28/-	12/6	80/-
" 650	" "	W "		1/-		28/-	2/6	80/-
" 651	5 "	K			12/-	1/3		28/-
" 652	8" Vase	W 2454		1/6		56/-	35/-	£8 15
" 653	5" Glow Bow	W 2287	12	2/-		46/-	12/6	£7
" 654	9" Vase	W 2431		1/6		66/-	33/-	£10.10
" 655	6" "	W 2413		1/6		25/-	5/-	45/ 40/
" 656	6 "	W 2484	14	1/6		44/6	3/6	105/-
" 657	6½ Vase	W 2449	14	1/6		21/6	5/-	70/ 60/
" 658	7" "	W 2479	14	1/6		37/6	5/-	£6

248

No.	Articles	W.No.	Per Turn	Bruns	Eng	Elbod	Pauls	Sale
9159	6½ Vase	W2451	14	1/6		34/6	5/-	84/-
9160	3½ Vase	W246		1/-		28/6	15/6	£5
9661	1½ "	W.2484		1/6		46/6	9/6	£7.6
662	Plate	W2438				2/6	5/6	16/-
to "	Low Comport	"				3/-	6/6	21/-
" "	Tall "	"				3/6	7/6	30/-
663	4" Bowl	W2502		1/6		46/6		£6.10
664	7" "	W2465		1/6		60/-	29/6	£8.00 £7.10
665	" "	W2464		1/6		38/6	18/-	£5.10 7.10
666	6" Vase	W.2350		9		8/6	1/6	90/- 25/-
667	4" Globe Bowl	W.2509		1/-		56/6		£6.10
668	" "	W2508		1/-		68/6		£7.17
669	" "	W2506		1/-		80/-	5/6	£11.11
670	6½ Vase	J		1/-	18/6	18/-	2/-	63/-
671	9" "			1/3		3/-	2/6	16/6
672	3½ Globe Bowl				50/-		1/6	84/-
673	9" Vase					4/6	2/6	22/6
674	9" Vase	W2203		1/-		5/6	2/6	21/-
75	6" Bowl	K		1/-	25/-		5/6	60/-

Number	Articles	W. Number	Per cases	Brushing &c	Engr.	Etching	Pottery	Sale
3676	9½ Vase	Faun		1/-	40/-	33/-	8/6	105/-
" 677	8" Hd Vase			1/6	15/-	12/-	21/-	£5.5.0
" 678	9" Vase			1/3	50/-	30/-	2/6	£7. [6.10.0]
" 679	10" "			1/6	26/-	20/-	30/-	£6-6.0
" 680	4" Globe Bowl	W 2505		1/-		44/-	16/6	£7-10-0
" 681	4" Hd Vase	W as J. 24	30			19/-	1/6	44/-
" 682	4" Globe Bowl	W 2507				80/-		£10-10-0
" 683	Salad Bowl	W 2613				7/6	6/6	35/-
" 684	Lamp body	" 3552	Plain o/4 cut ?			13/6	2/6	30/- [57.12]
" 685	"	W 2536	"	" 6		12/6	2/6	28/-
" 686	"	W 2535	"	" 6		10/-	2/6	25/-
" 687	8½ Vase	W 2600				98/-	18/-	£15.
" 688	10" Vase	Kritschman		1/6	7/6		2/6	
" 689	9" Flat Side Vase	K.		2/-	132/-	40/-		£25.
" 689½	"	"		2/-	130/-	40/-		£25.
" 690	10" Vase	Painted Forged	Plain 6/6				8/-	18/6
" 691	9" "	"	" 4/6				5/6	13/-
" 692	6" "	"	" 1/6				2/-	4/-
" 693	6" "	"	" 2/-				2/-	4/6

250

Number	Article	W Number	Per Turne	Wash	Eng?	Etch?	Painting	Sale
J.694	6½ Vase	Painted forget me nots	Plum 4/6				2/-	7/-
J.695	4½ Bowl	"	" 1/-				1/6	3/6
" 696	4 " "	"	" 1/3				1/6	3/9
" 697	4 " "	"	" 1/-				2/3	4/3
" 698	5 " Vase	"	" 1/3				1/3	3/3
" 699	3½ Globe Toilet	"	" ? 1/3				1/3	3/9
" "	3in "	"	"				1/-	3/3
" "	2½ "	"	"				9/-	2/6
" 700.	4in Vase	"	" 1/0				1/3	3/-
" 701	5 " "	"	" 1/-				1/-	2/6
" 702	4½ Sprinkler	"	" 10				10	2/-
" 703	3½ Bowl	"	" 1/-				1/-	2/6
" 704	Ginger		1/3				1/6	3/6
" 705	Violet		2/-				8	3/3
" 706	10 inch Salad Bowl					15/-	3/-	40/-
" 707	9in Vase	W 2202		1/6	3/6	4/6	3/-	26/-
" 708	" "	" 2201		1/6	3/6	4/3	3/-	25/-
" 709	" "	2202½		1/6	3/6	4/3	3/-	25/-
" 710	" "	Fritsch		1/6	5/-	2/6	3/-	36/-

Number	Article	W. Warre	Pattern	Brushing	Eng 9.	Etching	Painting	Sale
J. 711.	5 in Vase			1/6	6/-		1/6	20/-
„ 712	6 in Vase			1/6	8/6		1/6	25/-
„ 713								
„ 714	3/S Mug 2/S „	W.2627				2/6 3/-	3/6 5/-	13/6 18/-
„ 715	9 in Vase	W 2570		1/6		72/-	..	£ 12.
„ 716	Tankard	W 2613		1/6		4/6	8/6	30/-
„ 717	„	„				„	..	30/-
„ 718	Melon shape Claret in	W 2619			)	4/6	13 3589 6/6	28/-
„ 719	3 1/2 Goblet Toilet	W 2621 a				2/-	2/6	12/-
„ 720	9 in Plate							
„	Four Compote							
„	Tale „							
„ 721	10 in Berry plain		20					15/-
„ 722	9 in Vase							30/-
J. 723	7 1/2 in Ivory piece at bottom „	W 2597				5/-	10/6	42/-
J. 724	6 1/2 Vase Ivory polished	W. 2691				4/6		12/-
J. 725	6 side Vase					Wordall Estimat 39/-		70/3
J. 726	7 in Vase	W2286				W. 13/-	5/6	50/-
J. 727	8 1/2 in Bowl Painted Blackberry	B 4059	30				5/-	10/6

Number	Article	W/Number	Per Turner	Brushing &c	Eng g	Clay Paint	Sale
J.728	5½ in Bowl painted	B.4058				2/9	6/6
J.729	Vase painted for set men	B.4060				4/3	4/6
J.730	Vase painted & creepers	B.4061				2/6	6/6
J.731	2 H⁴ Vase painted		24			1/6	8/6
J.732	Bamboo 7in Vase		80			1/6	5/-
..34	2 H⁴ Vase Painted Lilac		18			2/-	12/6
..735	G. Vase			1/6	3/-	6/- 10/6	42/-

Article	No	Description	Price
1 Vase	W467	Lemon on Ruby	£31.10
1 "	W780	Amber & White on Brown	£50
1 "	I258	White on Brown	£50
1 "	W882	Amber & White on Brown	£25
1 "	W914	White on Topaz	£15
1 "	W907	White on Ruby	£15
1 "	W908	" " "	£25
1 "	I355	Ruby on Jade	£65
1 "	I230	Amber	£3.3
1 "	I166	Blue	60/-
1 "	I164	Amber	45/-
1 "	W868	White & Green & Brown	£14
1 "	I260	Green & White on Ruby	£68
1 "	W868	White & Green on Brown	£14
1 "	W904	White on Topay	£4
1 Plate	W371	" " Ruby	£8.8
1 Vase	W380	White & Green on Amber	£24
1 "	I154	White on Brown	84/-
1 "	I245	White & Blue on Amber	70/-
1 "	W369	White on Amber	60/-
1 "	W927	Blue	47/6
1 "	I180	Ruby	55/-
1 "	W919	"	22/6
1 "	W918	Amber	21/-
1 "	I230	"	63/-
1 "	I166	Blue	60/-
1 "	I164	Amber	45/-
1 "	W681	White on Ruby	£30
1 "	I367	" "	£18.18

Prices of Cameo Vases & & no Photographs

sent to Winckley Hoo

21/1/85

1	"	W841	" " Amber	£15.15
1	"	W880	" " Ruby	£5.1.0
1	"	W701	Pink & White on Blue	£75..
1	"	W28	White on Dk Blue	£18..
1	"	W95	" " Brown	£22.10
1	"	W404	Lemon on Ruby	£22.10
1	"	W59	White on Amber	£15.
1	"	W60	" " "	£18.18
1	"	W33	" " "	£55
1	"	W926	" " Ruby	£16.16
1	"	W950	" " Topay	£19.18
1	"	W723	" " Amber	84/-
1	"	W906	" " Ruby	£8..
1	"	W863	" " Topay	84/-
1	"	W959	" " Amber	65/-
1	"	W960	" " Ruby	65/-

Article	No	Description	Price
1 Vase	W961	White on Topay	60/-
1 Plaque	W733	" " Brown	£63
1 "	W824	" " "	£75
1 Lamp Complete	W379	Lemon on Ruby	£45
1 " "	W48	White on Dk Blue	£16.16
1 " "	W692	" " Green	£30
1 Vase	W362	" " Ruby	84/-
1 "	W338	" " Topay	£8.8
1 "	W489	" " Ruby	£12.15
1 "	W881	" " "	£28
1 "	W929	" " Brown	£9.9
1 Toilet	W293	" " Ruby	£9.9
1 "	W235	" " Blue	65/-
1 "	W234	" " Ruby	65/-

as sen't to Australia Feb/1891

2 Vases	Bamboo	✓ 9 364	80 Turn. Dec'd Forget me not	1/6	
2	-	✓ 9 363	80 - -	1/3	5/
2	-	✓ 9 214 .	70 - -	1/3	4/
2	-	✓ 9 454 .	85 - -	3/	8/6
2	-	✓ 9 593	50 - -	2/6	7/
2	~	✓ 9 358	50. - -	2/6	7/6
1	-	15847.	Burmese 2/. -	1/3	3/6
2	-	14389.	Plain 4/6 . -	1/3	5/6
3	-	14301	-	1/-	3/9
2	-	-	-	8ᵈ	2/6

256

FIGURAL SKETCHES

W. 2582

Cost. pp - pr - x.
10 per liw
cost pp. pi. x
sale £ 0x.

S1

W 2801
White on Brown
W 2795 shope
"Carinna"

W 2804
White on Brown, Psyche

Figure
on W 2721

S2

W 2803
White on Brown
"Clochis
Cost 1 - l. d.

S3

W 2841
White on Brown
"Harmony"

S4

W. 2728
White on Brown

Natures Mirror
S5

W. 2731   cost £24 - h. ×
White on Brown   Sale

Fethered Favourite
S6

W. 2730
White on Brown
(Subject Pandora)

S7

W. 2725
White on Blue

S8

258

C192. Vase, 3 inches; striking geometric design. (Authors' collection)

C193. Vase, 10 inches, attributed to Stevens & Williams; African tulip. (Collection of Leo Kaplan Antiques)

C194. Vase, 5¾ inches, signed "Thomas Webb & Sons"; fuchsia decoration. (Private collection)

259

C195. Vase, 5½ inches, signed "Thomas Webb & Sons, Gem Cameo"; stylized fish motif. (Private collection)

C196. Vase, 2¼ inches, with strawberries on an engraved ground. (Private collection)

C197. Vase, 6 inches, signed "Thomas Webb & Sons, Gem Cameo"; passion flower motif. (Private collection)

C198. Vase, 6¼ inches, signed "Richardsons Cameo–Rich." (Collection of The Chrysler Museum of Art at Norfolk)

C199. Top of a walking stick, 1½ inches. (Private collection)

C200. Vase, 6½ inches, white on pink on gold. (Private collection)

C201. Vase, 4½ inches, with sunflower motif, signed "Webb." (Private collection)

C202. Vase, 9½ inches, signed "G. Woodall & Sons, Gem Cameo"; The Origin of Painting. *(Private collection)*

C203. Vase, 9½ inches, Origin of Painting, signed "G. Woodall 1887, Thomas Webb & Sons, Gem Cameo." *(Collection of James and Barbara Frambers)*

C210. Two perfumes with unusual enameled background; motifs are the Christmas rose and the cherry, 3½ inches. (Collection of Susan P. Kaplan, courtesy of Alan Kaplan)

C211. Perfumes, 3¾ inches, decorated with pears, a swan, and a brown monkey. (Collection of Susan P. Kaplan, courtesy of Alan Kaplan)

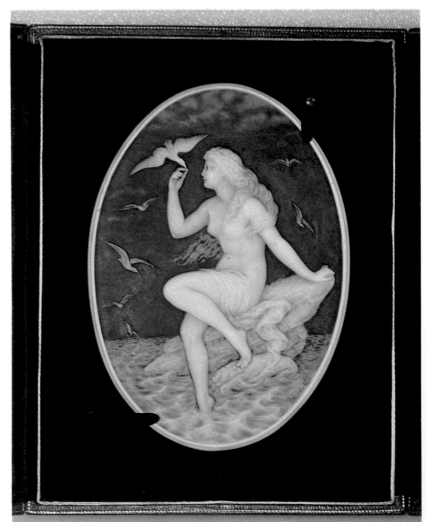

C212. Perfume bottle, 3½ inches, signed "Woodall." *(Private collection)*

C213. Framed panel, 6 inches, signed "Geo. Woodall."
Undine GW 31. *(Private collection)*

266

C214. Vase, 6½ inches, with overall floral decoration, signed "Thomas Webb & Sons, Gem Cameo." *(Private collection)*

C215. Vase, 6½ inches, with poppy motif; signed "Tiffany & Co., Paris Exhibition, Thomas Webb & Sons." *(Private collection)*

C216. Rambler rose vase, 4½ inches. *(Private collection)*

C217. Ivory decanter, 8 inches; signed "Thomas Webb & Sons, Gem Cameo." Melon-skin finish; the handle forms the melon stem. *(Private collection)*

C218. Vase, 7¼ inches, with iris, clematis, and bumblebee motifs, signed "Thomas Webb & Sons, Gem Cameo." *(Private collection)*

C219. Dolce Relievo covered jar, 7¼ inches, purple on cream ground; attributed to Stevens & Williams. *(Private collection)*

C220. Vase, 4 inches, with morning-glory design; signed "Webb." *(Authors' collection)*

C221. Vase, 8½ inches, with petunia motif, unfinished white casing over blue over brown. Acquired from Beatrice Alice Woodall, Kingswinford, England. *(Private collection)*

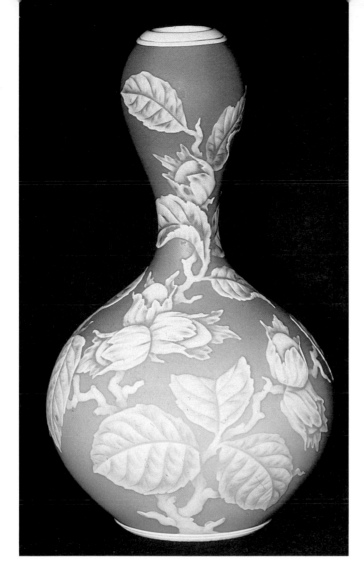

C222. Vase, 9 inches, in double gourd shape; signed "Thomas Webb & Sons, Gem Cameo." *(Private collection)*

C223. Vase, 9 inches, with apple blossom motif; signed "Thomas Webb & Sons, Gem Cameo." *(Private collection)*

C224. Perfume bottle with fine matching stopper, 4½ inches; signed "Thomas Webb & Sons, Gem Cameo." *(Private collection)*

269

C225. Anemone-decorated inkwell, 4¼ inches. *(Private collection)*

C226. Cologne bottle, 6½ inches. Floral design on the silver top matches the cameo body. *(Private collection)*

C227. Vase, 8 inches; signed "G. Woodall, Thomas Webb & Sons"; white on brown. *(Collection of Hilda and Hugh Creighton)*

C228. Vase, 5½ inches, with morning glory, signed Thomas Webb & Sons." *(Private collection)*

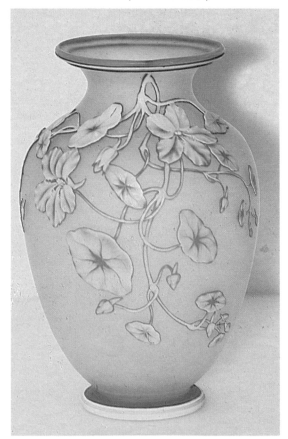

C229. Vase, 7¼ inches, with palm trees and bamboo, signed "Thomas Webb & Sons, Gem Cameo." *(Private collection)*

C230. Vase, 9 inches, signed "Thomas Webb & Sons, Cameo"; blackberry cameo on engraved red ground. *(Collection of Leo Kaplan Antiques, courtesy of Alan Kaplan)*

C231. Vase, 5¾ inches, with stylized roses; signed "Thomas Webb & Sons, Gem Cameo." *(Private collection)*

C232. Vase, 5 inches, with soft yellow rim and heavy carving of peaches, cherries, pears, and cattails around the bottom; signed "Tiffany & Co., Paris Exhibition 1889, Thomas Webb & Sons, Gem Cameo." *(Private collection)*

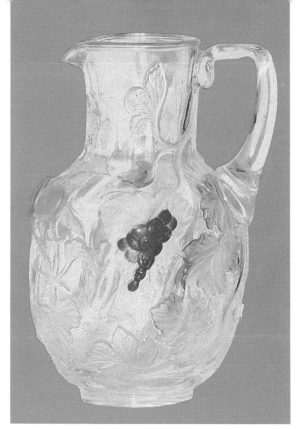

C233. Pitcher, 5½ inches, with raspberry, lemon, cherry, and butterfly decoration; signed "Webb." *(Private collection)*

C234. Vase, 5¾ inches, with passion-flower motif; signed "Thomas Webb & Sons." *(Collection of Willard Levin Antiques)*

C235. Vase, 8½ inches, rainbow cameo on diamond-quilted mother-of-pearl; attributed to Thomas Webb. *(Private collection)*

C236. Vase, 6 inches. Sixteen insects, including bees, butterflies, and dragonflies, are carved on this fine piece. *(Private collection)*

C237. Bamboo-shaped vase, 9 inches, with blackberry decoration. *(Private collection)*

C238. Vase, 5¾ inches, with sweet peas; signed "Thomas Webb & Sons, Gem Cameo." *(Private collection)*

C239. Lamp base, 10¾ inches, showing a female figure, along with an assortment of crocodiles, squirrels, serpents, a mongoose, clouds, and an owl, in addition to an arrow pointing to midnight. Signed "Thomas Webb & Sons, Gem Cameo." *(Private collection)*

C240. Plaque, 6 inches, white on brown, signed "Geo. Woodall." *(Collection of Howard and Paula Ellman)*

274

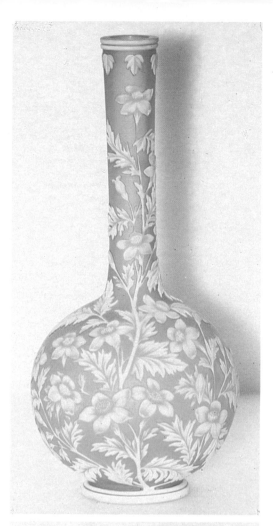

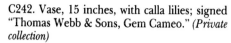

C241. Anemone vase, 9½ inches; signed "Thomas Webb & Sons." (*Private collection*)

C242. Vase, 15 inches, with calla lilies; signed "Thomas Webb & Sons, Gem Cameo." (*Private collection*)

C243. Vase, 8½ inches, with petunia motif; signed "Thomas Webb & Sons, Gem Cameo." (*Private collection*)

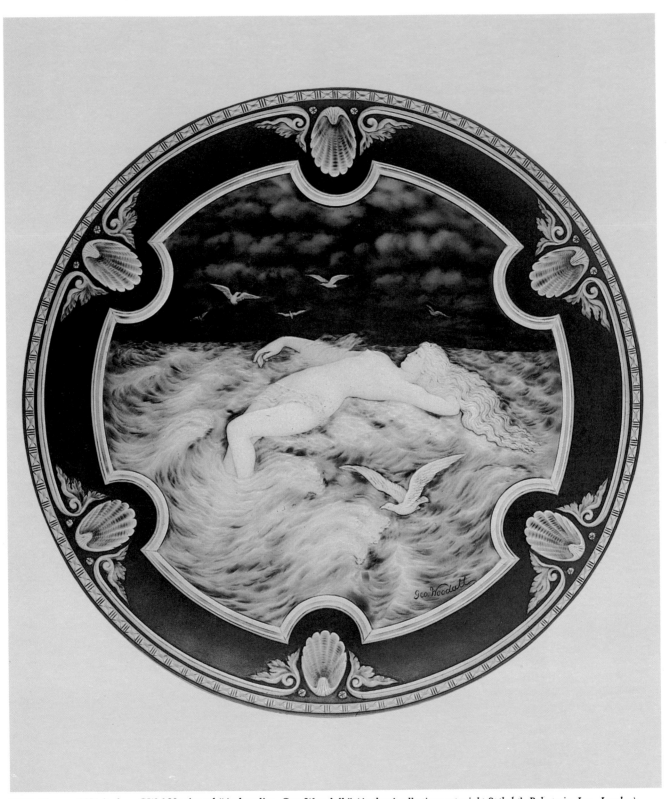

C244. Plaque, 10⅝ inches, GW 160; signed "Aphrodite, Geo Woodall." *(Authors' collection; copyright Sotheby's Belgravia, Inc., London)*

276

C245. Vase, 8 inches, with reindeer scene, signed "G. Woodall, Thomas Webb & Sons, Gem Cameo." *(Private collection)*

C246. Vase, 8¾ inches, carved and gilded; appliqués and marquetry techniques. *(Collection of Leo Kaplan Antiques, courtesy of Alan Kaplan)*

277

C247. Plaque, 6¼ inches; signed "Geo. Woodall, Thomas Webb & Sons, Gem Cameo." The back of the leather case is impressed "Alice Woodall"; front of the case impressed "*Song of the sea*, George Woodall." *(Private collection)*

C248. Oval portrait plaque, signed "F. Kretschman." *(Private collection)*

C249. Vase, 18¼ inches, with decoration of wheat, poppies, and foxglove; signed "Thomas Webb & Sons, Gem Cameo, Tiffany Exhibition 1889." *(Private collection)*

C250. Vase, 7 inches, with wild-rose motif; signed "Stevens & Williams, Art Glass, Stourbridge, England." *(Private collection)*

279

C251. Plaque known only as Venus and Cupid, 18¼ inches, signed "Geo. Woodall." *(Collection of The Corning Museum of Glass)*

C252. Vase, 7¾ inches, with unusual carving of a bird on an apple tree. *(Collection of Minna Rosenblatt Antiques)*

C253. Vase, 9 inches, in orchid pattern, signed "Webb." *(Collection of Leo Kaplan Antiques, courtesy of Alan Kaplan)*

C254. Vase, 9 inches, signed "Stevens & Williams, Art Glass." *(Private collection)*

C255. Vase, 8¼ inches, with gloxinias; signed "Thomas Webb & Sons, Gem Cameo." *(Private collection)*

C256. Vase, 7¼ inches, with passion-flower motif and unusual carving on the neck; signed "Thomas Webb & Sons, Gem Cameo." *(Private collection)*

C257. Vase, 7½ inches, with overall carving of pansies; signed "Thomas Webb & Sons." *(Collection of Minna Rosenblatt Antiques)*

C258. Two-handled vase, 11 inches, signed "Nature's Mirror, T. & G. Woodall," W 2728. (Authors' collection)

283

C259. Cameo rose pitcher, 6¼ inches; signed "Thomas Webb & Sons, Gem Cameo." *(Private collection)*

C260. Vase with white cameo grapes on a purple ground. *(Private collection)*

C261. Vase, 7 inches, with allover Christmas-rose decoration. *(Private collection)*

C262. Vase, 8 inches, with cineraria, bees, and butterfly; signed "Thomas Webb & Sons, Gem Cameo." *(Private collection)*

C263. Vase, 8½ inches, showing Pandora; gold-plated and engraved ring base; signed "G. Woodall, Paris Exhibition 1889, Thomas Webb & Sons, Gem Cameo." *(Currier Gallery of Art)*

285

C264. Clematis cameo teapot, 3¾ inches. *(Private collection)*

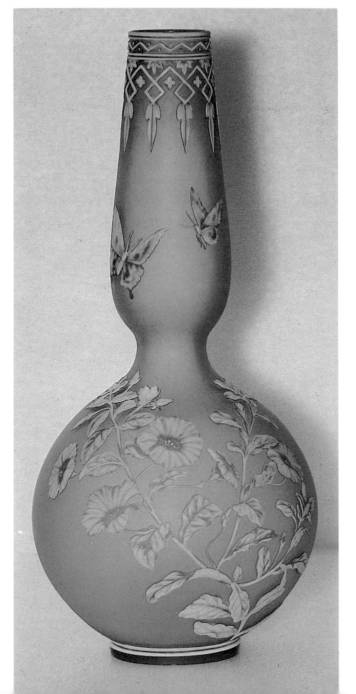

C265. Vase, 13¼ inches, with Canterbury-bells motif; signed "Stevens & Williams, Art Glass, England." *(Private collection)*

C266. Vase, 12 inches, with butterflies and morning glories; signed "Thomas Webb & Sons, Gem Cameo." *(Private collection)*

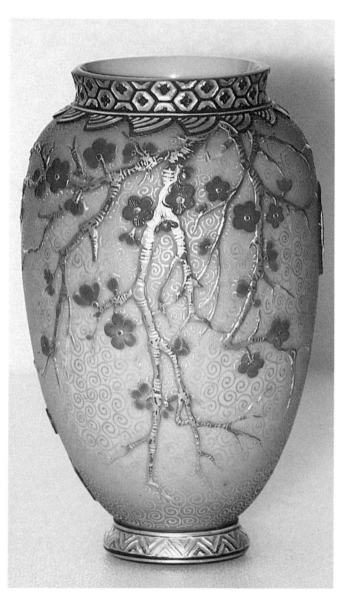

C267. Plaque, 12 inches, signed "Geo. Woodall, Poetry." *(Collection of Leo Kaplan Antiques, courtesy of Alan Kaplan)*

C268. Vase, 5½ inches, with prunus blossoms; signed "Thomas Webb & Sons, Gem Cameo," attributed to Jules Barbe. *(Private collection)*

287

C269. Vase, 10¾ inches, with female figure and narcissus; signed "Geo. Woodall, Webb, Thomas Webb & Sons, Gem Cameo." W 3111. *(Courtesy of Elliot and Enid Wysor)*

C270. Vase with calla-lily decoration. *(Private collection)*

288

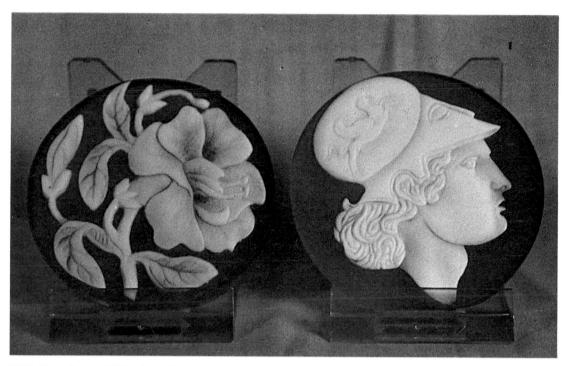

C271. Two plaques, 2½ inches, white on brown floral decoration, white on red portrait of Minerva. *(Collection of Leo Kaplan Antiques, courtesy of Alan Kaplan)*

C272. Vase, 11½ inches, with passion-flower motif, white on amethyst, on blue ground; signed "Thomas Webb & Sons, Gem Cameo." *(Private collection)*

C273. Vase, 5 inches, with polished white roses on a pale celadon-green ground; carving under the base; signed "Webb." *(Formerly in the collection of Beatrice Alice Woodall; now in a private collection)*

C274. Bowl, 4¾ inches, with carving of waves and fish; signed "Stevens & Williams 1901." *(Authors' collection)*

C275. Plaque, 6 inches, depicting Putti fishing; signed "T. & G. Woodall." *(Private collection)*

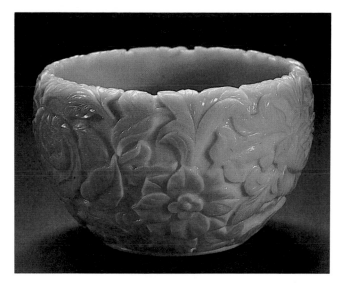

C276. Bowl, 3¾ inches, with allover floral carving on simulated jade ground in the Chinese Ch'ien-lung style; signed "Webb." *(Private collection)*

C277. Vase, 14½ inches, signed "Thomas Webb & Sons"; attributed to William Fritsche. *(Collection of Leo Kaplan Antiques, courtesy of Alan Kaplan)*

C278. Vase, 10 inches, gold fired on rose cameo glass on an opal ground; attributed to Stevens & Williams. *(Private collection)*

C279. Vase, 14 inches, by George Woodall on bronze dolphin base—an outstanding creation in cameo carving—signed "Antarctic." *(Collection of The Chrysler Museum of Art at Norfolk)*

C280. Vase, 2½ inches, with lacy allover decoration, even on the bottom; signed "Thomas Webb & Sons, Gem Cameo." *(Private collection)*

292

C281. Vase, 6¼ inches, with bridal-lace opal cameo on a topaz ground. *(Private collection)*

C282. Vase, 8 inches, with a finely depicted chrysanthemum. *(Private collection)*

C283. Curio vase, 4¾ inches, depicting on reverse people fleeing in a boat from a fire-breathing dragon, in the Oriental style; signed "Webb." *(Private collection)*

C284. Vase, 4 inches, with continuous cameo decoration of different flowers. *(Private collection)*

293

C285. Plaque, 9¼ inches, with fanciful peacocks, stylized floral design, and scrollwork; signed "Thomas Webb & Sons, Gem Cameo." *(Private collection)*

C286. Vase, 14½ inches, with honeysuckles; signed "Thomas Webb & Sons, Gem Cameo." *(Private collection)*

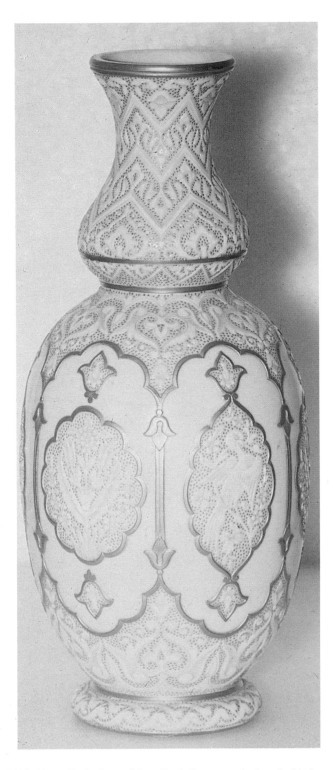

C287. Perfume bottle, with matching stopper, 5½ inches, carved on the bottom as well; signed "Thomas Webb & Sons, Gem Cameo." *(Private collection)*

C288. Vase, 8¾ inches, with stylized flowers and phoenix birds, with gold and ivory stippling; signed "Tiffany & Co., Paris Exhibition 1889, Webb." *(Private collection)*

C289. Vase, 5¾ inches, white on pink on chartreuse; signed "Stevens & Williams, F. Carder." *(Collection of Rockwell-Corning Museum)*

C290. Bluebird vase, 6 inches, white on red on green. *(Collection of Leo Kaplan Antiques)*

C291. Cameo biscuit jars, 6 inches; the one at right is signed "Webb" on the leaf. *(Collection of Leo Kaplan Antiques, courtesy of Alan Kaplan)*

C292. Pilgrim bottle, 10½ inches, signed "Thomas Webb & Sons, Gem Cameo." *(Private collection)*

C293. *Left to right:* Vase with gold ground and orchid motif; vase, signed "Webb," gazania motif; blue vase, 5¼ inches, with magnolias, signed "Webb." *(Collection of Leo Kaplan Antiques, courtesy of Alan Kaplan)*

C294. Jar and cover, 14 inches, signed "T. & G. Woodall, Webb, Dancing Girls." *(Courtesy of Alan Kaplan)*

C295. Vase, 8¾ inches, with applied colored glass carved in the Oriental manner, signed "Webb." *(Collection of Leo Kaplan Antiques, courtesy of Alan Kaplan)*

C296. Vase, 7 inches, with water scenes, willow trees, birds, prunus blossoms, chrysanthemums, dragonflies, and water lilies, signed "Thomas Webb & Sons, Gem Cameo." *(Private collection)*

C297. Epergne, 10½ inches, with morning glories, on a mirrored base. *(Private collection)*

299

300

C298. Two-handled vase, 15¾ inches, showing Cupid and Psyche, W 2609; signed "G. Woodall, Tiffany & Co., Paris Exhibition 1889, Thomas Webb & Sons, Gem Cameo." *(Authors' collection)*

C299. Orchid vase, 5½ inches, with carved scrollwork in the gold ground; signed "Thomas Webb & Sons," attributed to Jules Barbe. *(Private collection)*

C300. Vase, 6¾ inches, with hibiscus; signed "F. Carder, Stevens & Williams." *(Collection of Rockwell-Corning Museum)*

C301. Bowl, 5 inches, in the Oriental style, attributed to Stevens & Williams. *(Private collection)*

C302. Plaque, 16 inches, titled The Boxing Day Meet, signed "H. J. Boam"—a fine example of a respected artist's work. *(Collection of Leo Kaplan Antiques, courtesy of Alan Kaplan)*

C303. Vase, 11 inches, attributed to William Fritsche. *(Courtesy of Alan Kaplan)*

C304. Vase, 12 inches, signed "F. Carder, S & W.," with a typical Stevens & Williams neck. *(Collection of Rockwell-Corning Museum)*

C305. Two-handled vase, 15¾ inches, titled The Fruit Seller, W 2403; signed "G. Woodall, 1889, Thomas Webb & Sons, Gem Cameo." *(Authors' collection)*

C306. Vase, 8 inches, white on brown, signed "Geo. Woodall, Syrenea." *(Authors' collection)*

C307. Vase, 12½ inches, with lily decoration and unusual carving on the well-shaped neck. *(Collection of The Chrysler Museum of Art at Norfolk)*

C308. Vase, 8 inches, decorated with nicotiana, signed "Thomas Webb & Sons, Gem Cameo." *(Private collection)*

C309. Vase, 8½ inches, signed "Mischief," and "Geo. Woodall." *(Authors' collection; courtesy of Sotheby's Belgravia, Inc., London)*

W2802
Wandering Star   Wandering star

S9

W2516
White on Brown

S10

W2716. Flat side   W £0. pi.*
White on light Brown   Sale £0*. x .*
The Flower Gatherer

S11

W2660

Sale £nx

307

S12

Nº 2718
White on Brown
W £00 . L . x
sale £ pxl . x . x

DIANA AND NYMPH

S13

W 2714.
Dancing Girl. opalescent on Dark Brown
W. 2710. Ld . x x   Sale £ pi . x x

S14

W 2578
White & Blue on Red ground
— cost W £ L . h . x

S15

Sale 5 £0
W 2579.
Wcost L . h . x   £ pr . h . v
White Topaz Light Blue on Red ground

as 6578

Decorate
as 2578

S16

308

W 2609
White on Brown

White on Brown
W 2609

3 portion
Cost £ 25.
sale £di.

S17

W 2581
White & Red on a Blue Ground

Sold T46 g. pr. L.
Light W. Cost i. L. x

S18

W 2721
White on Brown
W £ h i. t

S19

W 2722
White on Brown

W p. p. 6/ x

W 2723
Shape & colour as 2722
subject a maid
of athens
Cott p.p. i. t
Sale of ps L. x

S20

309

W 2510
White on Brown

S21

H 2811
White on Green
on Flint

S22

W. 2043
Before the Race.
White on Brown
Cost. W. £ E.

3 Horses

S23

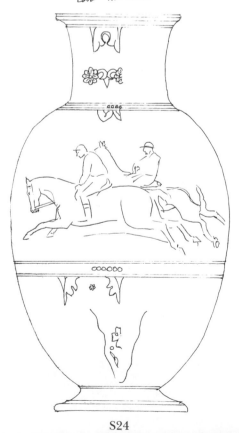

W 2179
The Race
White on Brown
Cost W. £ d. h. d.

S24

W. 2796
White on Brown

S25

W 2795 White on Brown
Pomond

S26

W 2797 WooB
oval
7½ x 5 in Cost c4/. sale £ pi.

March 1894

S27

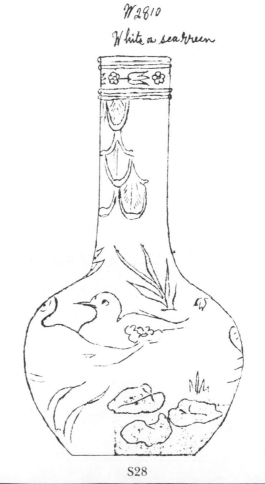

W 2810
White on sea green

S28

311

W2807
White on
Brown

EUTERPE   THALIA

S29

W2822
(At the Portal)

White on Brown

dull made pillar
Ground bright

S30

White on Brown
spring
& autumn

W3160

S31

"Pharoah's Daughter"

S32

S33

S34

S35

S36

313

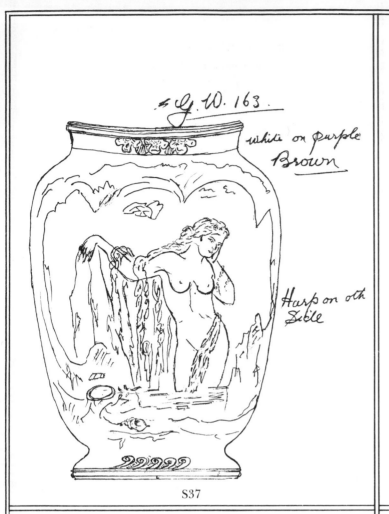

G. W. 163.

white on purple
Brown

Harp on oth
Side

S37

W. 1476. Cost m.fd / Ph. / x
The Milkmaid
Light Blue Ground
dark Blue & White outside

a Vase of
flowers on
reverse side

S38

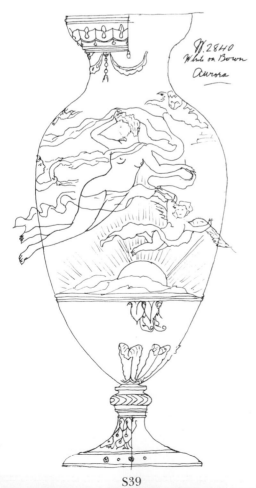

W 2840
White on Brown
Aurora

S39

W 2580
W. Cost fd   T. fle £ pr. h. x.
White & Blue on a red Ground

water

A plaque or two vases, Nos. of Vases
W 2580, 2580, 2578, 2579

S40

314

N2831
PSYCHE

S41

N2828 White on Brown
DANCING GIRL

S42

N2830 White on Brown
VESTAL

S43

N2827 White on Brown
HEBE

S44

315

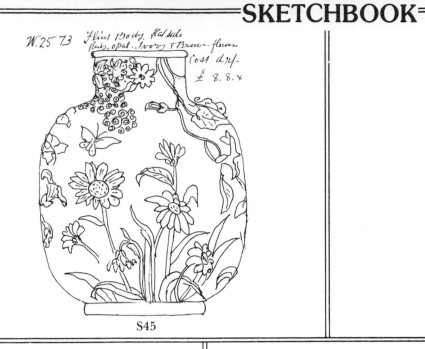

W.25.73 Flint Body. flat side
Rus, opal, Ivory & Brown flowers
Cost d,14/-
£ 8.8.4

S45

Jade Flatsum.
W2428

S46

W.2635
Scent Jar flowers
Dark Brown

S47

W2651
Flint Cameo
Sale 2/4/

S48

W.2662 Flint Cameo
Sale 0X/-

S49

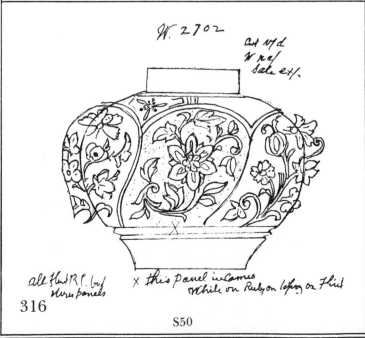

W. 2702
Cut N/d
N red
Sale e4/-

All Flint R.P. but
three panels

X this Panel in Cameo
White on Ruby on topay or Flint

316

S50

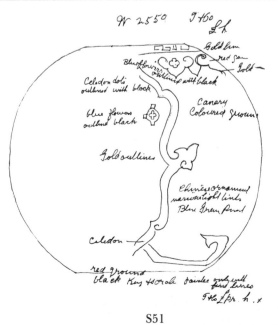

W 2550   9460
£4
Gold rim
red Jan
Gold—
Blue flowers outlined with black
Celodon dots
outlined with black
Canary
Coloured ground
blue flowers
outlined black
Gold outlines
Chinese ornament
narrow/roll lines
Blue Green Rim
Celodon
red ground
black Key & scroll painted only with
fine lines
9460 £Rr. h. x

S51

W.2661
Flim Cameo
vi/-sale

S52

February 1901
4-3259

Green on Betmet

S53

F.115
Fritsche 15
Green on opal   Green decoration
& Gold body thin box
EO-15/
Eng 15/   5.5.0
x Sell   P. 1/6
Eg. 8/6

S54

W.2537
Brown on Topaz
W.ri/.   Sale dof
Title

S55

W.2812
Light Brown on opal

S56

W.3164
White on light Blue

n.4

3

3

S57

W.3170
White on Light Blue

unsaleable
of size

20

S58

W.3165   White on Yellow
on White

no.5

S59

317

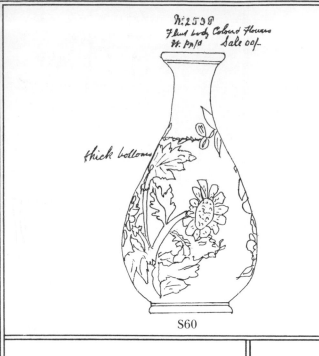

№ 2538
Flint body Coloured Flowers
W. Pn/d   Sale 00/-

thick bottoms

S60

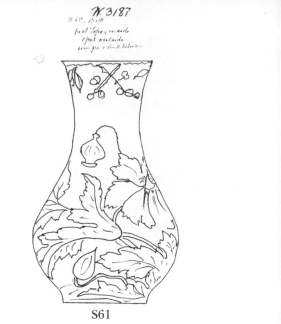

№ 3187

S61

№ 2815
White on Blue on Light Green

S62

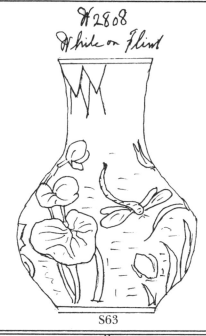

№ 2808
White on Flint

S63

White on Ruby

№ 2818

S64

№ 2816
White on Sea Green
part Eng^d & part Cameo

Cut into Center

S65

№ 2809

Cut by
White on
Lavender
on Flint

S66

318

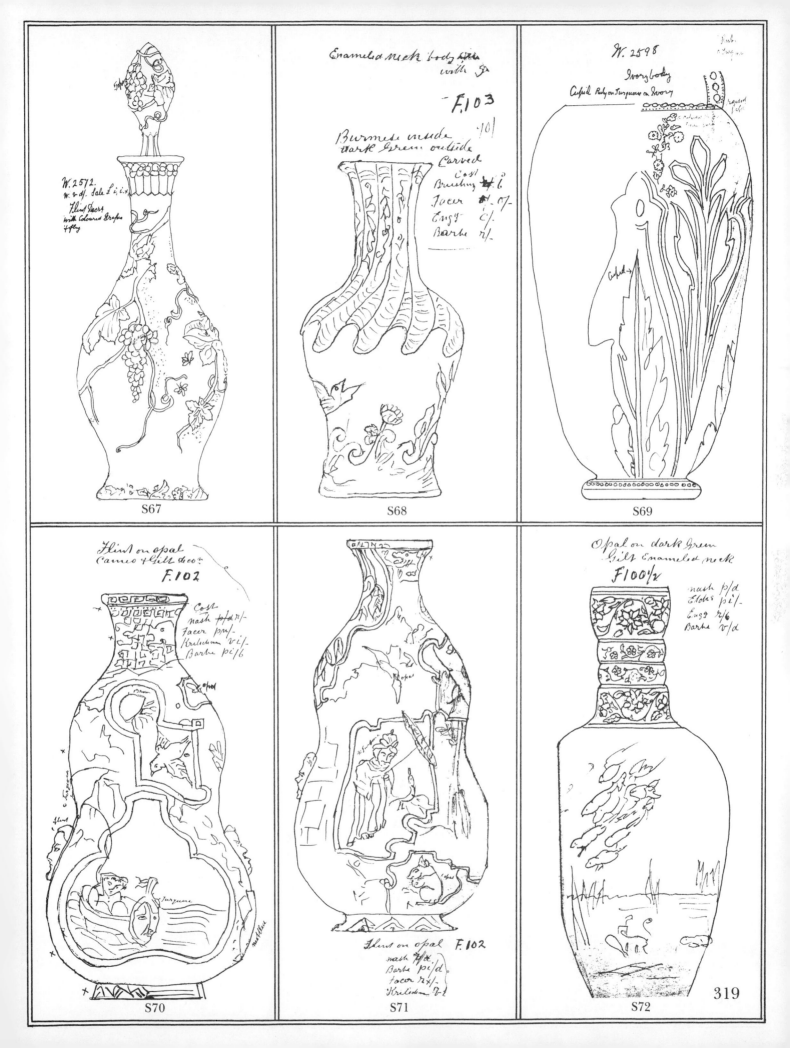

S67

S68

S69

S70

S71

S72

319

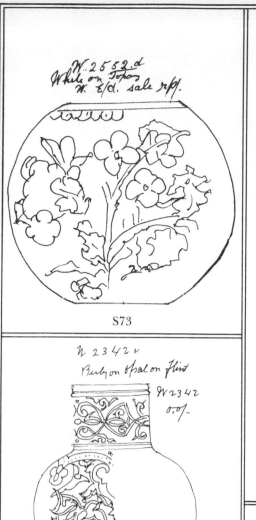

W. 2552 d
While on Topas
W. E/d. sale r/s/.

S73

W. 2729
Brown on Green on Flint
W. pm. sale i4.

S74

W. 3207
While on Brown

S75

N 2342 r
Ruby on Opal on Flint
W 2342
o.o/.

S76

W 2336 ✓
Opal on Flint
W 2336
Cost OE/d

3

S77

W. 2468
Ivory on Ruby

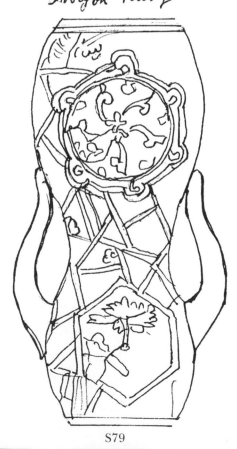

W. 2604 Co
sale £ h.

Ivory
Bird

Puce

Black Boy
on Ivory

320

S78

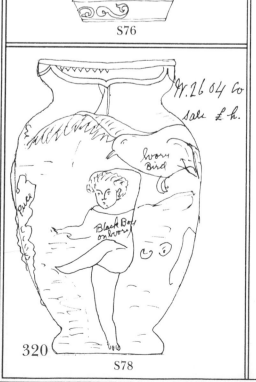

S79

W 2779
White on Black

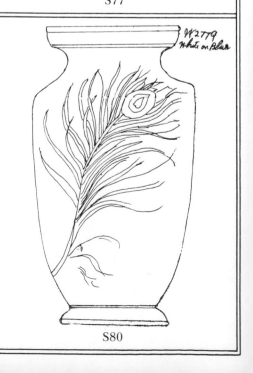

S80

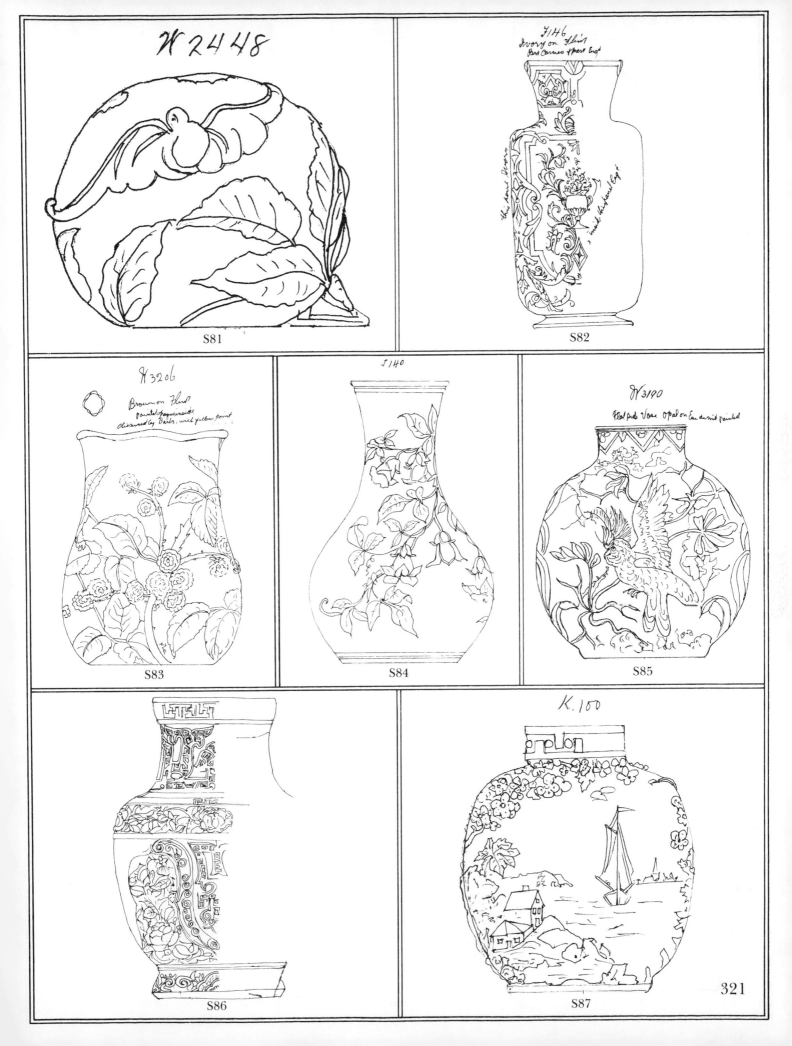

H 2448

S81

7146
Ivory on Flint
Bas Carved & best Engd

S82

H 3206

Brown on Flint
painted & opaque inside
disanned by Barbi, with yellow point

S83

J 140

S84

H 3190

Flat ends Vase Opal on Eau de nil painted

S85

S86

K.100

S87

321

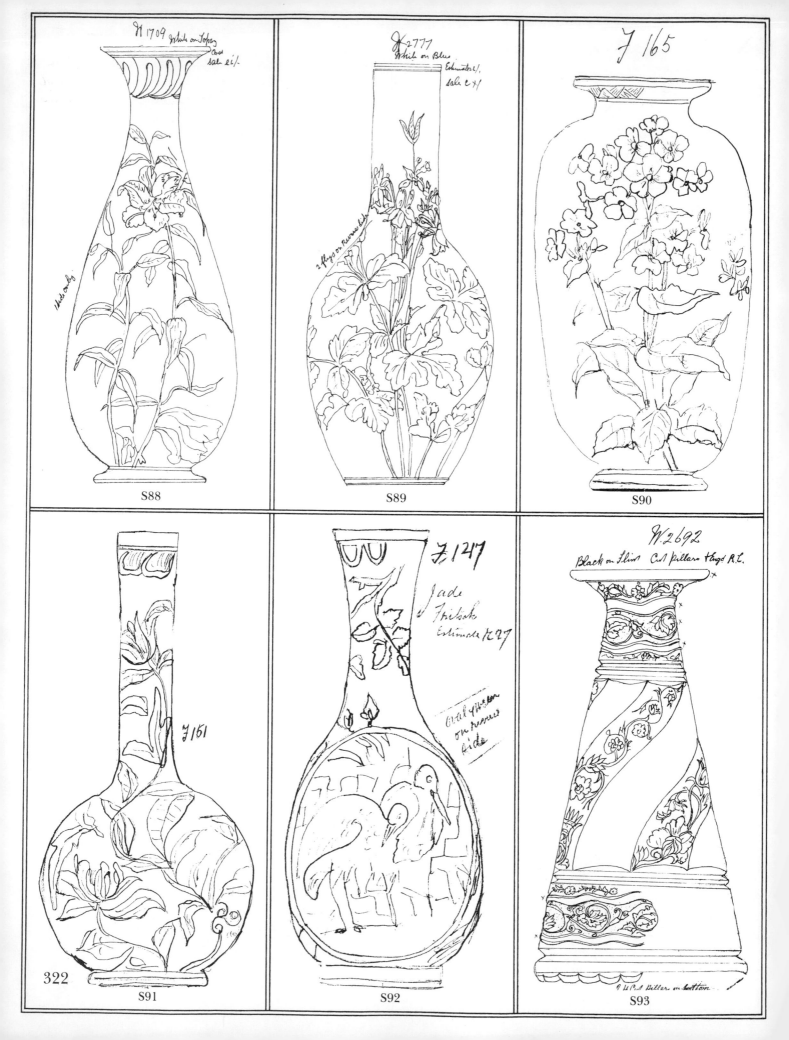

S88

S89

S90

322

S91

S92

S93

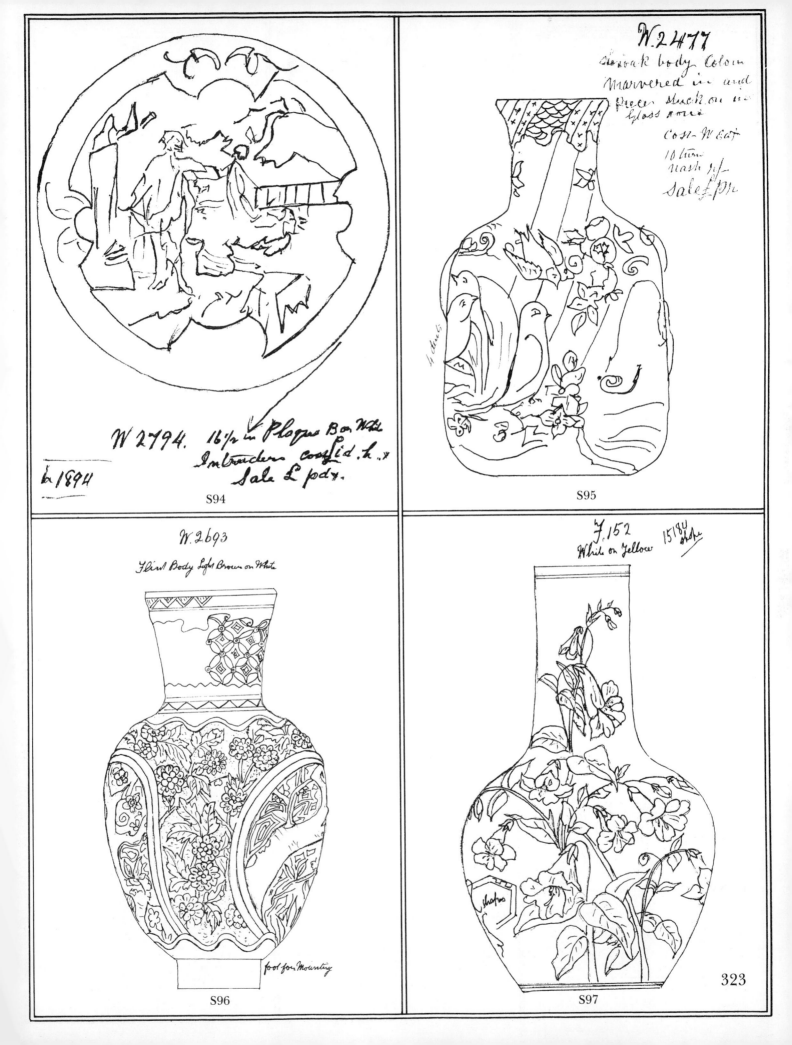

W 2794. 16½ in Plaque Bm White
Intruders cool/id. h. *
Sale £ pdr.

b 1894

S94

W.2477
slovak body Colour
Marvered in and
Pieces stuck on in
Glass once
Coss-W Eat
10 turn
nash p/
Sale/pn

S95

W. 2693
Flint Body Light Brown on White

foot for Mounting

S96

F. 152   15184
White on Yellow   sold

323

S97

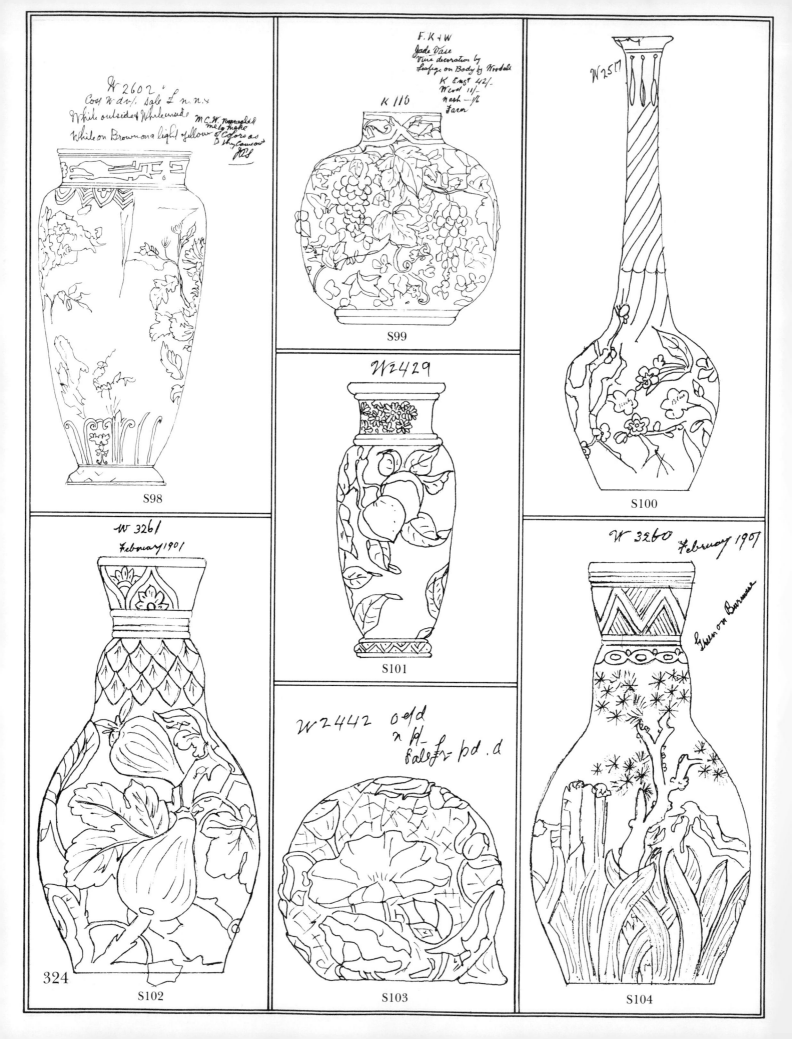

W 2602
Cost W dw/. Sale £ n. n. x
White outside & White inside
White on Brown on a light yellow
M C H reynolds
melo make
of Colors as
B the Cameo
HS

S98

F K + W
Jade Vase
Vine decoration by
Leafage on Body by Woodall
K Engt 42/-
Wcott 11/-
nash — 1/6
£ a on

K 110

S99

W 2429

S101

W 2517

S100

W 3261
February 1901

S102

W 2442 old
n 19
Sale £r– pd. d

S103

W 3260 February 1901

Green on Burmese

S104

324

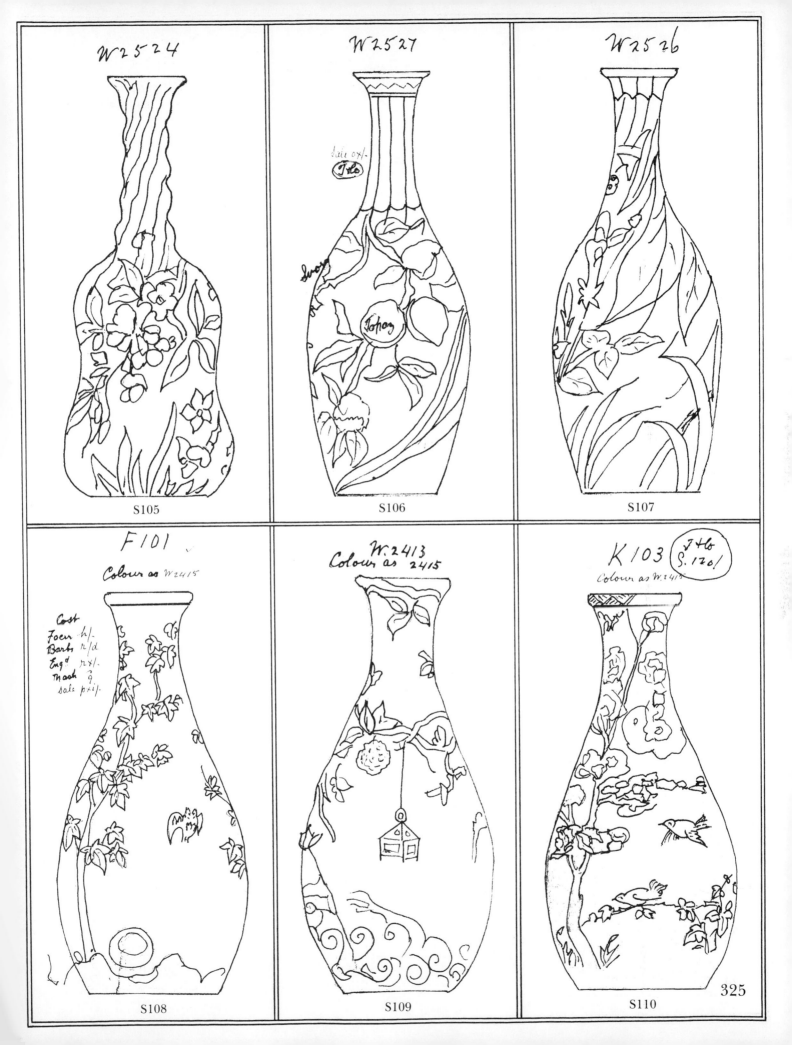

W 2524

S105

W 2527

dato o8/-

Ivory

tohoz

S106

W 2526

S107

F 101

Colour as W2415

Cost
Focu   h/.
Barts n/d
Eng⁴   nx/.
Mask   3
sale   px8/.

S108

W. 2413
Colour as 2415

S109

K 103   *346*
         S. 1201

Colour as W2415

S110

325

W 2415

Burmese body Ruby & Brown Fish
" & in Vases

S111

W 2400
White on Yellow

S112

W 2423
Colour as W 2415

Cost
W vi/.
n à
B 2/.

S113

W 2778
White on Blue
Edwards Oct.
Sale oct.

S114

W 2430

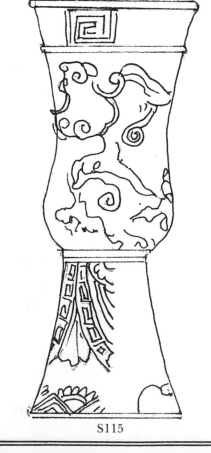

S115

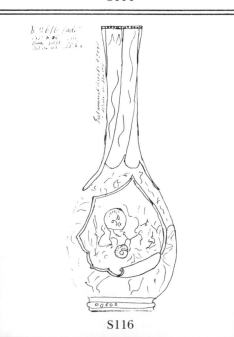

S116

W.2441

S117

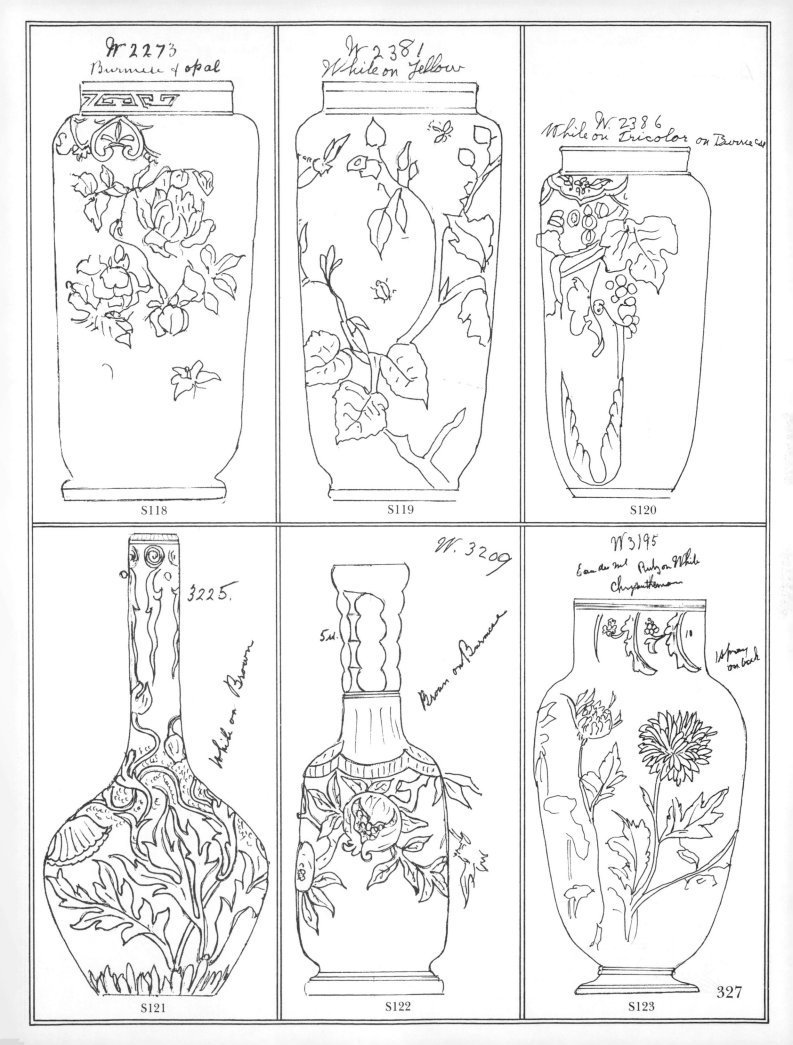

W 2273
Burmese & opal

S118

W 2381
White on Yellow

S119

W 2386
White on Tricolor on Burmese

S120

3225.
White on Brown

S121

W 3209
5.u.
Brown on Burmese

S122

W 3195
Eau de nil Ruby on White
Chrysanthemum
1st spray on back

327

S123

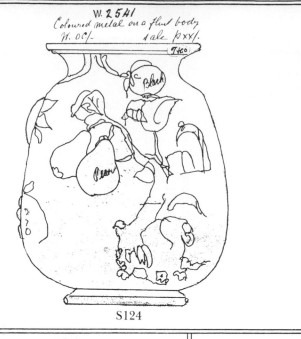

W. 2541
Coloured metal on a flint body
W. OC/.   sale pxx/.
7+co

S124

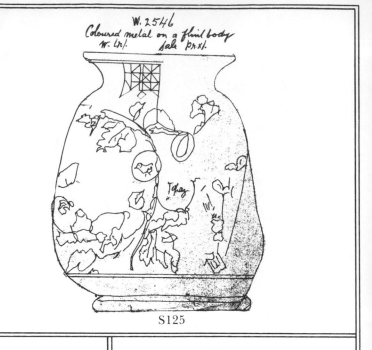

W. 2546
Coloured metal on a flint body
W. 4/.   sale prx/.

S125

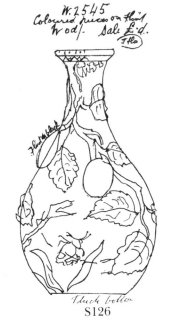

W. 2545
Coloured pieces on flint
W od/.   sale £id.
7+co

S126

W. 2542
Black on Ivory
W. or/d   sale nx/.

S127

W. 3201
White or yellow white inside

S128

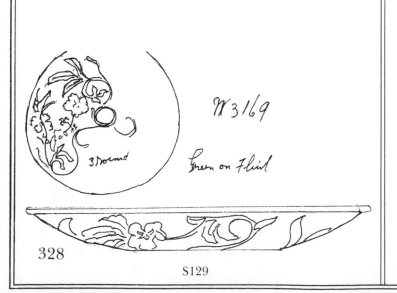

328

W 3169

Green on Flint

S129

W. 3185
"Toilet of Venus"

S130

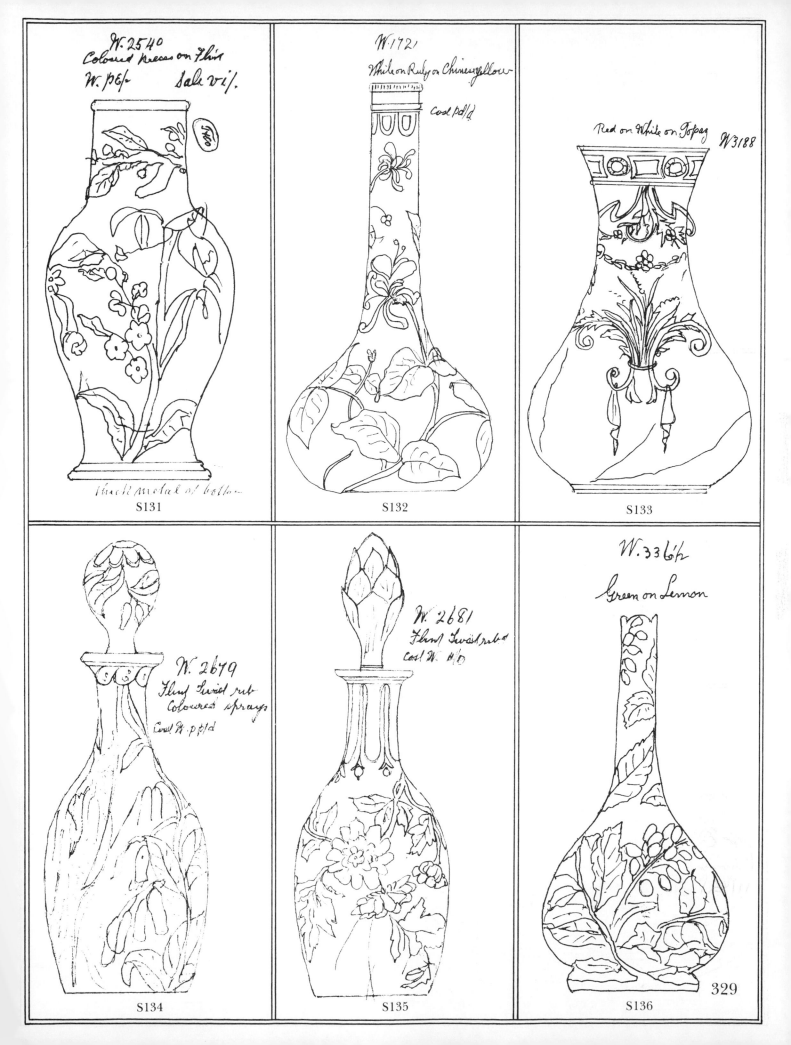

W.2540
Coloured pieces on Flint
W. p£/-   Sale vi/.

2540

thick metal at bottom
S131

W.1721
White on Ruby on Chinese yellow
                    Cost pd/d
S132

Red on White on Topaz   W.3188
S133

W.2679
Flint Twist rib
Coloured sprays
Cost N. p p/d
S134

W.2681
Flint Twist ribbed
Cost W. H/o
S135

W.336½
Green on Lemon

329

S136

W2748

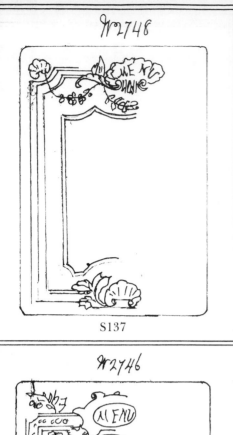

S137

W2715

Thin Body
Green decoration
Vine in relief
Sale d. b.

S138

W2749

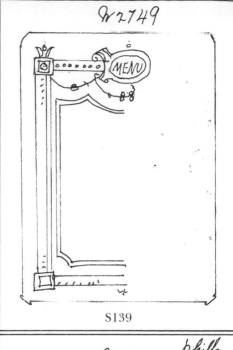

MENU

S139

W2746

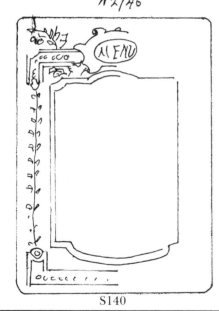

MENU

S140

W2483

Ivory Ground
Green outside
with colours

S143

W2747   Phillou
Nov 3 92

MENU

S141

J.180   12 Flutes   Enamel Pearls

4 Feathers

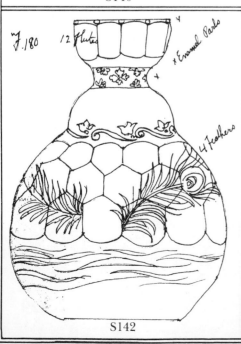

S142

W.3198

Small Spray on reverse side

S144

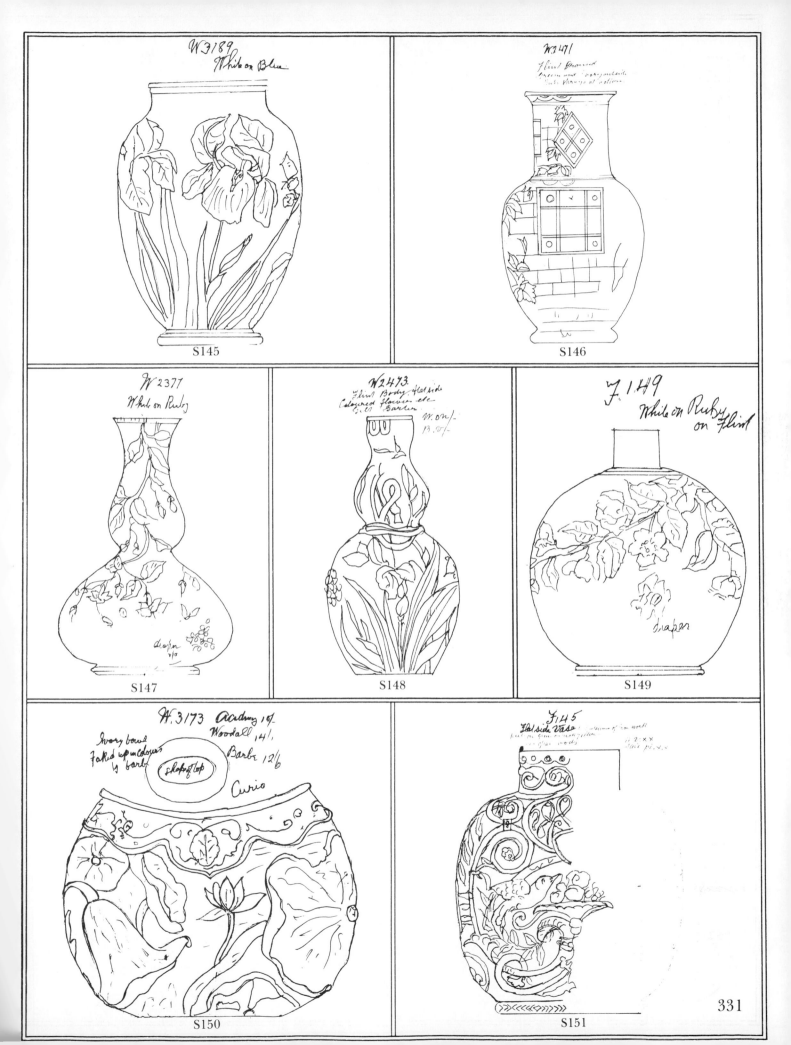

W3189
White on Blue

S145

W2471
Flint Ground
(handwritten notes)

S146

W2377
White on Ruby

draper
v/o

S147

W2473.
Flint Body, Flat side
Coloured flowers etc.
Barber
W. on /-
B. /-

S148

F.1449
White on Ruby
on Flint

draper

S149

W.3173   Academy 10/-
Woodall 14/-
Ivory bowl
Faked up in colours   Barber 12/6
by barber
shape of top
Curio

S150

F.145
Flat side Vase *(handwritten notes)*

S151

331

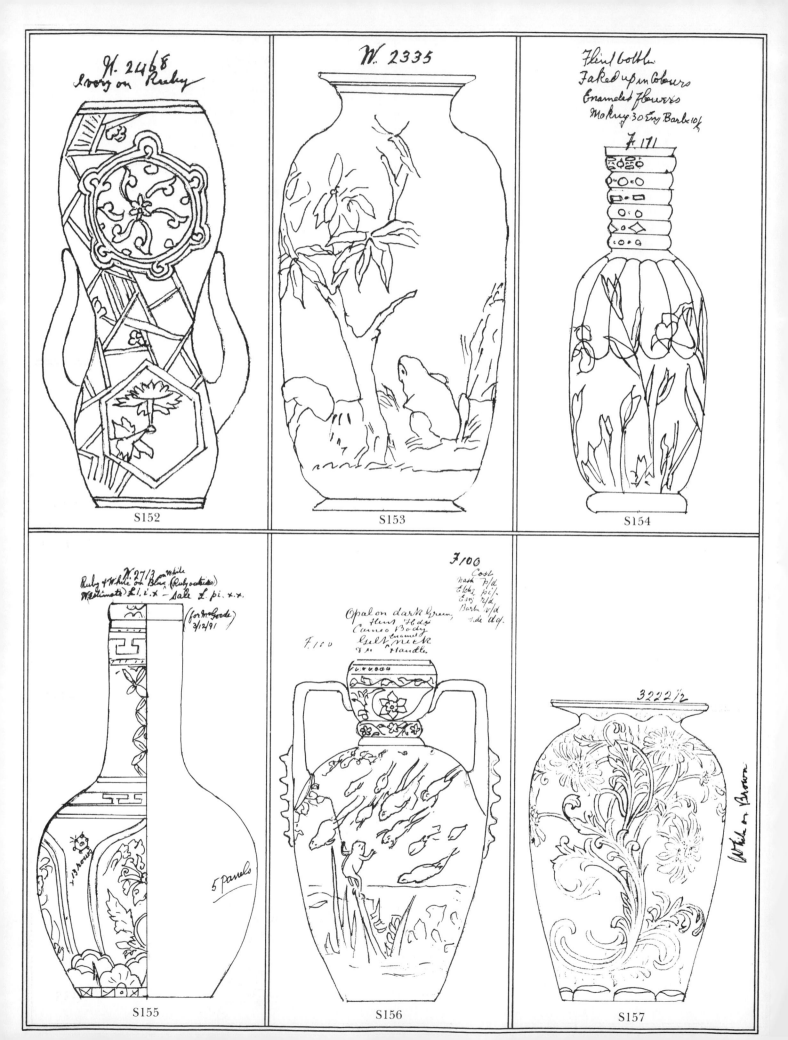

W. 24/8
Ivory on Ruby

S152

W. 2335

S153

Flint bottle
Faked up in Colours
Enameled flowers
Mo Ruy 30 Eng Barbe 10/

F 171

S154

Ruby & White on Blue (Ruby outside)
M estimate £1.1.x – Sale £.pi.x.x.
(for Mr Goode)
3/12/91
W. 27/3 white
5 Panels

S155

F 100
Cost
nash r/d
Etche pi/
Eng r/d
Barbe r/d
Sale 11/-

Opal on dark Green,
flint body
Cameo Body
Gilt neck
& in handle Enamel
F 100

S156

3222/2
White on Brown

S157

W2420 (con ?) Jade

S158

Jade
W2421
con R.V/d.

S159

W256
Jumb.

S160

W3151
Red on Rich Topaz

S161

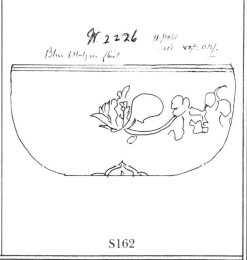

W2226   W pold
Blue & Ruby on flint   Jade xxf - 0%/.

S162

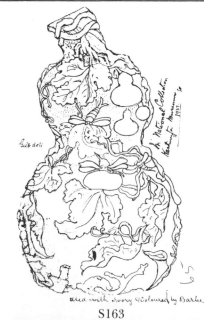

Gilt dots

In McComas Collection
Winch. Fr. Museum
1931

red with Ivory & Coloured by Barbe

S163

F129
White on Blue

disper. r?

S164

333

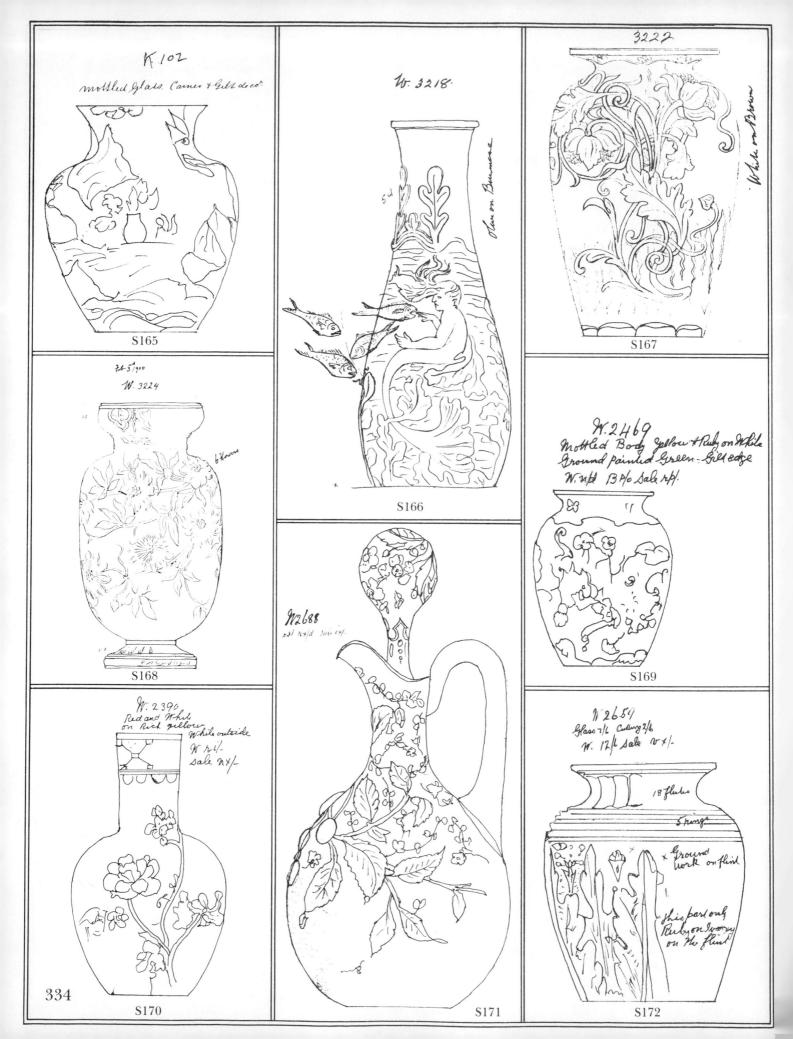

K.102

mottled Glass. Cameo & Gilt decd.

S165

W. 3218.

S166

3222

White on Brown

S167

Feb 3 1900
W. 3224

S168

W. 2469
Mottled Body Yellow & Ruby on White
Ground painted Green - Gilt edge
W. n/d 13 4/o Sale n/-

S169

W. 2688

W. 2390
Red and White
on Rich yellow
White outside
W. n/-
sale n x/-

S170

S171

W 2659
Glass 7/6 Cutting 2/6
W. 12/6 Sale v x/-

18 flutes
5 rings
Ground
work on flint

this part only
Ruby on Ivory
on the flint

S172

334

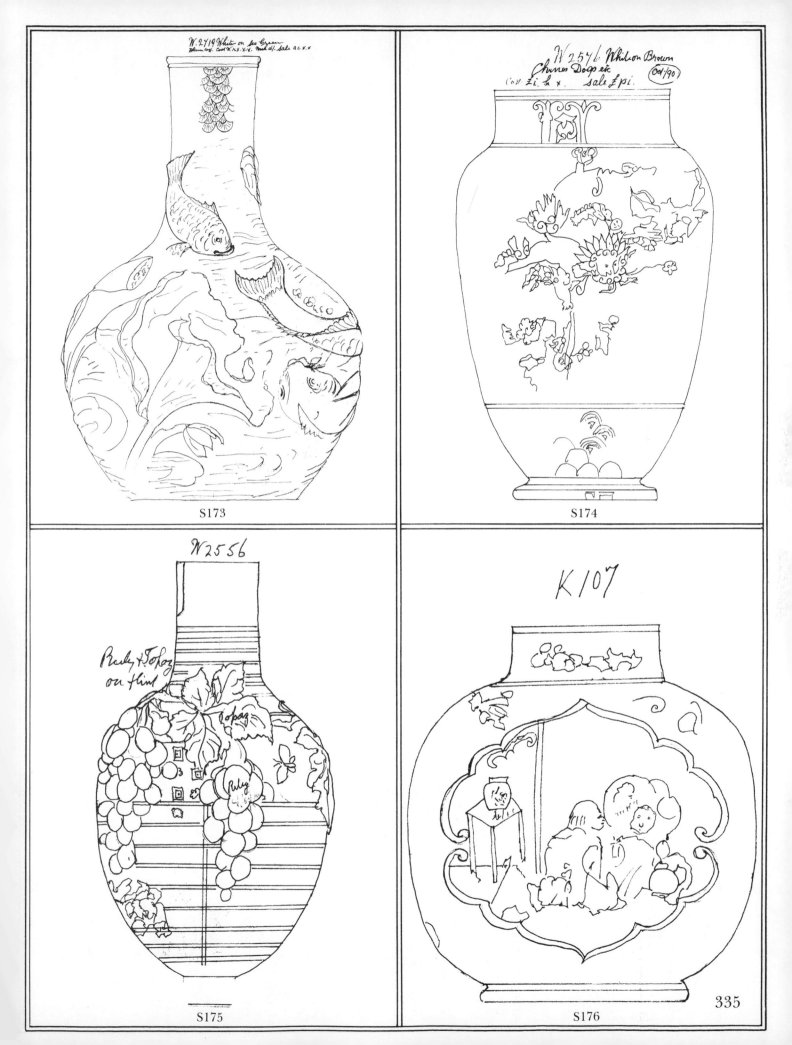

S173

S174

S175

S176

335

W 24145 Flint Carved

-glass-

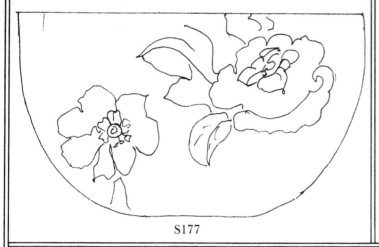

S177

K. 111

Black on Ivory

Black ground

S178

W 2552

Tumbler 9 -

S179

W 2601

While on Blue

S180

W 2654

Light Jade Ground

S181

J 138

White on Ruby on Topaz
H. 11   sale 54/.

S182

W 2591
White on Topaz & flint
Cost r/r
Sale 13

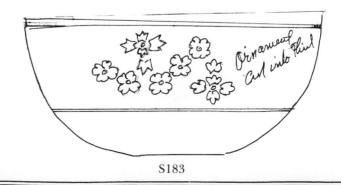

_Ornament
cut into flint_

S183

336

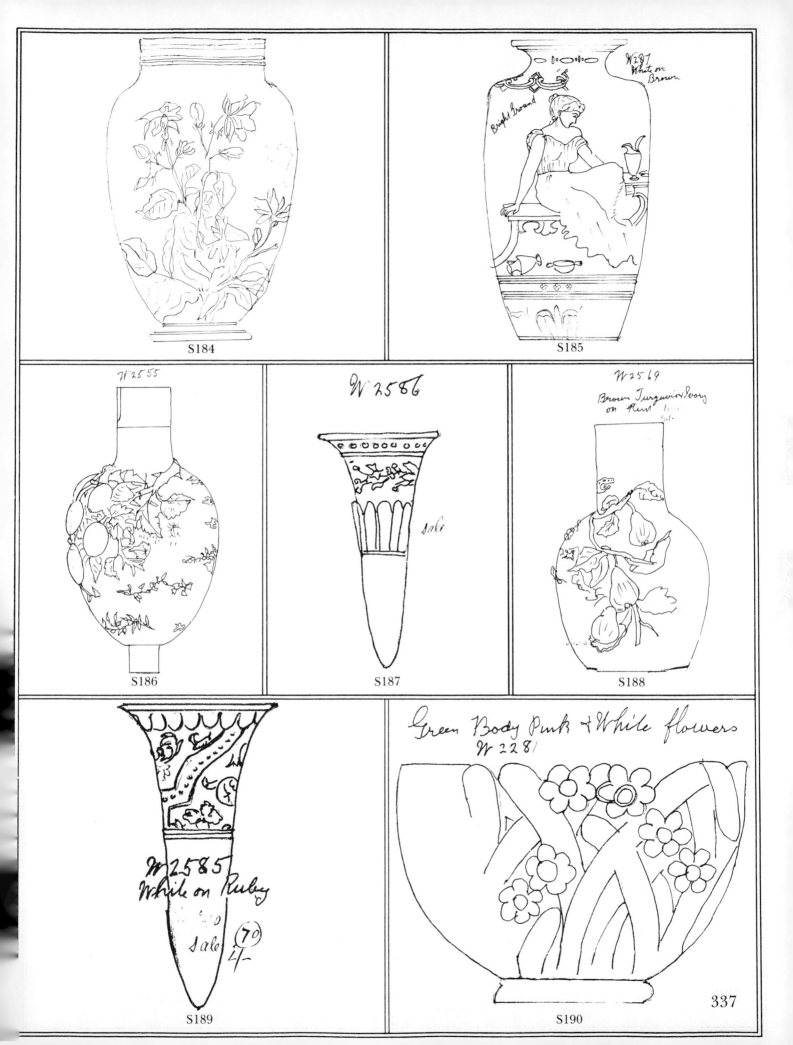

S184

S185

W2555

S186

W2586

S187

W2569

S188

W2585
White on Ruby

sale 70
4-

S189

Green Body Pink + White flowers
W2281

S190

337

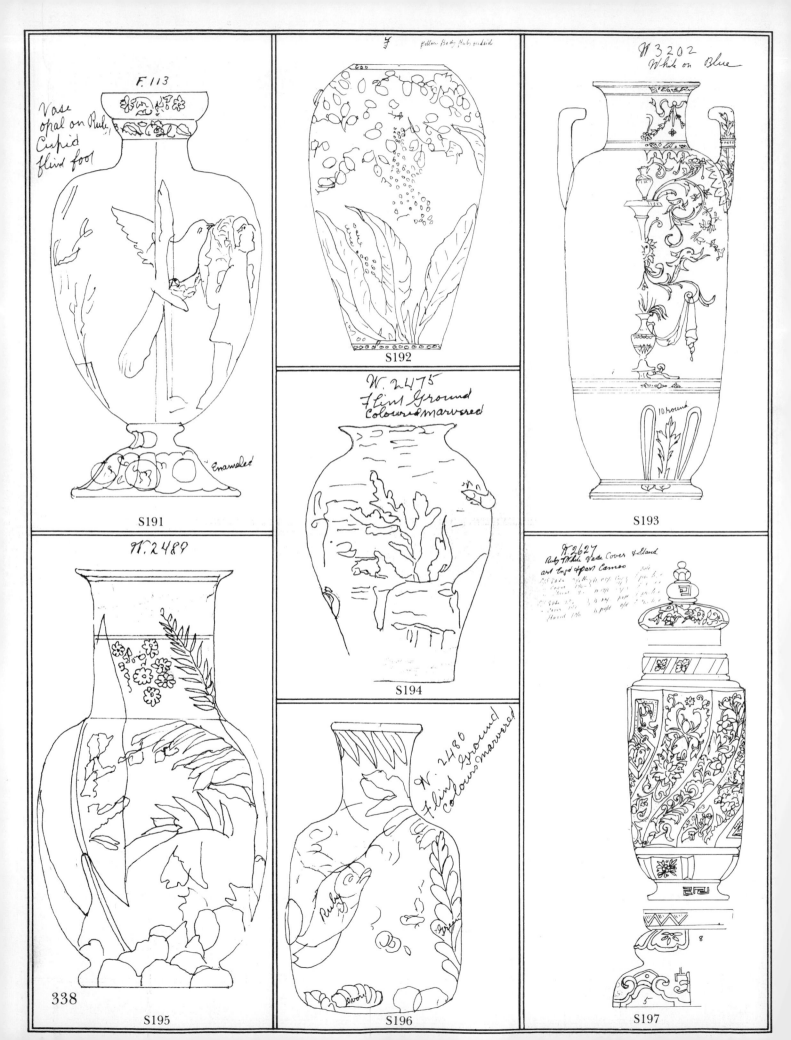

F. 113

Vase
opal on Ruby
Cupid
flint foot

Enameled

S191

yellow Body Rub: imbeded

S192

W. 2489

338

S195

W. 2475
Flint Ground
Colours marvered

S194

W. 2480
Flint Ground
Colours marvered

Ruby

S196

W. 3202
White on Blue

10 round

S193

W. 2627
Ruby & White Vase Cover & Stand
art cut opart Cameo

S197

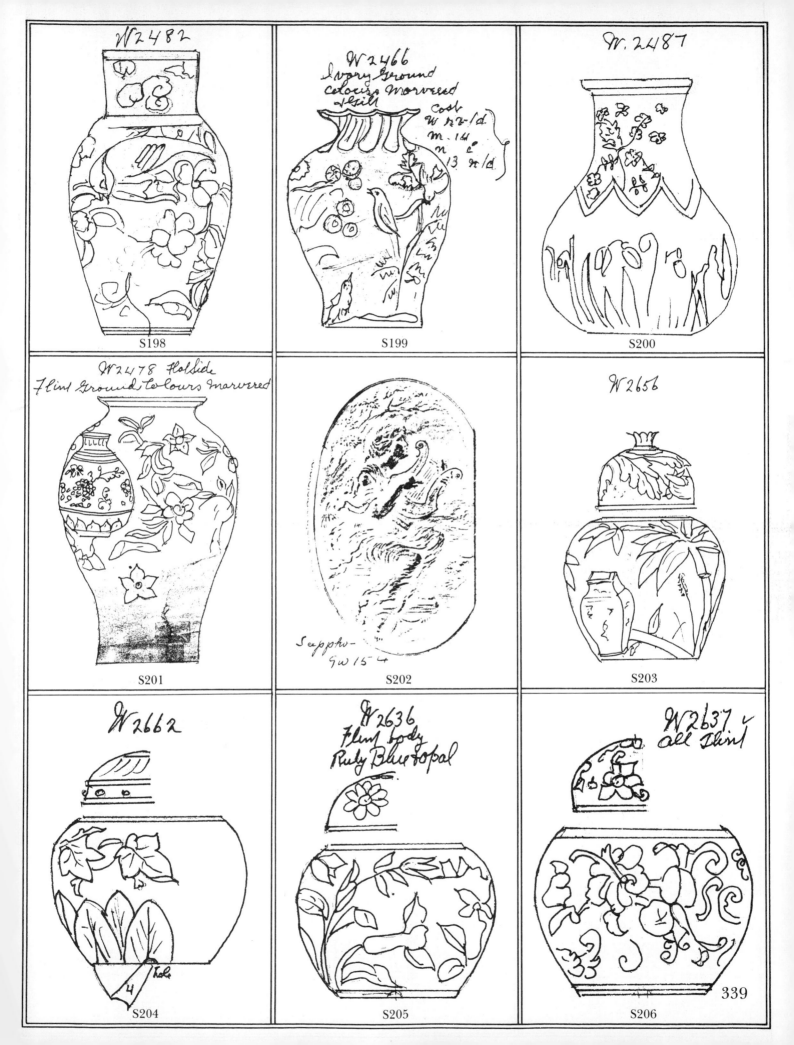

W2482

S198

W2466
Ivory Ground
colours Marvered
+ gill

cost
W 22-/d.
m. 14°
n 13 x/d

S199

W. 2487

S200

W2478 Flatside
Flint Ground colours Marvered

S201

Sappho-
GW 15-4

S202

W 2656

S203

W 2662

S204

W 2636
Flint body
Ruby Blue & opal

S205

W 2637 +
all flint

339

S206

W.2658
cost

Light Brown on White
on Black on Glass body.

S207

Fritsch 111.
Green Mother Glass or Jade T lot side
Cost £ 35/-
Cost 2/6
Glass 15/-
sale £ 2. 6. x.

another flower
Jade Brown

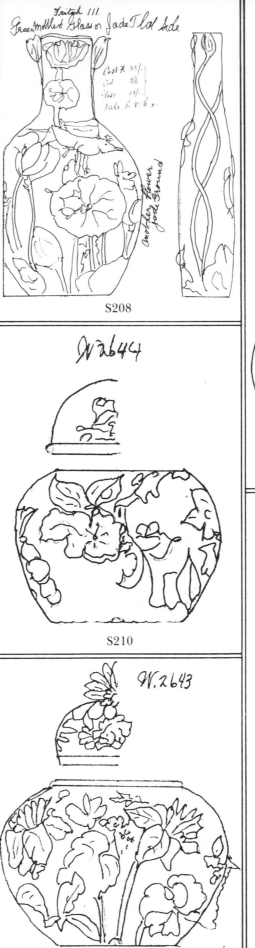

S208

W.2644

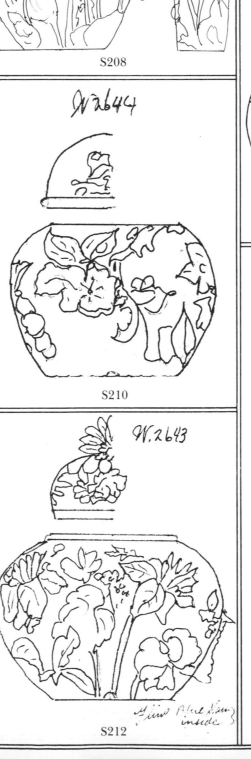

S210

W.2643

Glass Blue Lining
inside

S212

W.3192
White or Purple

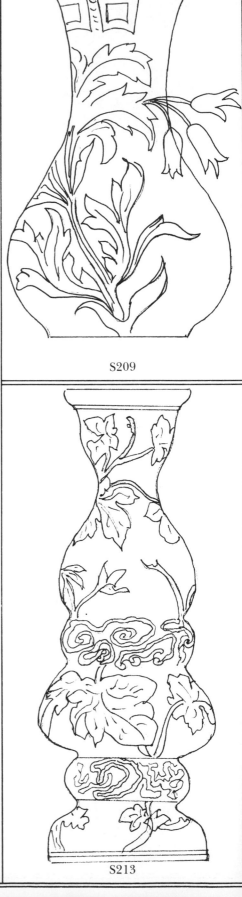

S209

W.3203

340

S211

S213

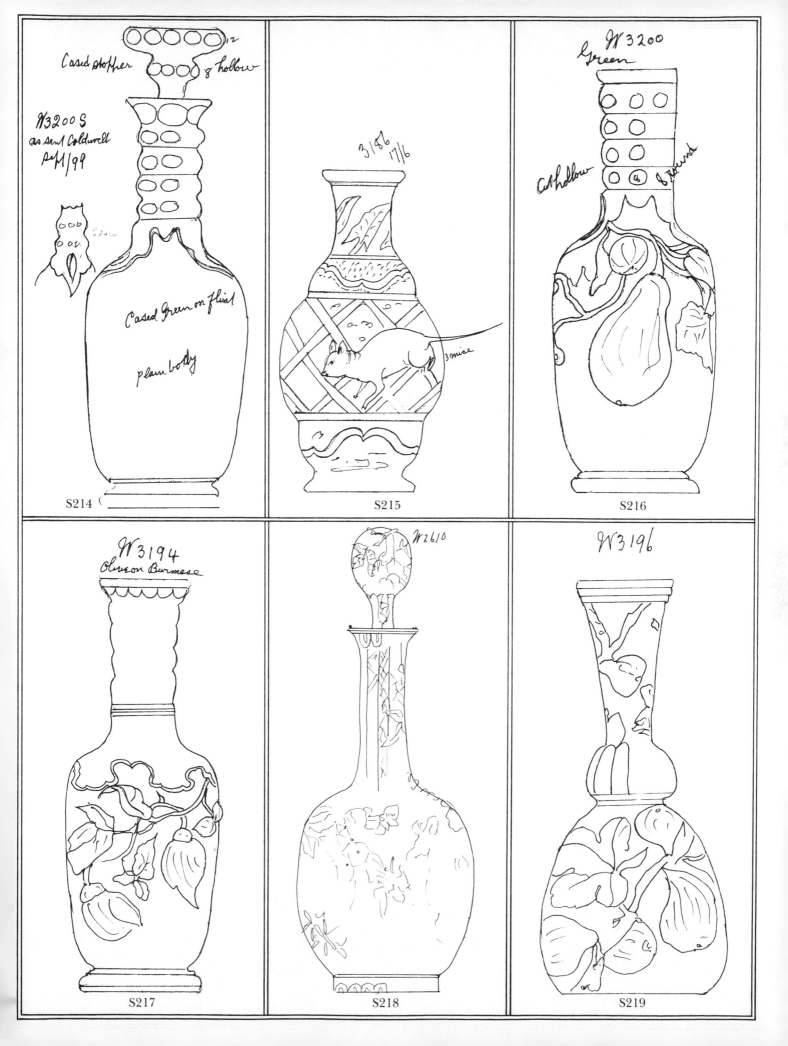

Cased stopper   12   8 hollow

W3200 S
as sent Caldwell
Sept/99

Cased Green on Flint

plain body

S214

3/86 17/16

3 mice

S215

W3200
Green

Cut hollow   8 round

S216

W3194
Olive on Burmese

S217

W2610

S218

W3196

S219

W.2530

S220

W.2531

S221

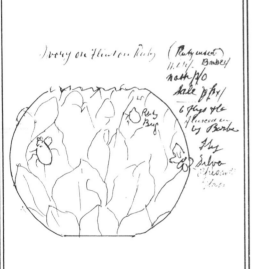

Ivory on Flint on Ruby (Ruby used)
W.E.W. Barbes
nash p/o
Sale pp x/
6 plys 4 lc
fluxed in
by Barbe
flux
Silver
Chestnut

S222

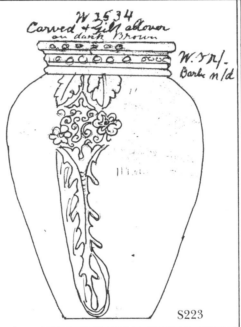

W.3534
Carved & gilt allover
on dark Brown

W.3r/-
Barbe n/d

S223

W.2533 n pp/d.
Brown on Ivory on Flint

S224

W2477
oak body color
thinnered in and
Pieces thick
Glost fire

cost W 6½

10 turn
nash f/.
Sale f pn.

S225

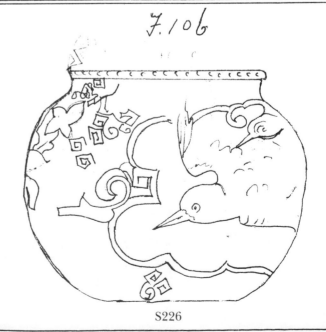

F.106

S226

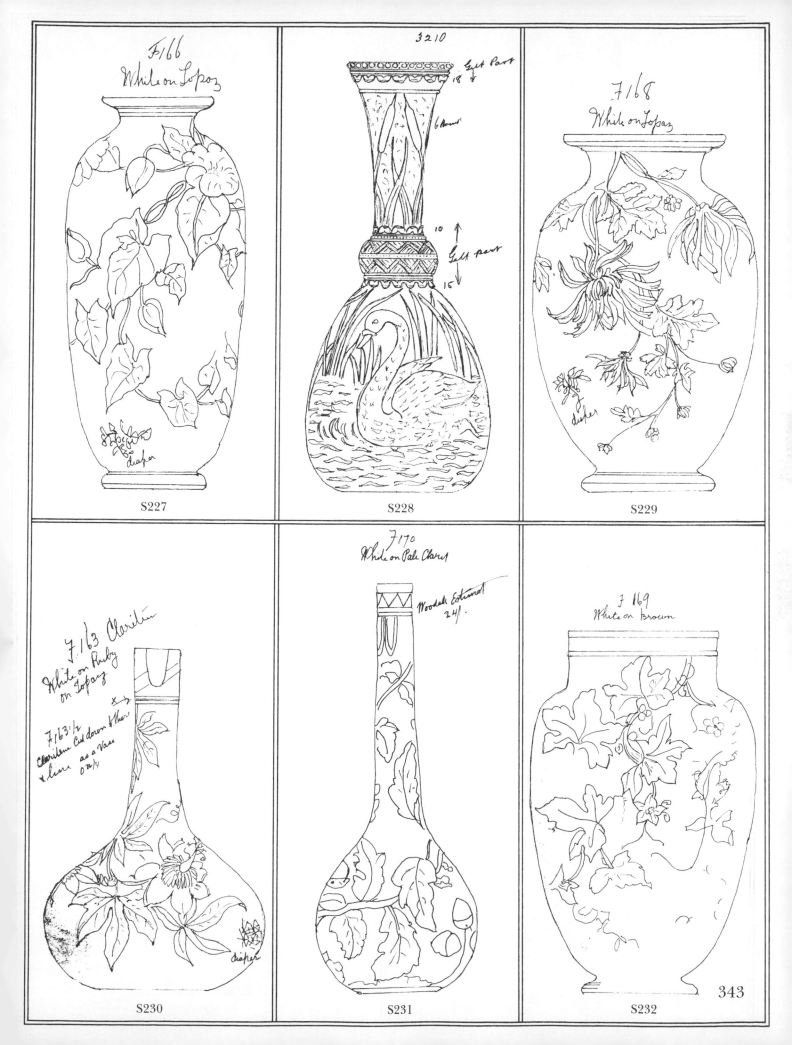

F166
White on Topaz

S227

3210

Gilt Part
18 ♦

6 round

10
Gilt Part
15

S228

F168
White on Topaz

diaper

S229

F163 Claritin
White on Ruby
on Topaz

F163½
Claritin Cut down & there
+ Line   as a Vase
on ¼

S230

F170
White on Pale Claret

Woodall Estimate
24/.

S231

F169
White on Brown

343

S232

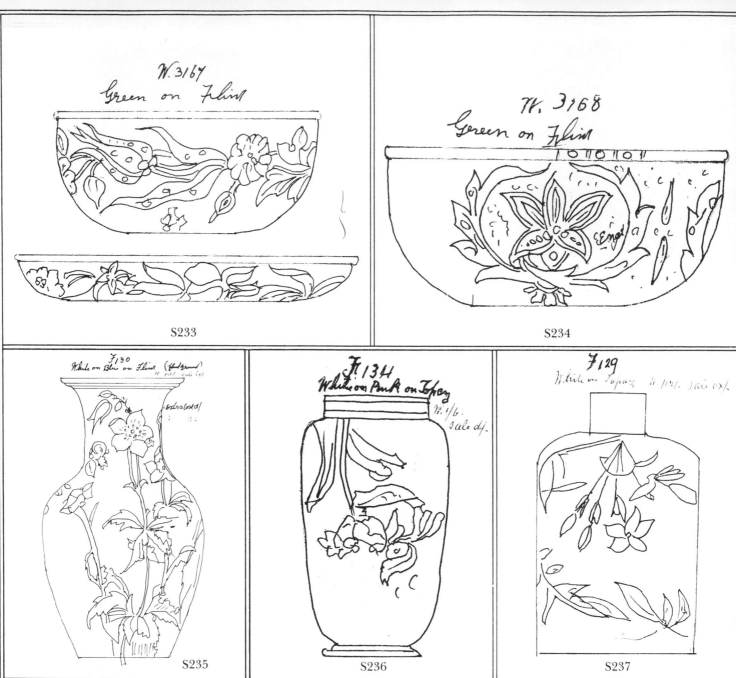

W. 3167
Green on Flint

S233

W. 3168
Green on Flint

Engd a

S234

F 130
White on Blue on Flint (Hard ground)
W. 14/. sale 14/.
Extra Gold/

S235

F. 134
White on Pink on Topaz
W. 1/6.
sale d/.

S236

F 129
White on Topaz   W. 12/. sale 9/.

S237

F. 127
White on Ruby on Blue
W. blank in 25/.
" " sale 24/.

S238

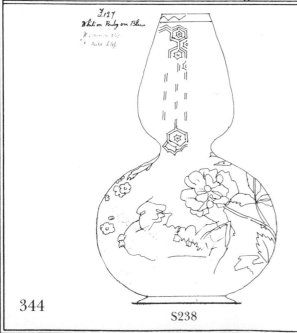

344

F. 128
White on Topaz
W. 14/. sale 24/.

S239

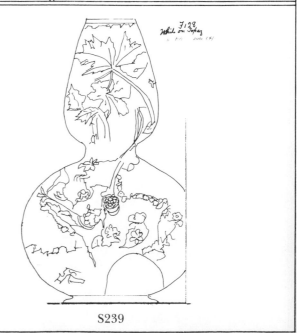

7.150
White on Ruby

S240

7.118
White & light Blue on Ruby (Ruby made)
(14m) Woodalls Estimate e/f sale £ h.h.v

S241

7161
White on Blue

S242

7148
White on Blue

S243

7.137
White on Ruby on Topaz West sale pit

S244

3217
Shape of lip

S245

345

7147
White on Yellow

S246

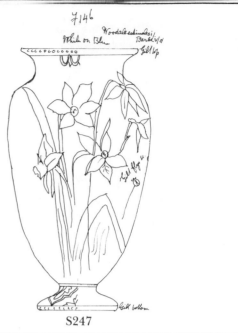

7146
White on Blue   Woodaleschinedai/
                     Barsled/d
                     fill lip

fell lip 4.

fell bottom

S247

7124
White on Ruby   W. Eston e/d
                     Jo. n x/.

S248

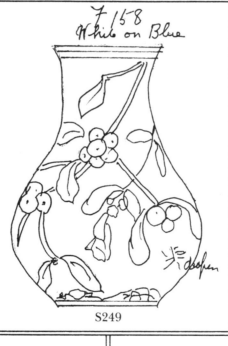

7158
White on Blue

draper

S249

7159
White on Topaz

draper

S250

S251

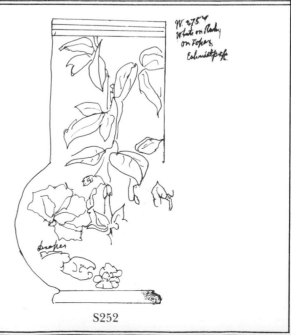

W. 275 4
White on Ruby
on Topaz
Cshmistt pfe

draper

S252

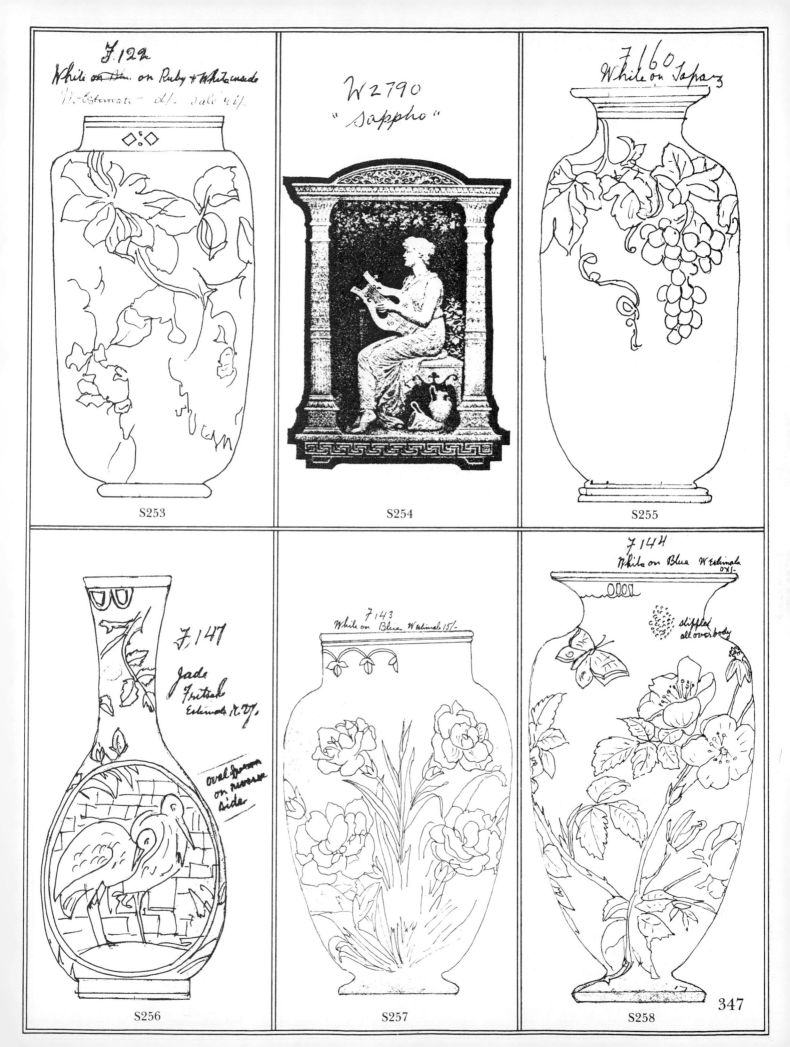

F.122
White on Blue on Ruby & White cased
W. Estimate - d/- Sale 4/-

S253

W2790
"Sappho"

S254

F160
White on Topaz

S255

F.147
Jade
Fritsch
Estimate X. 27.

Oval shown
on reverse
side

S256

F.143
White on Blue W.Estimate 15/-

S257

F.144
White on Blue W Estimate
0/-

stippled
all over body

S258

347

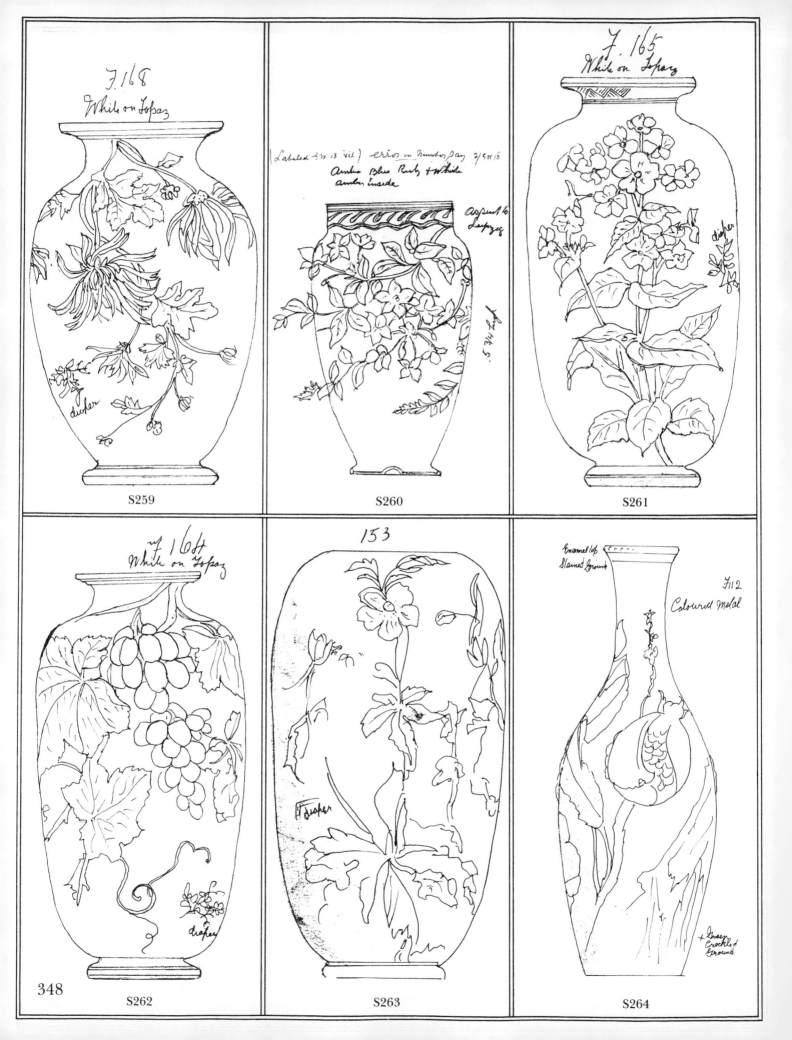

F.168
White on Topaz

S259

(Labeled 3 N 18 vit) error in number, say 2/5 N 18
Amber Blue Ruby + White
amber inside

Appear to
Leipzig

.5 3/4 left

S260

F.165
White on Topaz

diaper

S261

F.164
White on Topaz

diaper

S262

153

diaper

S263

Enamelled
Stained Ground

F.112
Coloured Metal

+ Green
Crackled
Ground

S264

348

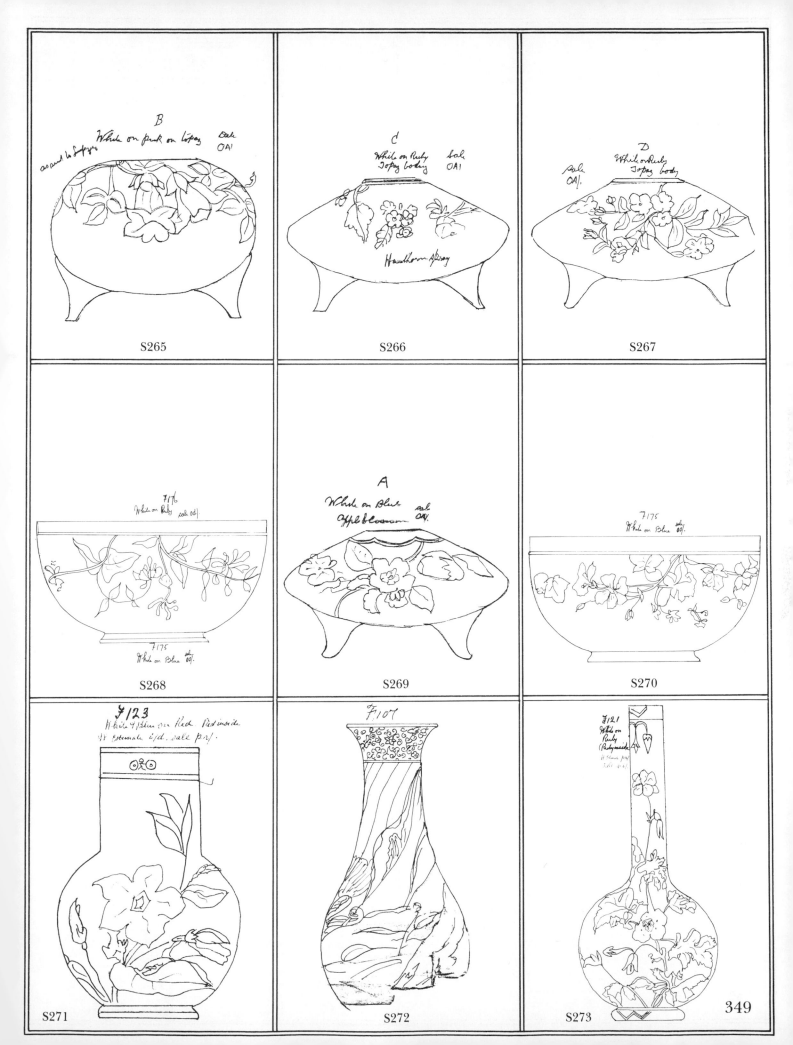

B
as used to Topes White on pink on Topaz   Sale OA1
S265

C
White on Ruby   Sale OA1
Topaz body
Hawthorn Spray
S266

D
Sale OA1   White on Ruby Topaz body
S267

7176
White on Ruby sale od/.
7175
White on Blue sale 00/.
S268

A
White on Blue sale OA/.
Apple blossom
S269

7175
White on Blue sale 00/.
S270

7123
White & Blue on Red Red inside.
If Extra male i/d. sale pr/.
S271

7107
S272

7121
White on Ruby
(Red inside)
If Extra pr/
sale 4 s/
S273

349

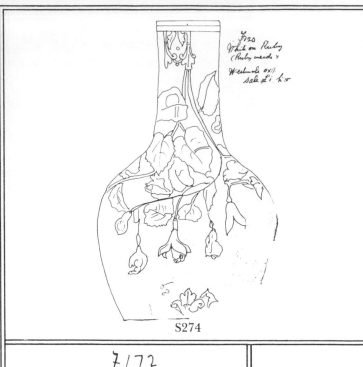

Fins
White on Ruby
(Ruby mode &
Weedmake oxll
sale £i.h.r

S274

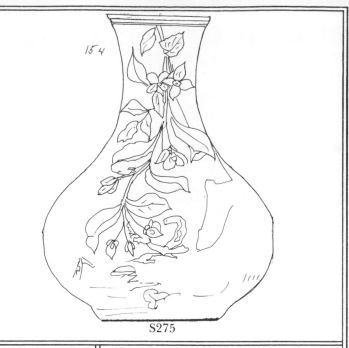

154

S275

7172
White on Blue

pm

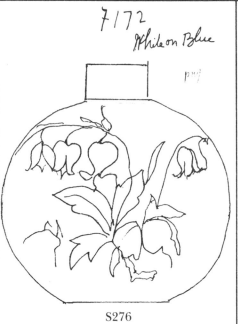

S276

W 3185

S277

7173

White on Blue

sale 1731

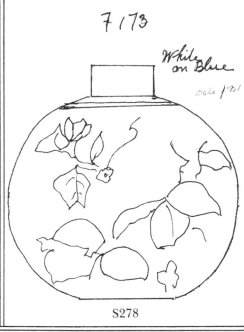

S278

156

S279

157

diaper

S280

350

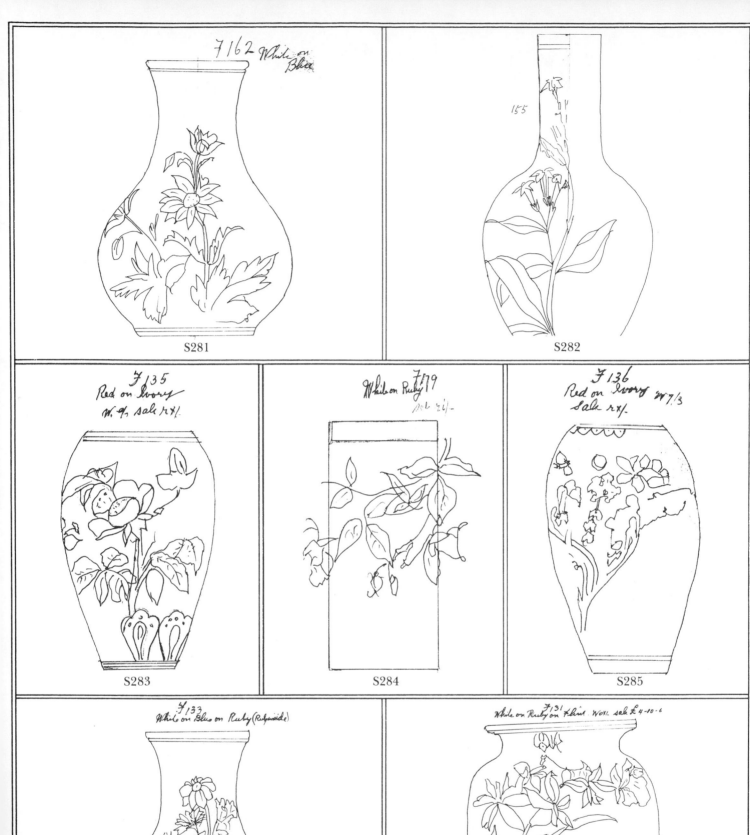

7162 White on Blue

S281

155

S282

7135
Red on Ivory
W. 9, sale rx/.

S283

White on Ruby 779
Nov 4/-

S284

7136
Red on Ivory W 7/3
Sale rx/.

S285

7133
White on Blue on Ruby (Rubyoxide)

S286

White on Ruby on Flint. Nov. sale £4-10-6
7131

S287

351

3226 17

S288

Venus
GW
156

S289

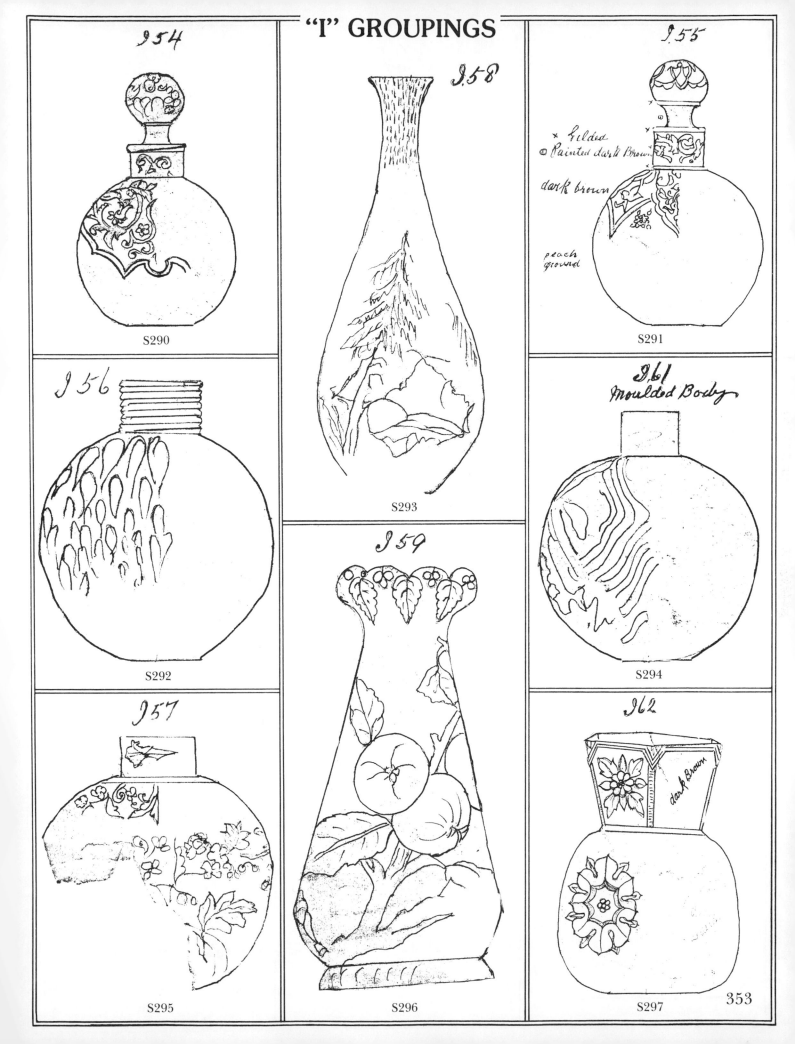

954

S290

958

S293

955

× Gilded

⊙ Painted dark Brown.

dark brown

peach ground

S291

956

S292

959

S296

961
moulded Body

S294

957

S295

962

dark Brown

S297

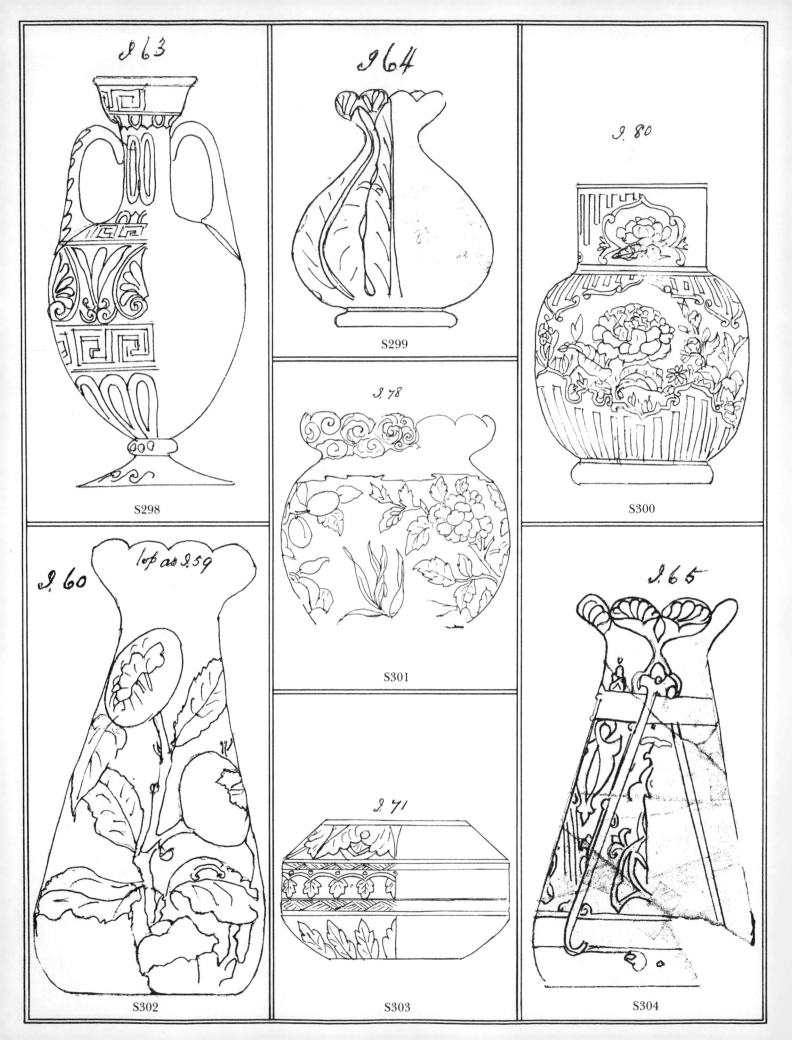

963

964

9.80

S298

S299

S300

9.78

S301

9.60   lop as 9.59

9.65

S302

9.71

S303

S304

976

S305

990

S306

993

S307

975
Dark Brown inside panels

S308

995

S309

984

S310

991

S311

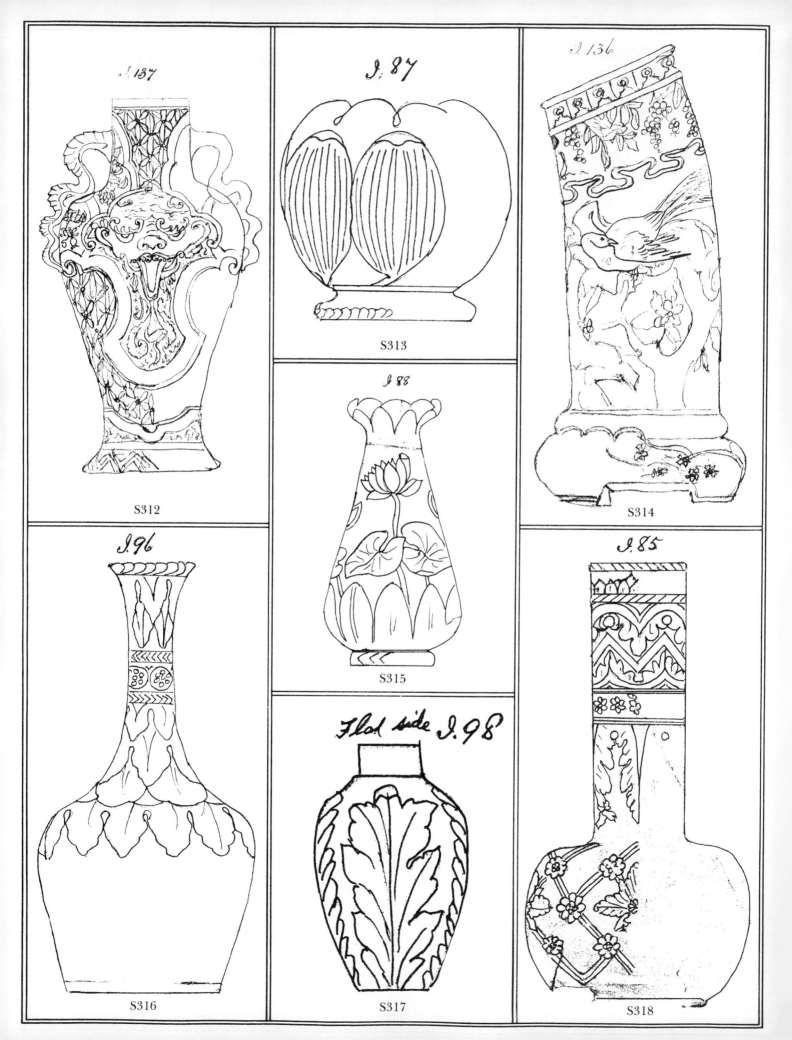

S.137

S312

J.87

S313

J.88

S315

J.136

S314

J.96

S316

Flat side J.98

S317

J.85

S318

9.165

S319

9.97

S322

9.166

S324

9145

S320

9170

S325

9146

S321

9164

S323

9.168

357

S326

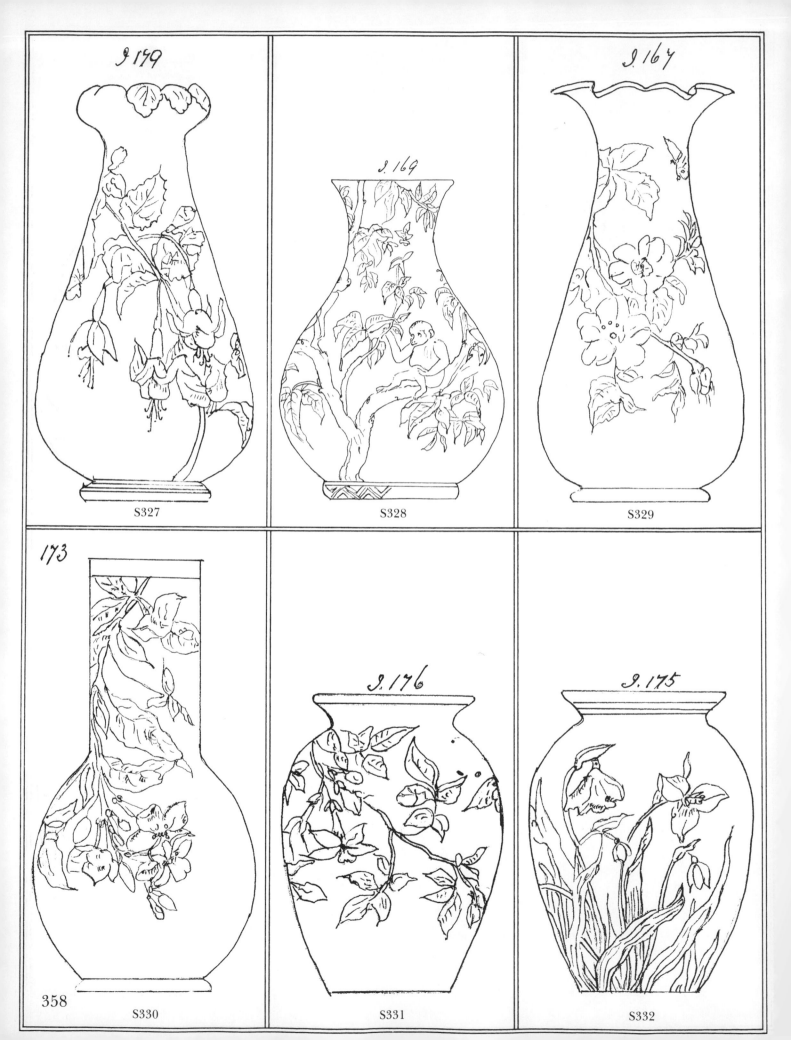

9 199

9 169

9 167

S327

S328

S329

173

9 176

9 175

358

S330

S331

S332

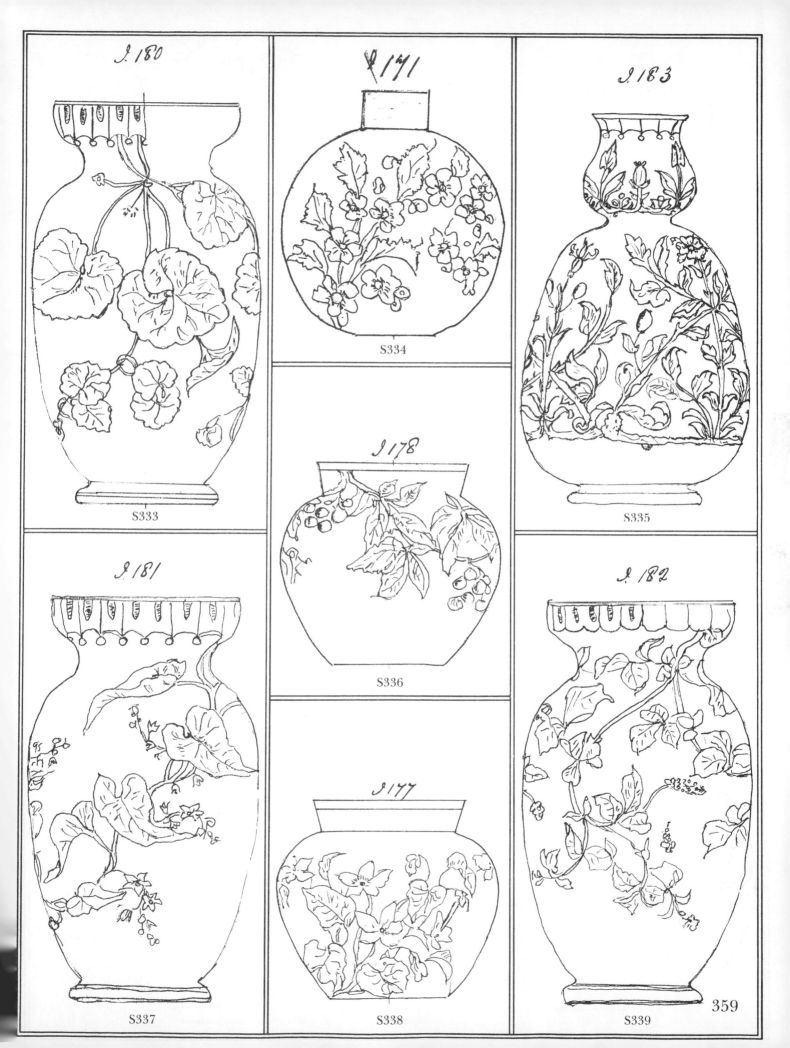

J. 180

S333

∮ 171

S334

J. 183

S335

J. 178

S336

J. 181

S337

J. 177

S338

J. 182

S339

359

S340

S341

S342

S343

S344

360

S345

S346

S.189

S197

S.190

S347

S348

S349

S191

S187

S350

S351

200

193

207

S352

S353

S354

361

209

199

S355

S356

206

Ɉ210

Ɉ204

S357

S358

S359

Ɉ203

Ɉ201

362

S360

S361

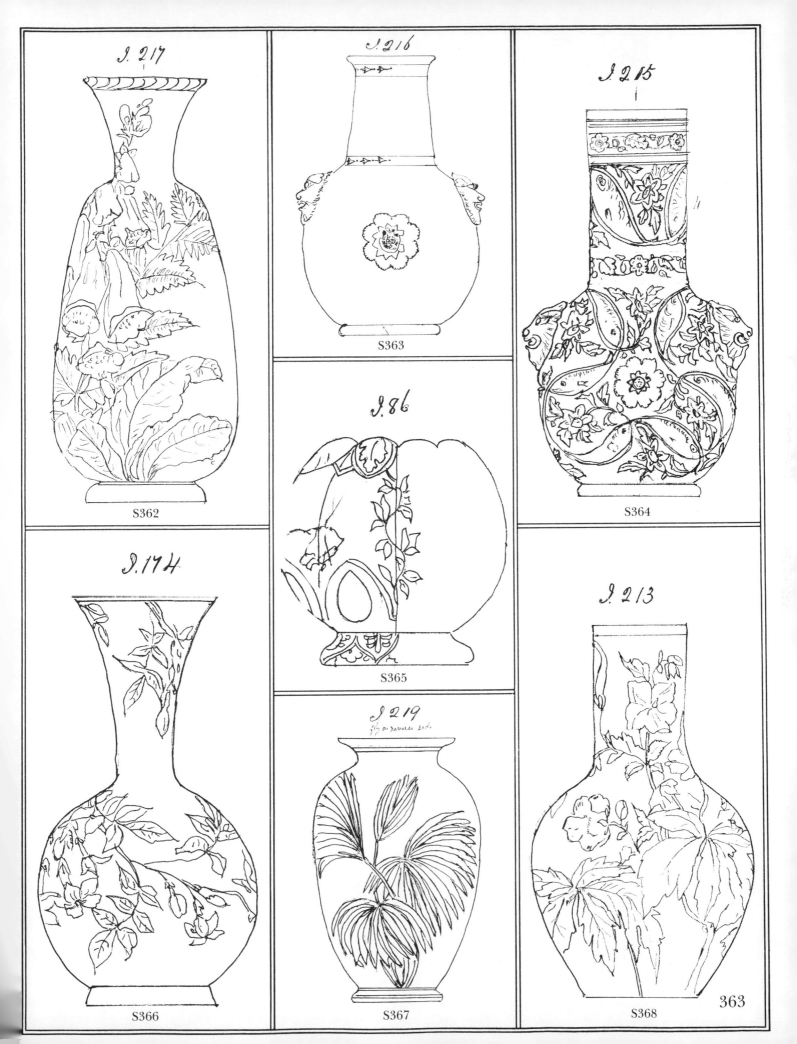

S. 217

S362

S. 216

S363

S. 86

S365

S. 174

S366

S. 219
fly on reverse side

S367

S. 215

S364

S. 213

S368

363

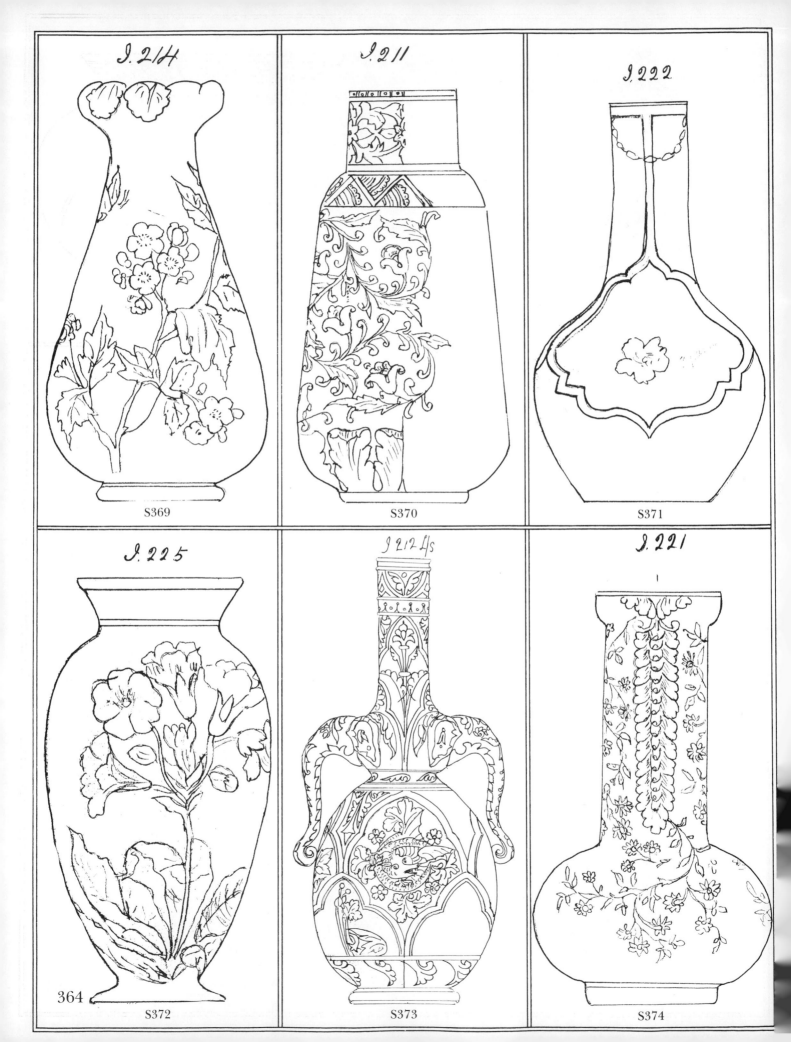

S369

S370

S371

S372

S373

S374

364

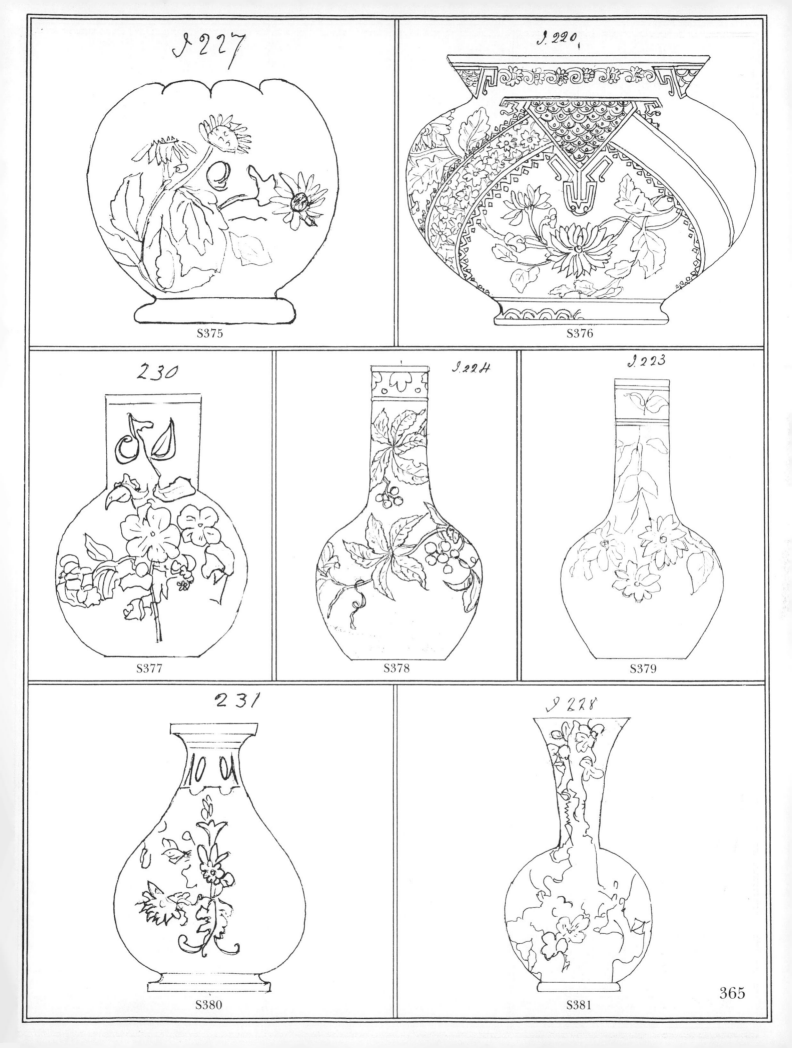

S375

S376

S377

S378

S379

S380

S381

365

232

S382

9226

S383

135

S384

241

S385

236

fly only on reverse side

366

S386

1234

S387

233

S388

S255

S389

S250

S390

S237

S391

S258

S392

S254

S393

S257

S394

S251

S395

367

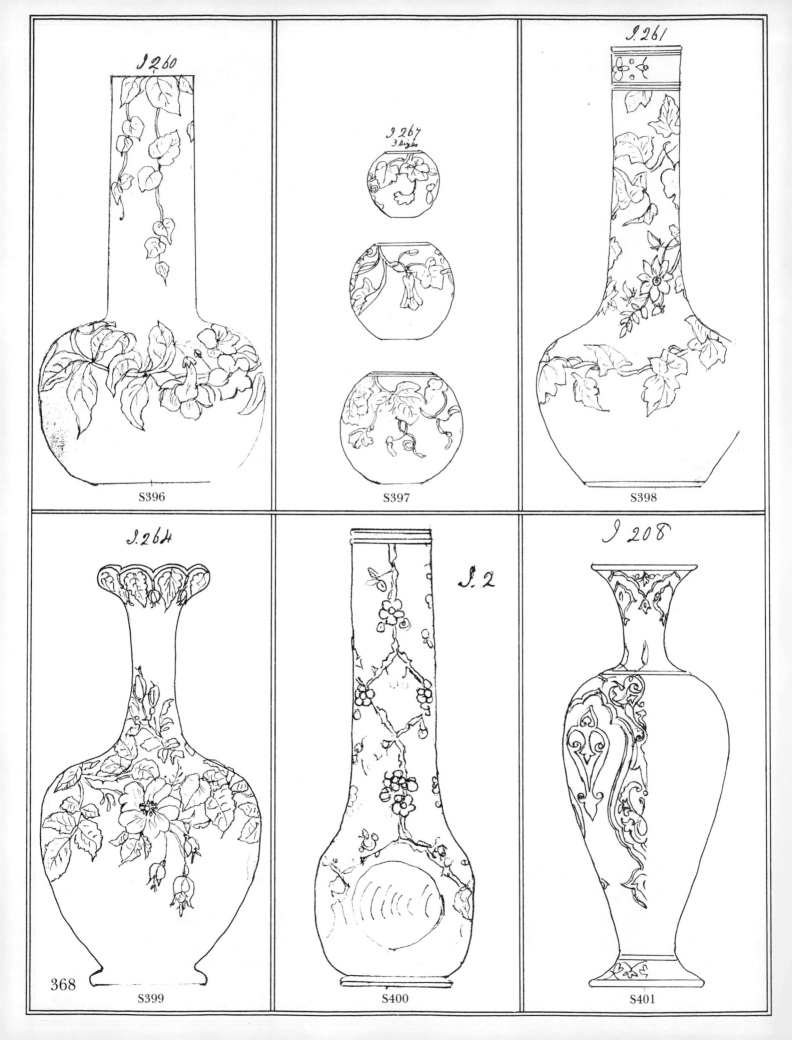

S396

S397

S398

S399

S400

S401

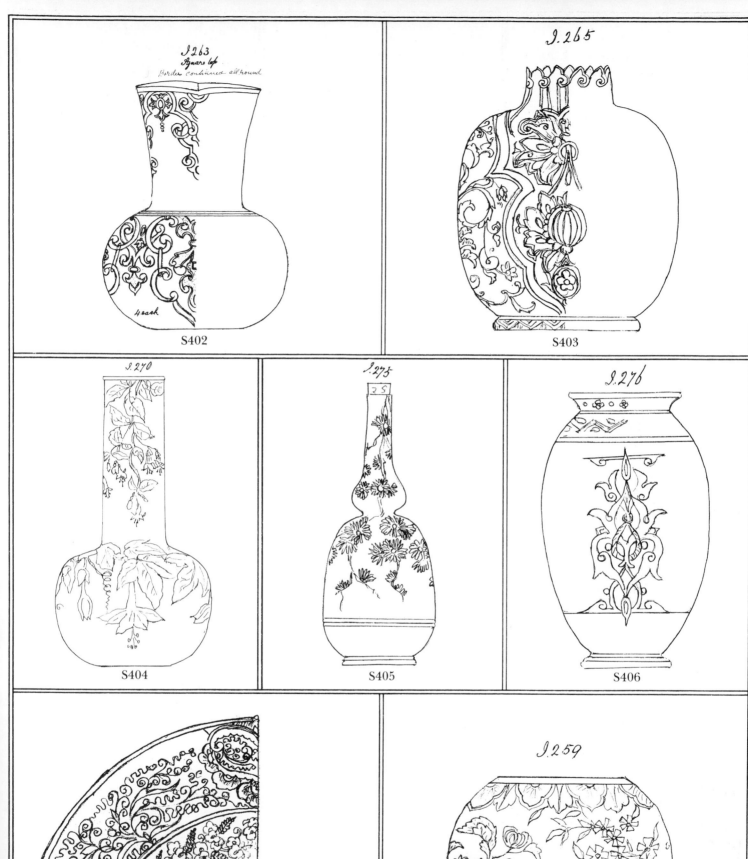

J263
Square top.
Border continued all round

4 each

S402

J.265

S403

J.270

S404

J.275

2S

S405

J.276

S406

J.262

8¼ in Rd Plate

S407

J.259

S408

S.274

S409

S.271

S410

S.273

S411

S.269

S412

S.272

S413

S.268

S414

370

C310. Vase, 7½ inches, signed "Thomas Webb & Sons, Gem Cameo, Tiffany & Co., Paris Exhibition 1889." *(Private collection)*

C311. Vase, 11 inches, signed "F. Carder, S & W." *(Collection of Rockwell-Corning Museum)*

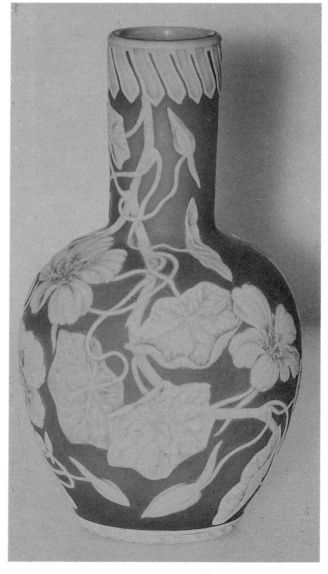

C312. Nasturtium-design vase, 6½ inches, white on antique gold; signed "Webb." *(Private collection)*

C314. Decanter, 9 inches, signed "Thomas Webb & Sons." Wild-rose decoration. *(Private collection)*

C313. Plaque, 6 inches, signed "Geo. Woodall." Feathered Favourites. *(Private collection)*

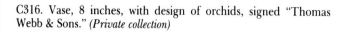

C315. Vase, 12 inches, signed "J. Millward, Stevens & Williams Ltd." (*Private collection*)

C316. Vase, 8 inches, with design of orchids, signed "Thomas Webb & Sons." (*Private collection*)

C317. Vase, 9¼ inches, with phlox, signed "Thomas Webb & Sons." (*Private collection*)

373

C318. Vase, 18 inches, signed "Tiffany & Co., Paris Exhibition 1889, Thomas Webb & Sons, Gem Cameo." *(Private collection)*

C319. Plaque, 2½ inches, signed "G. Woodall, William E. Gladstone, Thomas Webb & Sons, Gem Cameo." *(Private collection)*

374

C320. Daffodil vase, 9 inches, signed "Thomas Webb & Sons." *(Collection of Leo Kaplan Antiques, courtesy of Alan Kaplan)*

C321. Decanter, 14¼ inches, plum cameo carving on crystal ground. *(Collection of The Chrysler Museum of Art at Norfolk)*

C322. Vase, 10 inches, signed "Davis Collamore & Co., Paris Exhibition 1889, Thomas Webb & Sons, Gem Cameo." *(Courtesy of Alan Kaplan)*

C323. Dahlia-decorated vase, 7½ inches, signed "Tiffany & Co., Paris Exhibition 1889, Thomas Webb & Sons, Gem Cameo." *(Private collection)*

C324. Morning-glory vase, 13¼ inches, attributed to Thomas Webb & Sons. *(Authors' collection)*

C325. Vase, 8½ inches, with prunus blossoms, a typical Webb shape. Signed "Thomas Webb & Sons, Cameo." *(Private collection)* →

C326. Vase, 8¼ inches, signed "G. Woodall, Thomas Webb & Sons, Gem Cameo." *(Collection of Metropolitan Museum of Art)*

C327. Very rare figural perfume bottle, 4¼ inches. Attributed to Geo. Woodall. *(Private collection)*

C328. Vase, 10 inches, signed "Geo. Woodall." Phyllis. *(Courtesy of Alan Kaplan)*

C329. Silver-topped decanter, 9¼ inches, with passion flowers. *(Private collection)*

378

C330. Vase, 12 inches, with bird on a hammered red ground, signed "J. Millward." *(Courtesy of Alan Kaplan)*

C331. Vase, 7½ inches, with two children perched on an eagle, signed "Geo. Woodall, Loves Areo." *(Private collection)*

C332. Vase, 15 inches, with allover decoration; marked "WN." *(Private collection)*

C333. Plaque, 8 inches by 5¾ inches, W 2805; signed "Geo. Woodall." Nymph of the Sea. *(Courtesy of Alan Kaplan)*

C334. Cupid seated on rocks, 10⅛″, signed "G. Woodall, Thomas Webb & Sons, Gem Cameo." *(Courtesy of Sotheby Parke Bernet)*

C335. Vase, 10½ inches, with cherries; an outstanding conception. *(Courtesy of Christie's, London)*

C336. Three-part vase (base, body, and cover), 23 inches. Known as either the Dennis or the Pegasus vase. Signed "John Northwood, 1882." Undoubtedly this was one of the finest of Northwood's accomplishments. *(Gift from the John Gellatly Collection, courtesy of the Smithsonian Institution)*

C337. Plaque, 15 inches; signed "W. Northwood, Venus and Dancing Cupid 1888." *(Brierly Hill Glass Collection, courtesy of the Dudley Art Gallery)*

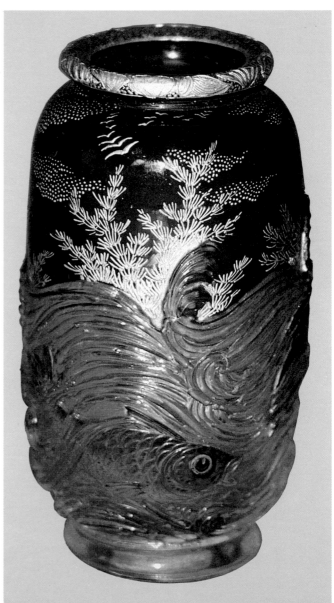

C338. Vase, 4½ inches, with fish and other marine motifs. *(Authors' collection)*

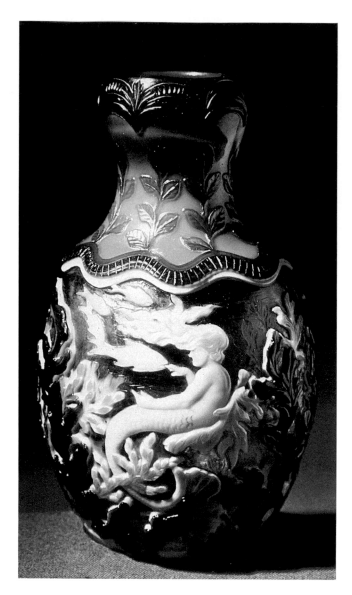

C339. Vase, 8 inches, with seaweed, fishes, and a sea nymph; W 3218. *(Courtesy of Christie's, London)*

C340. Vase, 9¾ inches, signed "J. Millward, Stevens & Williams Ltd., Brierly Hill." *(Private collection)*

C341. Vase, 9 inches, with dancing girl, signed "G. Woodall, Thomas Webb & Sons, Gem Cameo." *(Private collection)*

C342. Tapestry design oil lamp, 22 inches, attributed to Thomas Webb & Sons. (*Collection of Leo Kaplan Antiques, courtesy of Alan Kaplan*)

C343. Vase, 5¾ inches; in a striking color combination; attributed to Webb. (*Collection of the Milan Historical Museum*)

C544. Serving set, 12 inches; violet and rose motifs in an unusual application. (*Private collection*)

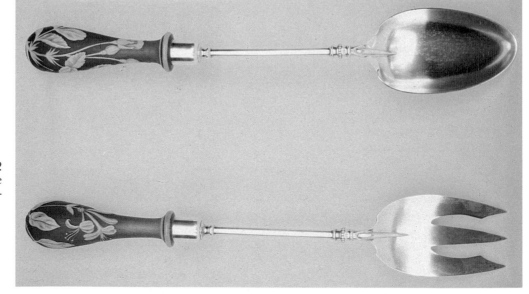

386

C345. Portrait of Queen Victoria, 6½ inches. *(Collection of the Currier Gallery of Art)*

C346. Vase, 12 inches, The Milkmaid; signed "G. Woodall." W 1776. *(Courtesy of Christie's, London)*

C347. An outstanding replica of a vase unearthed in Pompeii in 1834. The original is in the Naples Museum, supported on a silver base. *(Private collection)*

C348. Two-layered vase, 8 inches; the yellow glass inside was refired to shade to coral. *(Authors' collection)*

C349. Four-layered unfinished vase, 17½ inches, pink on white on blue, with clear lining. *(Authors' collection)*

C350. Two 18-inch colored plaques prior to cutting. Both have an opal layer on the other side for carving cameo decoration. *(Authors' collection)*

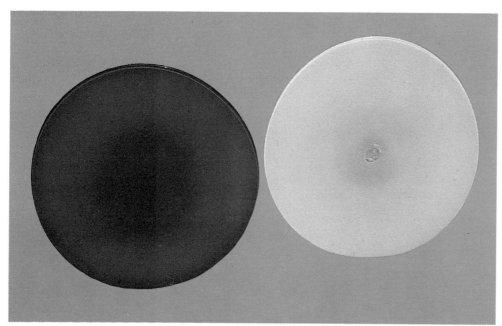

389

C351. Clematis-decorated vase, 5 inches, signed "Thomas Webb & Sons, Gem Cameo." *(Private collection)*

C352. Vase, 17 inches, signed "Paris Exhibition 1889, Thomas Webb & Sons, Gem Cameo." Cameo motifs include foxglove, butterfly, and bee. *(Private collection)*

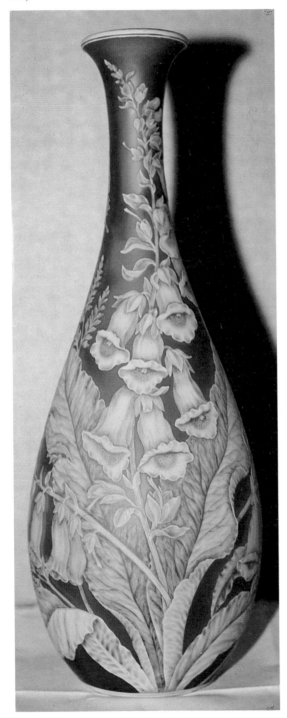

C353. Four-layered 12-inch vase signed "Thomas Webb & Sons." *(Private collection)* →

C354. An unusual piece in that the portrait of Queen Victoria appears as the lone subject. *(Private collection)*

C355. Oval bowl, 3¾ inches, signed "Thomas Webb & Sons, Gem." Carved fish and waves in blue-streaked waters. *(Collection of Lillian Nassau)*

C356. Vase, 14½ inches, with underwater motifs (whelk, conch, and scallop shells); signed "Thomas Webb & Sons, Gem Cameo." *(Private collection)*

C357. Vase, 12 inches, with blackberries; signed "Thomas Webb & Sons, Gem Cameo." *(Private collection)*

392

C358. Two-handled 16-inch vase, signed "G. Woodall, Tiffany & Co., Paris Exhibition 1889, Thomas Webb & Sons, Gem Cameo." *(Private collection)*

C359. Flask, 5¾", carved on both sides with figures, attributed to Thomas Webb & Co. *(Courtesy of Sotheby Parke Bernet)*

C360. Perfume bottle, 6 inches, signed "Tiffany & Co., Thomas Webb & Sons, Gem Cameo." Silver top is engraved "Isabel." *(Private collection)*

C361. Plaque, 10¾ inches, signed "Geo. Woodall." Syrene (also spelled "Siren"). *(Copyright Sotheby's Belgravia, Inc., London)*

C362. Vase, 11¼ inches, signed "Thomas Webb & Sons." It is an outstanding example of the technique of enameling with platinum and gold on ivory cameo. *(Private collection)*

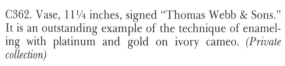

C363. Opal topaz flask, 5 inches, decorated with violets on both sides. *(Authors' collection)*

C364. Double gourd vase, 4¾ inches, decorated with poppies. *(Private collection)*

C365. Vase, 13½ inches, with blackberries; signed "Thomas Webb & Sons, Gem Cameo." *(Private collection)*

C366. Vase, 6½ inches, with allover leaf design; signed "Stevens & Williams, Stourbridge, Art Glass." *(Private collection)*

395

C367. Plaque, 13½ inches, signed "F. Carder, 1897." The Immortality of the Arts is one of the rare examples of Frederick Carder's great cameo work. *(Collection of The Corning Museum of Glass)*

C368. Vase, 10 inches, white on rose du Barry ground; attributed to Stevens & Williams. *(Collection of the Milan Historical Museum)*

C369. Vase, 10 inches, signed "Phyllis at the Fountain, T. & G. Woodall, Thomas Webb & Sons." W 2722. (*Private collection, photo courtesy of Dr. and Mrs. Jesse B. Foote*)

C370. Isaac Newton plaque, symbolic of science, signed "J. North-wood 1878." Diameter of the plaque is 7⅜ inches; with stand, 9¼ inches high. *(Copyright Sotheby's Belgravia, Inc., London)*

C371. The tazza with the Newton plaque attached, 9¼ inches; signed "J. Northwood 1878." *(Copyright Sotheby's Belgravia, Inc., London)*

C372. Portrait of John Flaxman, 9¼ inches, representing art, with hawthorn border; signed "JN [in monogram] 1880." *(Copyright Sotheby's Belgravia, Inc., London)*

C373. Portrait of William Shakespeare, 9¼ inches, symbolic of literature, in a border of acorns and oak leaves. Circa 1882. *(Copyright Sotheby's Belgravia, Inc., London)*

398

C378. Vase, 13 inches, signed "G. Woodall, Thomas Webb & Sons." Autumn. *(Courtesy of Charles E. Tuttle Co., publisher of the authors'* Art Glass Nouveau*)*

C379. Vase, 10¼ inches, with bird and cattails, signed "Paris Exhibition 1889, Thomas Webb & Sons, Gem Cameo." *(Private collection)*

401

C380. Vase, 9¼ inches, white on du Barry pink with grapes and vine motif, signed "Thomas Webb & Sons, Gem Cameo." *(Private collection)*

C381. Vase, 10 inches, with floral and insect motifs; signed "Thomas Webb & Sons, Gem Cameo." *(Private collection)*

C382. White on brown vase, 8 inches, signed "Thomas Webb & Sons, Gem Cameo." Ares, God of War. *(Authors' collection)*

C383. Vase, 12 inches, signed "Thomas Webb & Sons, Gem." Colors of glass layers are pink, white, yellow, blue, and cream. *(Private collection)*

C384. Vase with allover shell decoration, 14½ inches, signed "Thomas Webb & Sons, Gem Cameo, Paris Exhibition 1889." *(Private collection)*

C385. Vase, 7¾ inches, signed "F. Carder" and attributed to Stevens & Williams. *(Collection of Rockwell-Corning Museum)*

404

C387. Vase, 7 inches, The Flower Gatherer; signed "G. Woodall, Thomas Webb & Sons, Gem Cameo." White on topaz. *(Authors' collection)*

405

C388. Vase, 7 inches, signed "Webb"; cobalt blue cameo on engraved metallic ground; holly and berries motif. *(Private collection)*

C389. Twelve-inch claret jug with passion-flower motif; attributed to Stevens & Williams. *(Collection of Leo Kaplan Antiques)*

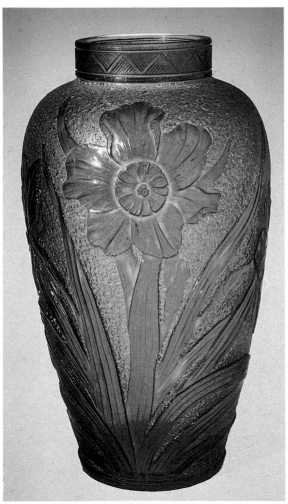

C390. Vase, 7½ inches, signed "F. Carder." *(Collection of Rockwell-Corning Museum)*

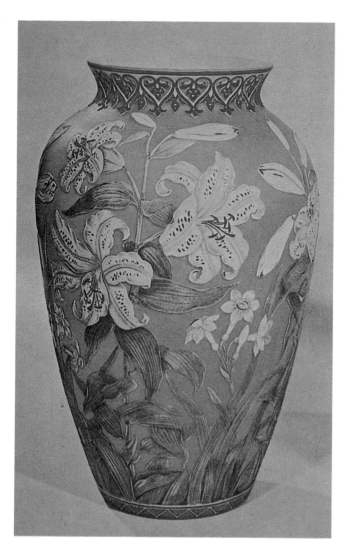

C391. Vase, 15½ inches; enamel decoration on three-color cameo. *(Courtesy of Charles E. Tuttle Co., publisher of the authors'* Carved and Decorated European Art Glass)

C392. Dancing Girl vase, 12 inches, signed "G. Woodall, Thomas Webb & Sons, Gem Cameo." *(Courtesy of Charles E. Tuttle Co., publisher of the authors'* Carved and Decorated European Art Glass)

C393. White-on-blue vase, 12 inches, signed "G. Woodall, Thomas Webb & Sons, Gem Cameo." *(Courtesy of Charles E. Tuttle Co., publisher of the authors'* Carved and Decorated European Art Glass)

C394. Plaque, 7¾ inches, Cupid on Panther, signed "Geo. Woodall." *(Courtesy of Charles E. Tuttle Co., publisher of the authors'* Art Glass Nouveau)

408

C395. A rare 6-inch mold-blown vase by Thomas Webb & Sons. Outstanding detail. *(Private collection)*

C396. Vase, 4¼ inches, signed "Thomas Webb & Sons, Paris Exhibition 1889." Fine green cameo on Burmese (yellow refired to red) ground. *(Private collection)*

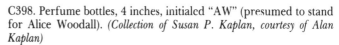

C397. Perfume bottles (largest 6 inches). Smallest has engraved "HB" superimposed, identified as the initials of Harriet Bott, wife of Thomas Bott, pâte-sur-pâte artist and maternal uncle of George Woodall. *(Private collection)*

C398. Perfume bottles, 4 inches, initialed "AW" (presumed to stand for Alice Woodall). *(Collection of Susan P. Kaplan, courtesy of Alan Kaplan)*

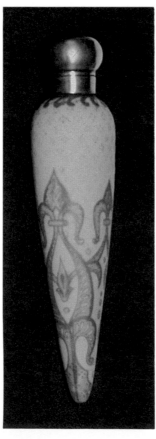

C399. Perfume bottle, 4 inches, attributed to Stevens & Williams. *(Collection of Susan P. Kaplan)*

C400. The famous Portland Vase, 10 inches, signed "John North-wood 1876." *(Copyright Sotheby's Belgravia, Inc., London)*

C400A. The Phrygian cap that appears at the bottom of the Portland Vase.

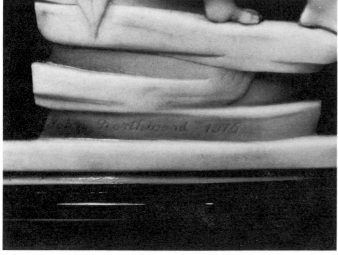

C400B. Signature on the Portland Vase

411

C401. Vase, 9 inches, with convolvulus motif, white on pink on chartreuse; signed "Thomas Webb & Sons." *(Private collection)*

C402. Large (14-inch) vase decorated with sunflowers, butterflies, and dragonfly. *(Private collection)*

C403. Vase, 9 inches, with iris; signed "Thomas Webb & Sons." *(Private collection)*

C404. Oval portrait of Bismarck, 7½ inches, signed "F. Kretschman 1886." Made at Thomas Webb & Sons. *(Private collection)*

C405. Vase, 6½ inches, with cameo-carved prunus blossoms and wheat on a Burmese ground; signed "Thomas Webb & Sons." *(Private collection)*

C406. One of a very few specially carved brooches, set in an oval gold setting. *(Private collection)*

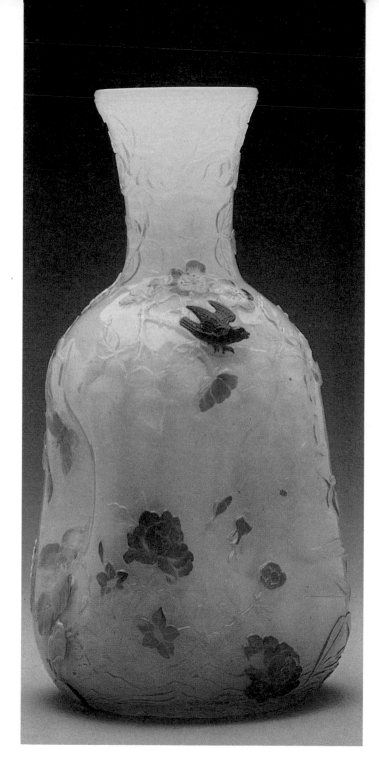

C407. Vase, 10¼ inches, signed "Webb," with cameo leaves, flowers, bird, and a butterfly. *(Collection of Lillian Nassau)*

C408. Four-color cameo punchbowl, 16 inches in height, produced by the "Woodall team"; signed "Thomas Webb & Sons." *(Courtesy of Charles E. Tuttle Co., publisher of the authors'* Carved and Decorated European Art Glass)

414

C416. Cabbage-rose vase, 9½ inches, signed "Thomas Webb & Sons, Gem Cameo." *(Private collection)*

C417. Morning-glory vase, 8 inches, signed "Thomas Webb & Sons, Gem Cameo." *(Private collection)*

C419. Vase, 12 inches, with Christmas roses, signed "Stevens & Williams Art Glass, Stourbridge, England." *(Private collection)*

C418. Pansy-motif vase, 6 inches, signed "Thomas Webb & Sons, Gem Cameo." *(Private collection)*

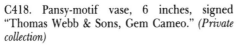

417

C420. White-on-blue vase, 8½ inches, signed "G. Woodall, Thomas Webb & Sons, Gem Cameo." *(Courtesy of Charles E. Tuttle Co., publisher of the authors'* Carved and Decorated European Art Glass)

C421. Plaque, 8¾ inches, white on red, of Joseph Silvers; Stevens & Williams collection; carved by Joshua Hodgetts 1926. *(Courtesy of Charles E. Tuttle Co., publisher of the authors'* Carved and Decorated European Art Glass)

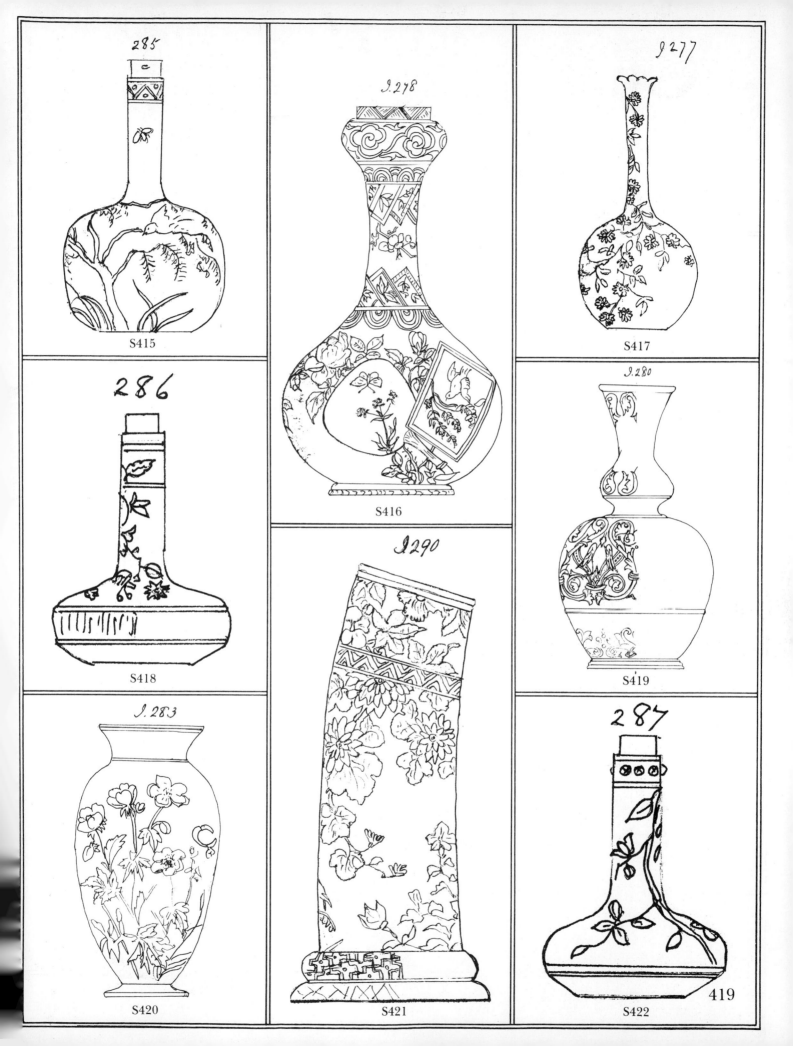

285

S415

J.278

S416

J277

S417

286

S418

J290

S421

J.280

S419

J.283

S420

287

419

S422

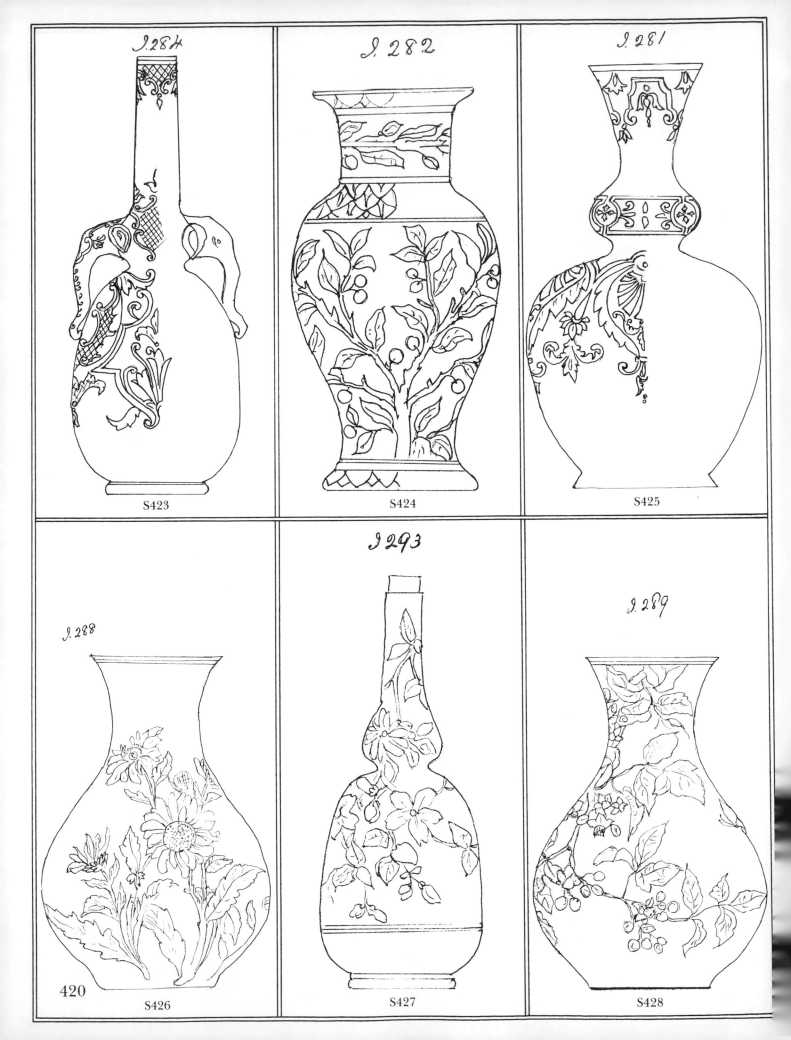

J.284

J.282

J.281

S423

S424

S425

J.288

J293

J.289

420

S426

S427

S428

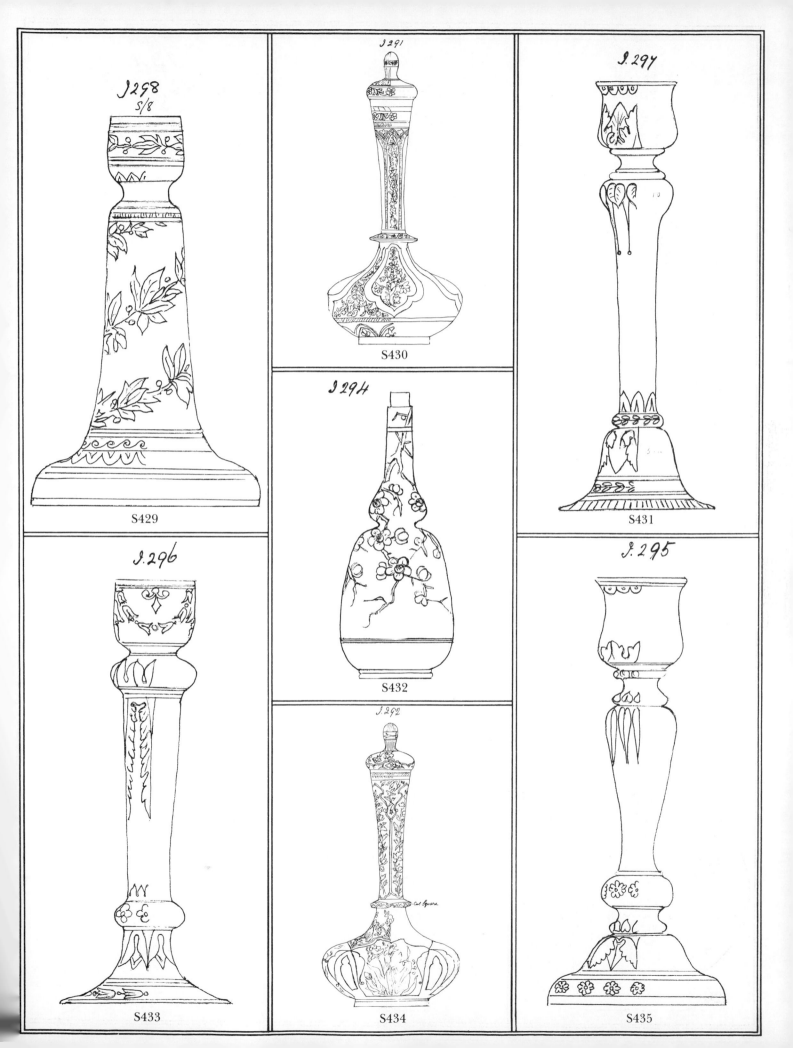

J 298
S/8
S429

J 291
S430

J 294
S432

J 292
S434

J. 297
S431

J. 296
S433

J. 295
S435

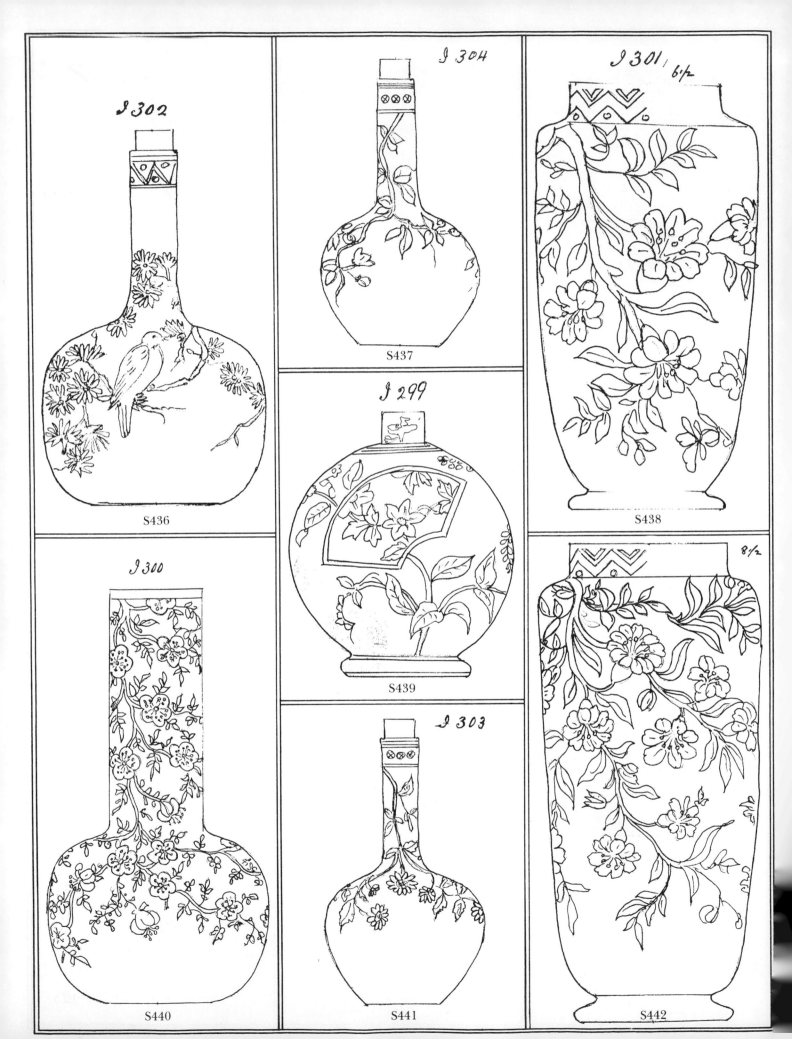

S302

S436

S304

S437

S301, 6½

S438

S299

S439

S300

S303

S441

S440

8½

S442

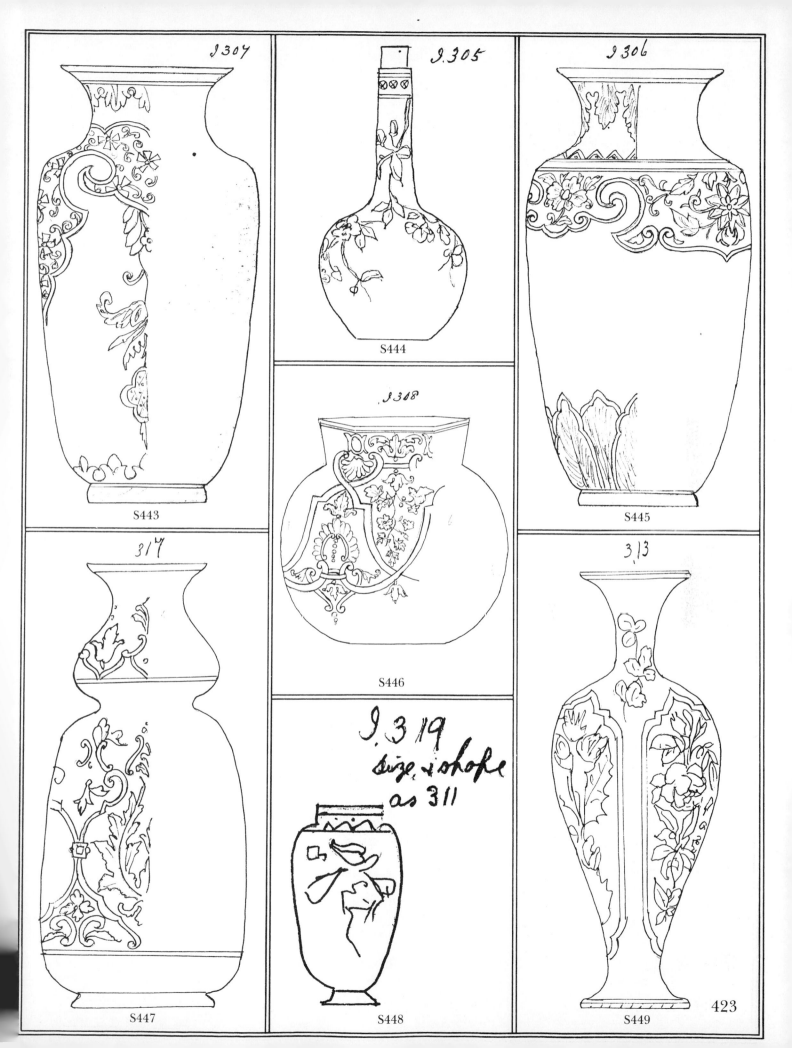

9307

9.305

9306

S443

S444

S445

9318

317

S446

3.13

9.319
size + shape
as 311

S447

S448

S449

423

312

314

320

S450

S451

S452

424

S453

321

S454

310

S455

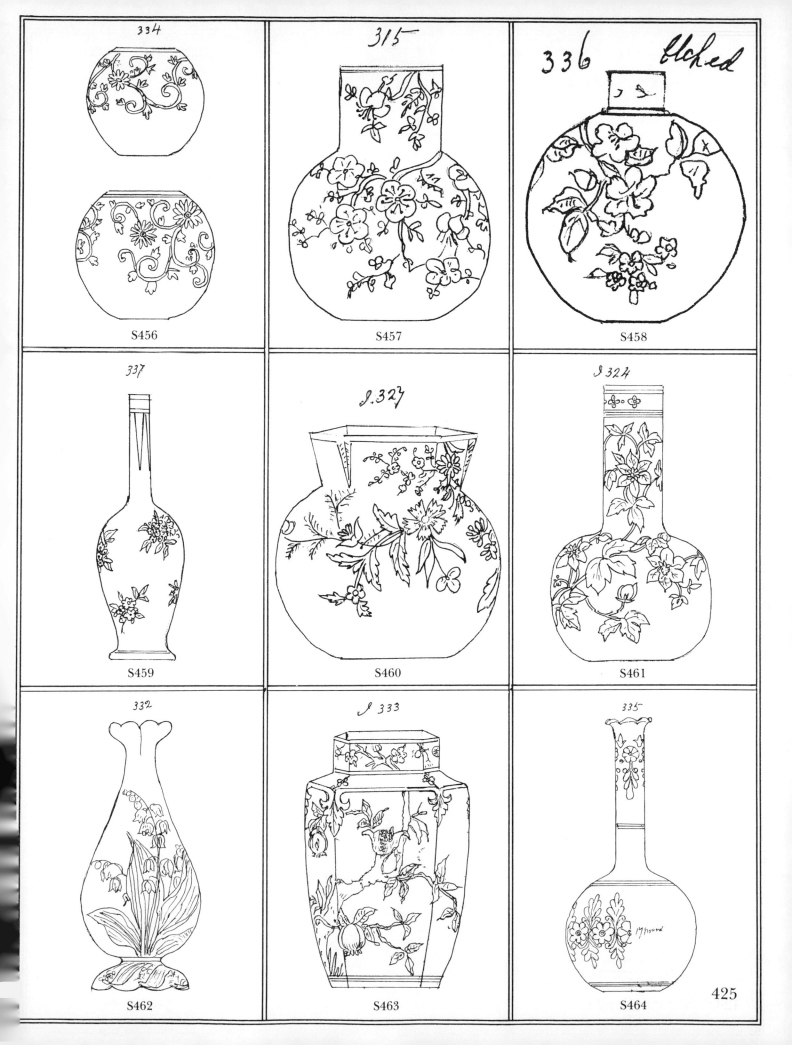

334

315

336 etched

S456

S457

S458

337

S.327

S324

S459

S460

S461

332

S333

335

S462

S463

S464

425

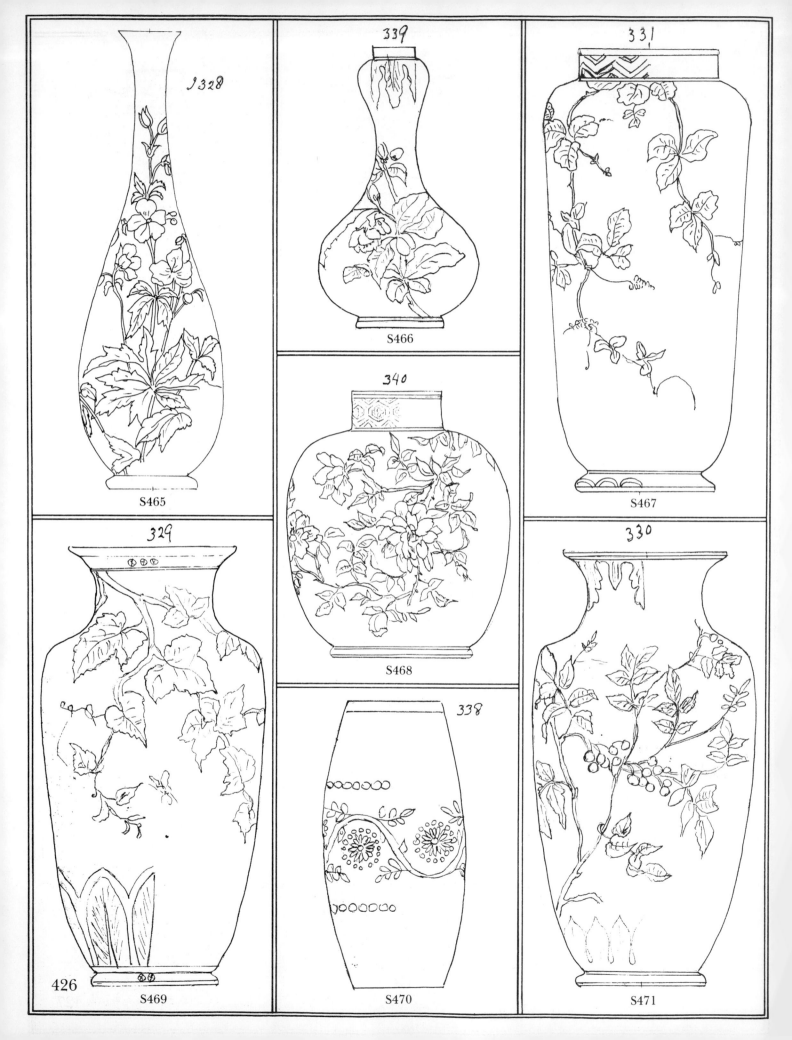

1328

339

331

S466

340

S467

S465

329

S468

330

426

338

S469

S470

S471

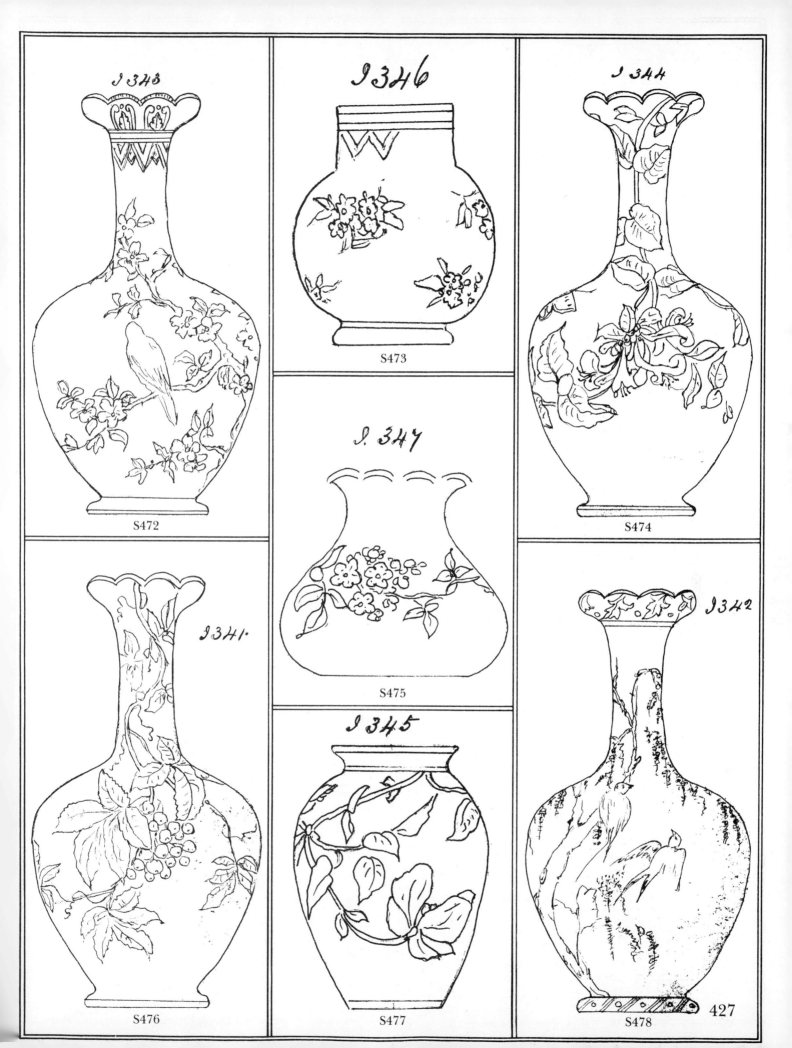

S472

S473

S475

S474

S476

S477

S478

427

S479

S480

S481

S482

S483

S484

S485

428

357

358

356

S486

S487

S488

359

355

360

this part as Bowl 220

S489

S490

S491

429

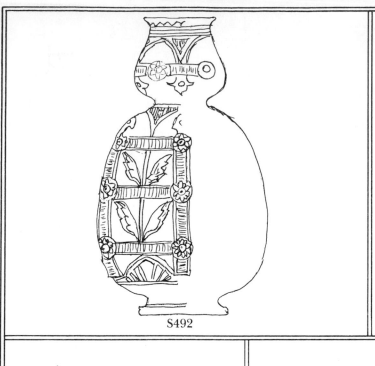

S492

368

S493

9.362

S494

371

S495

9.361

S496

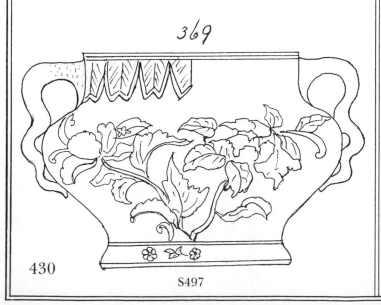

369

430

S497

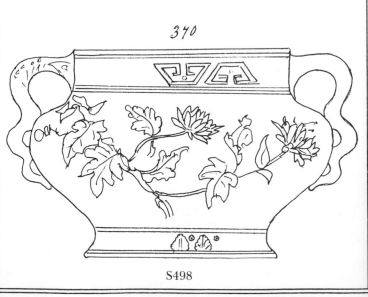

370

S498

372

S499

365

S500

9 376

S501

shape of top

363

S502

366

S503

364

S504

431

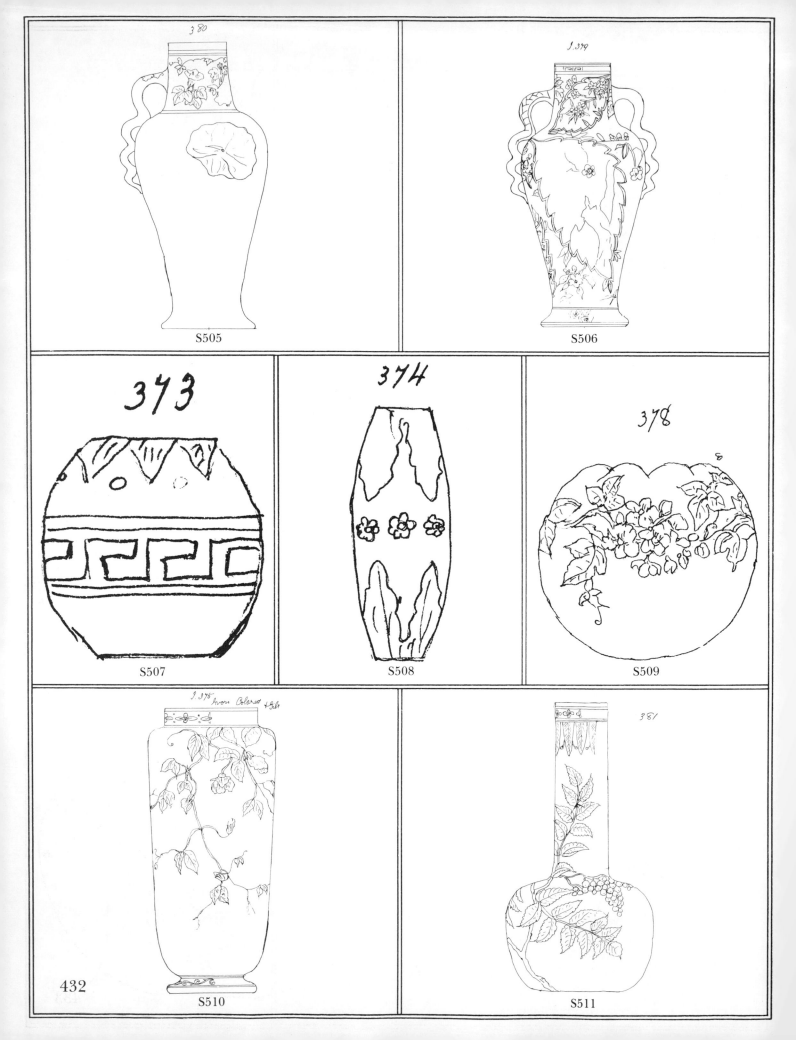

380

S505

9.379

S506

343

S507

374

S508

378

S509

9.375 *ivory colored + gilt*

S510

432

381

S511

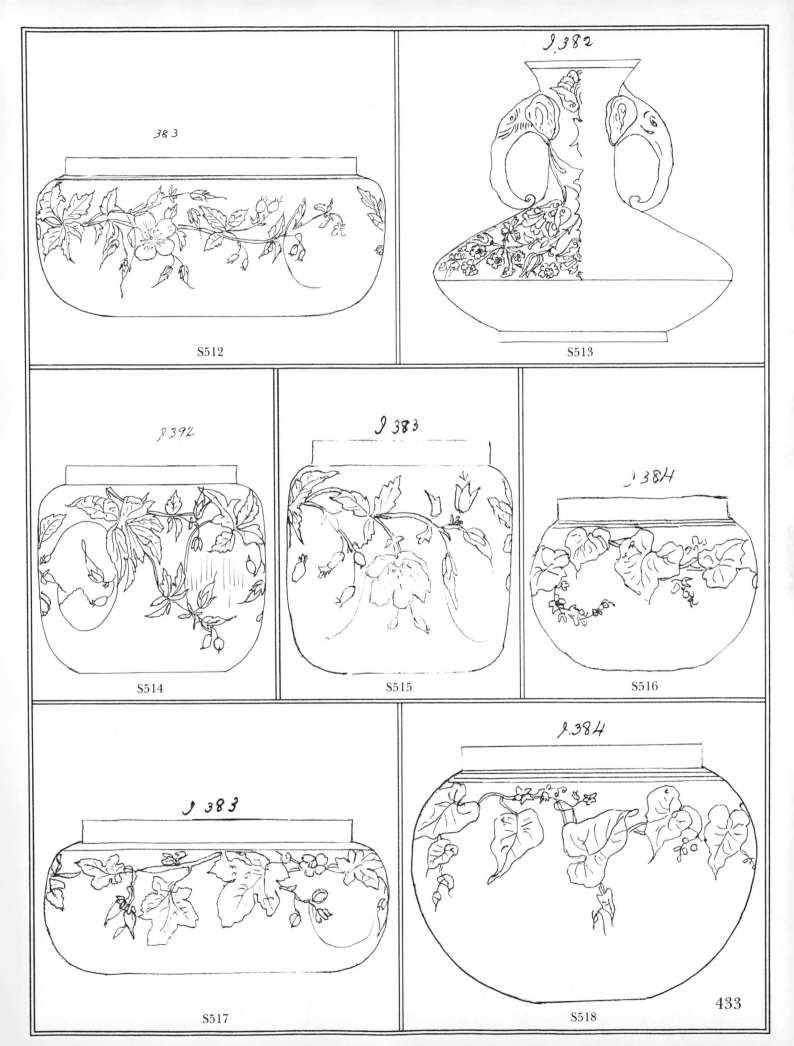

383

S512

9.382

S513

9.392

S514

9 383

S515

9 384

S516

9 383

S517

9.384

S518

433

S389

S519

S391

S520

S391

S522

S390

S521

S393

S523

S385

S524

S386

S525

9396

S526

9.408

S527

229

S529

9397

S528

9388

S530

9.395

S531

9.398

S532

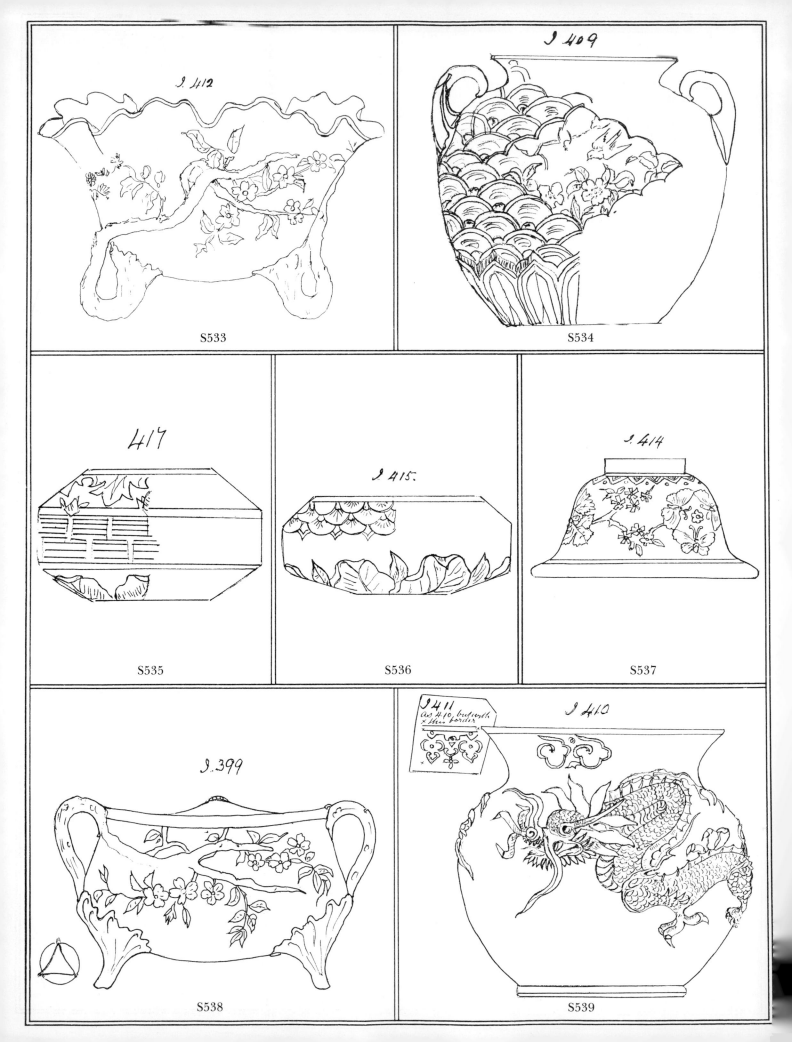

9.412

S533

9.409

S534

417

S535

9.415.

S536

9.414

S537

9.399

S538

9.411
As 4.10, but with
x this border

9.410

S539

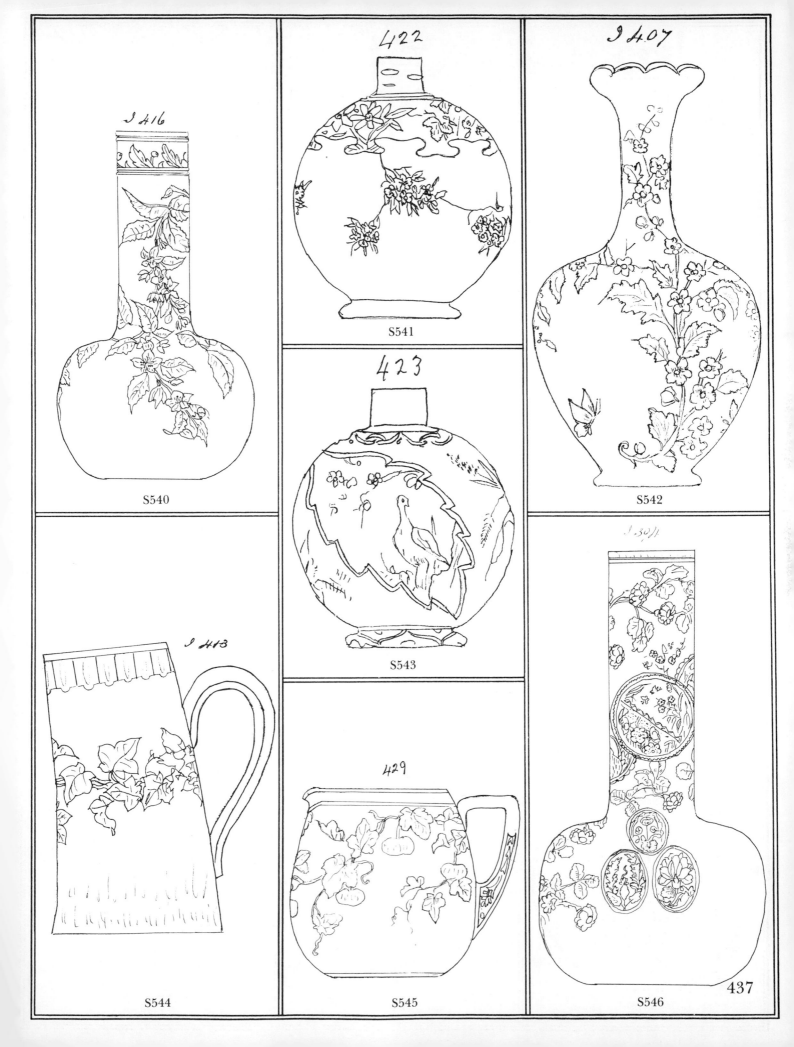

S416

422

9407

S540

S541

423

S542

9413

S543

429

S544

S545

S546

437

406

402

405

S547

S548

S549

404

401

406

S550

S551

S552

405

238

239

438

S553

S554

S555

418
S556

419
S557

420
S558

428
S559

424
S560

421
S561

439

S562

S563

S564

S565

S566

S567

S568

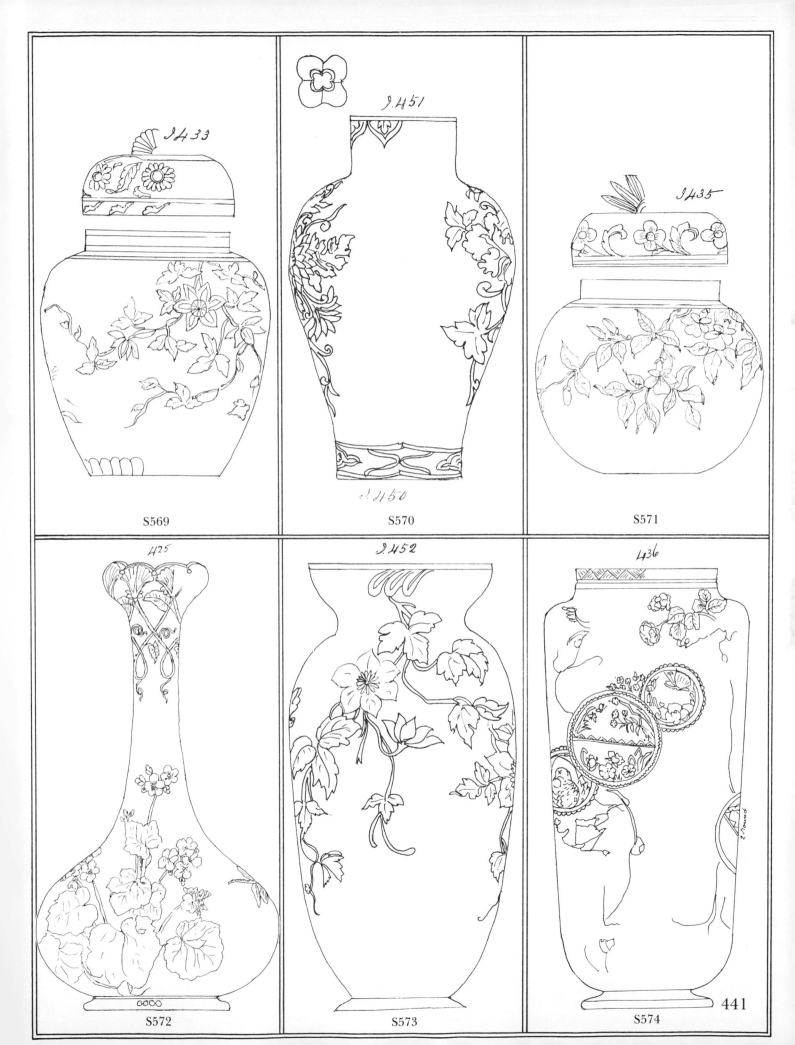

S569   S570   S571

S572   S573   S574

441

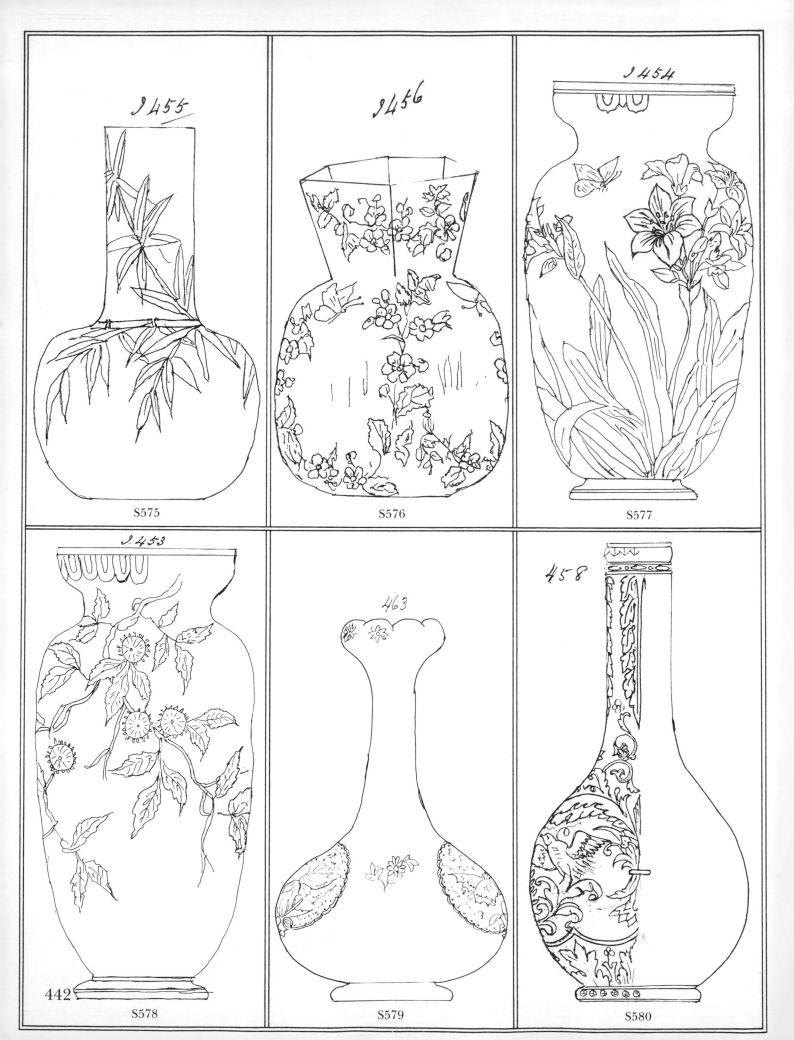

9455

9456

9454

S575

S576

S577

9.453

463

45-8

442

S578

S579

S580

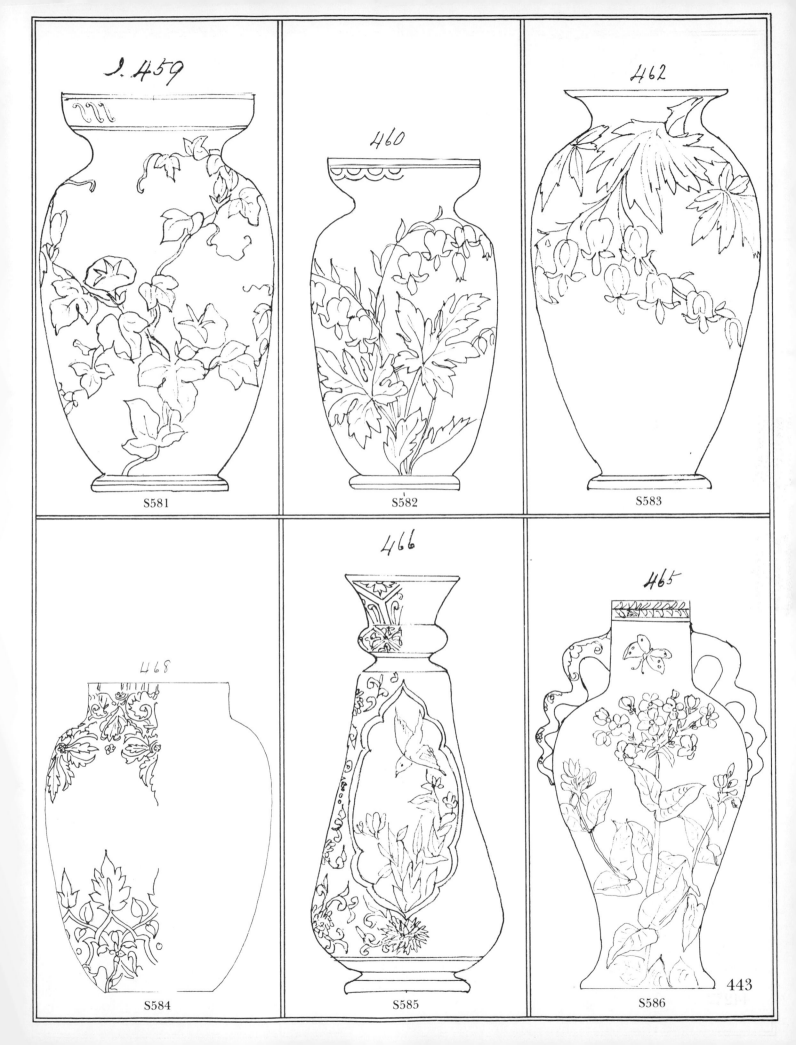

ɔ. 459

460

462

S581

S582

S583

466

465

468

443

S584

S585

S586

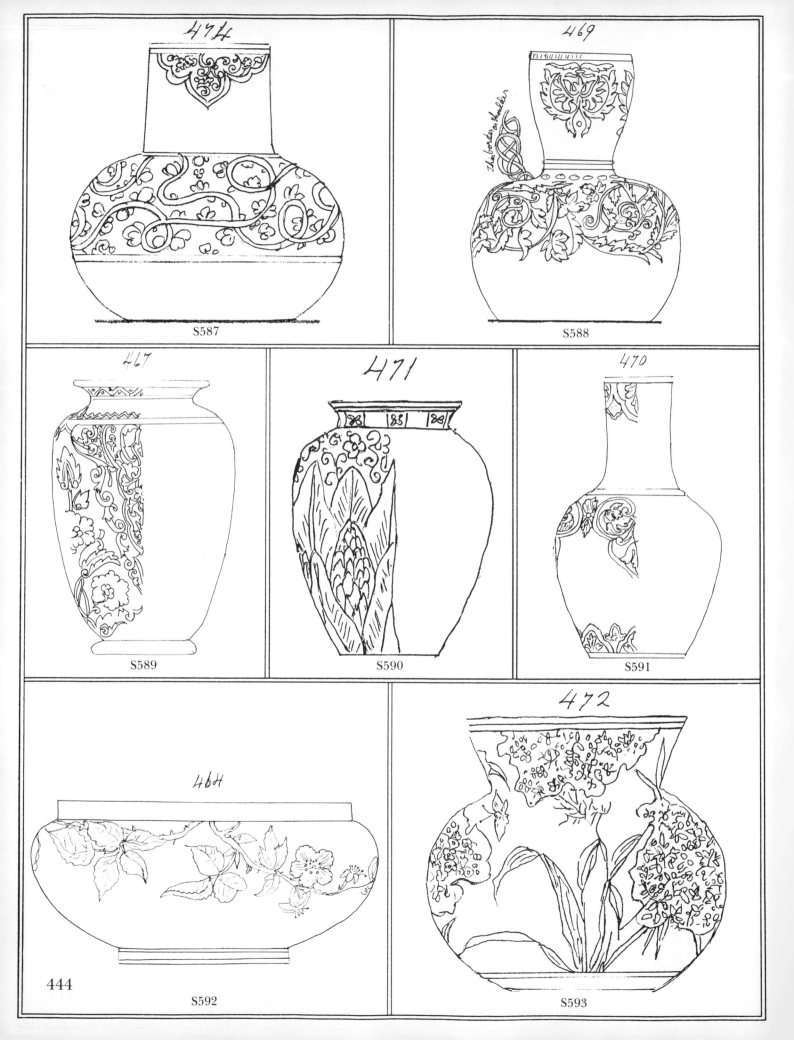

474

S587

469

S588

467

S589

471

S590

470

S591

464

472

444

S592

S593

495

S594

9511

S595

492

S596

491

S597

498

S598

9.480

S599

494

S600

445

Grod

497

of this Vase) body of
Reverse side, decor as Jug, 493?

9513

S601

9509

S602

S603

S501

9570

S604

S605

9508

9505

446

S606

S607

S608

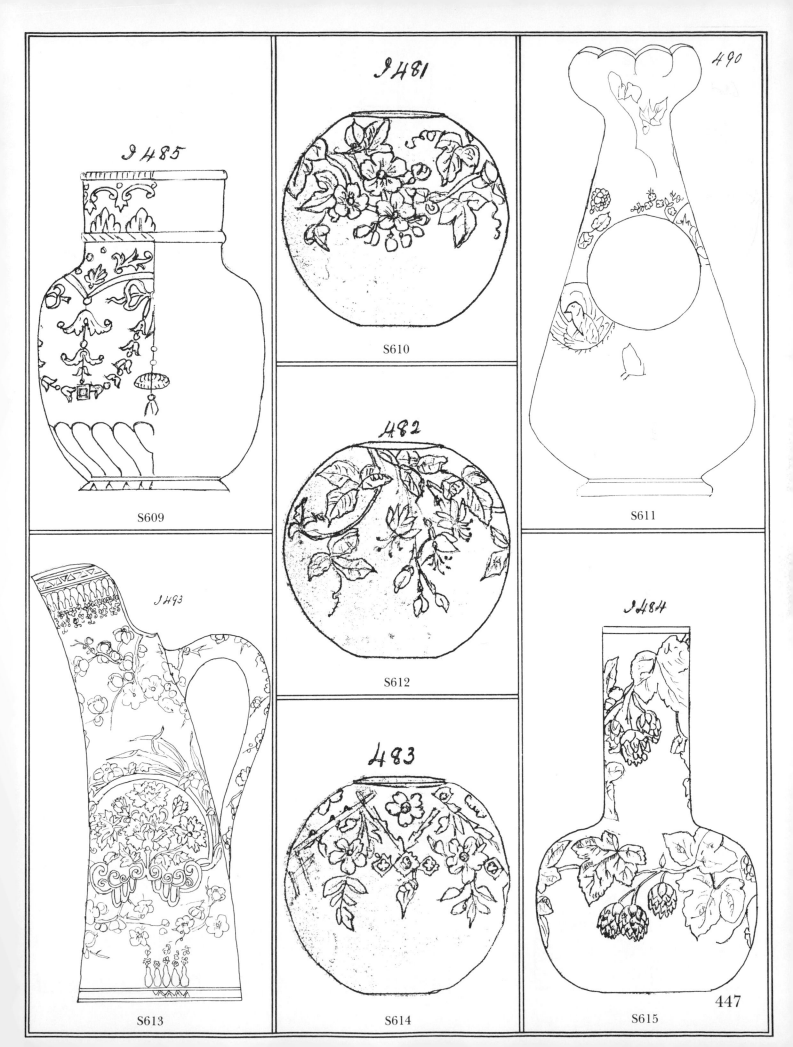

S609

S610

S611

S612

S613

S614

S615

447

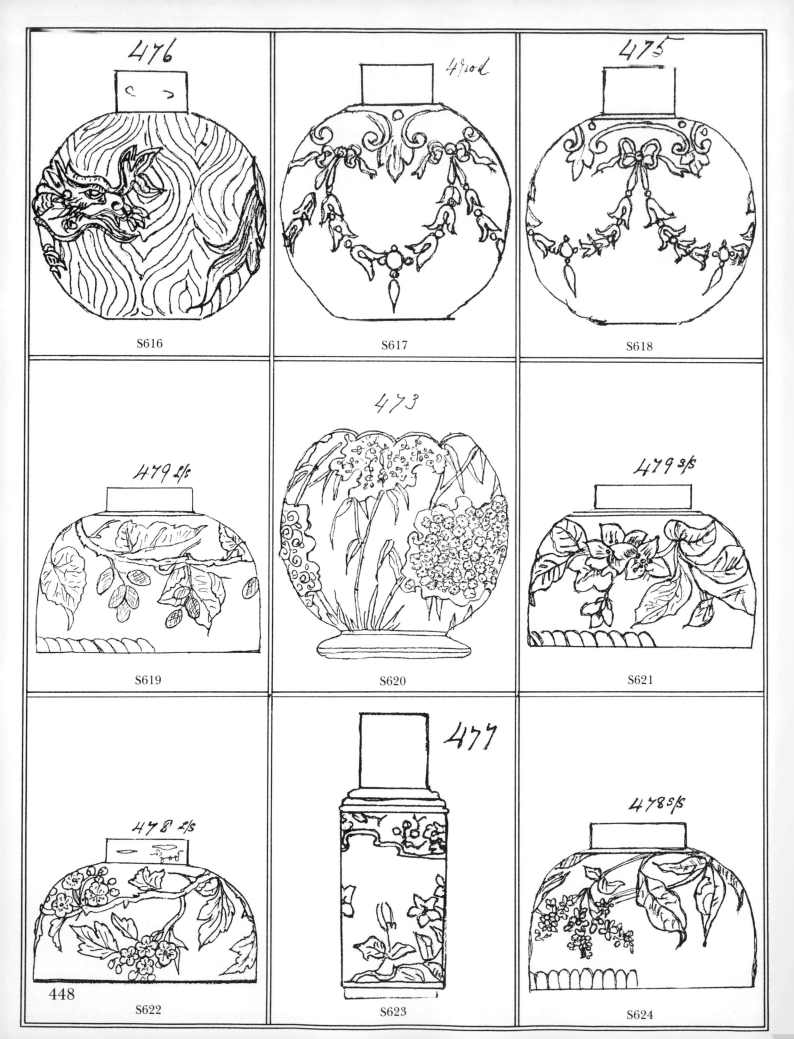

476

472d

475

S616

S617

S618

473

479 2/s

479 3/s

S619

S620

S621

477

478 2/s

478 s/s

448

S622

S623

S624

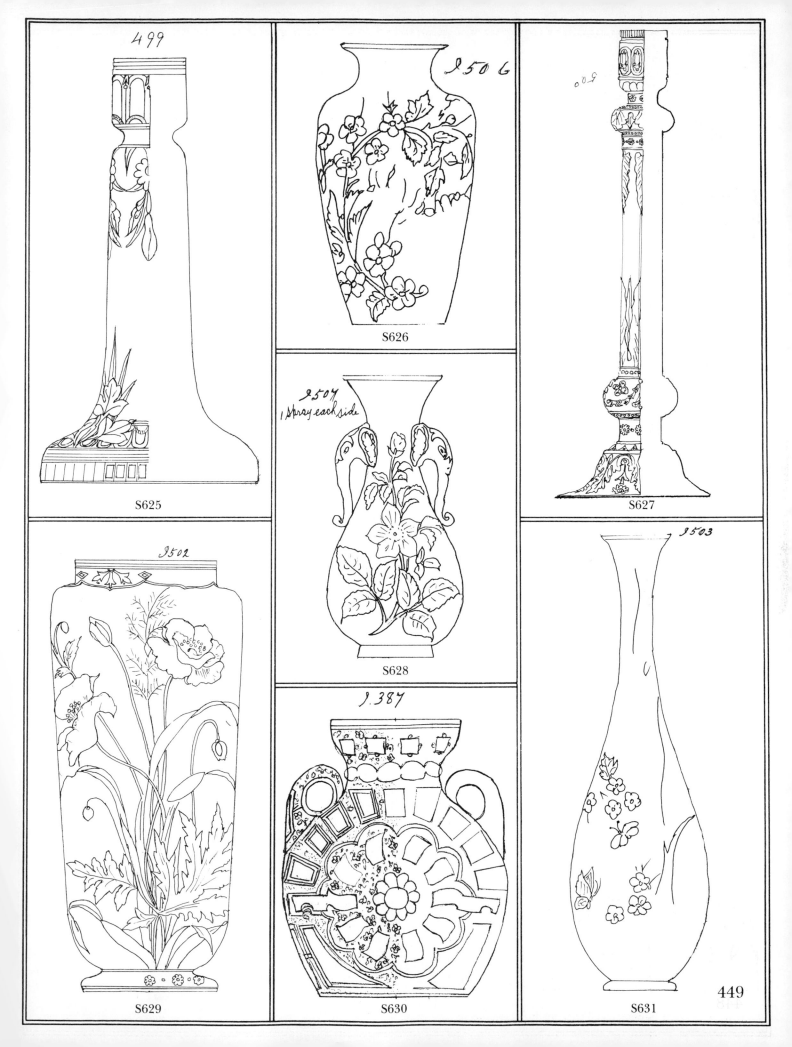

499

S625

9506

S626

9507
1 spray each side

S628

1.387

S630

009

S627

9502

S629

9503

S631

449

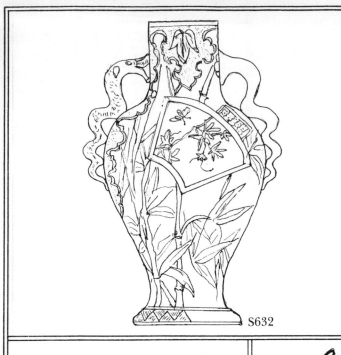

S632

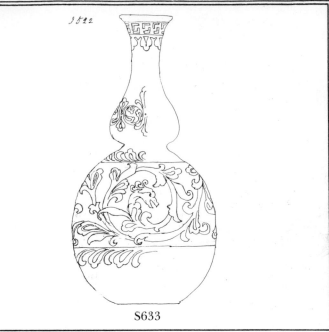

9522

S633

9536

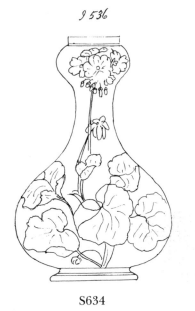

S634

I 5 36½

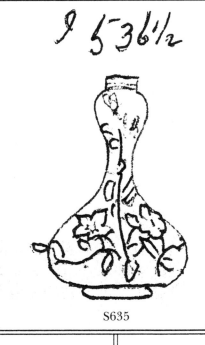

S635

9517

S636

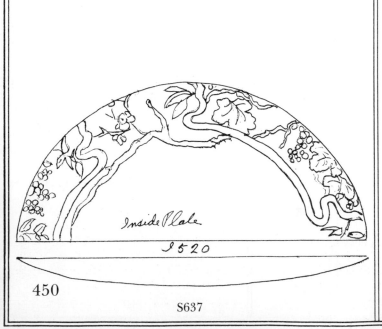

Inside Plate

9520

450

S637

9516

S638

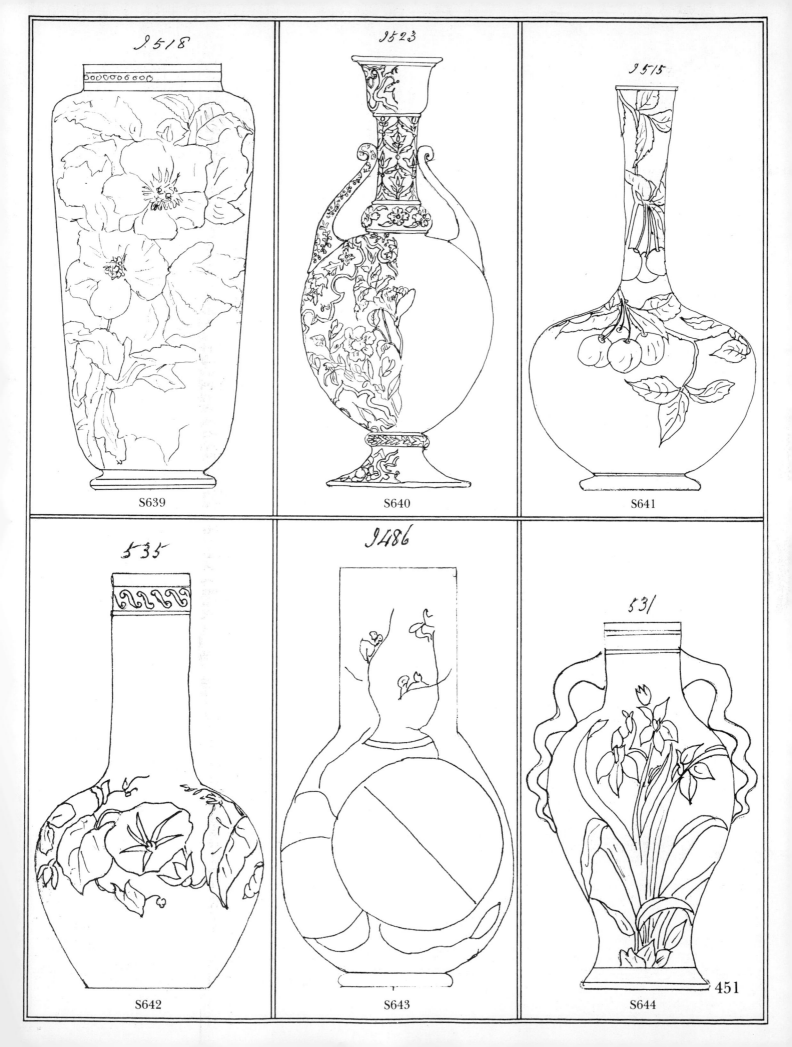

9518

9523

9515

S639

S640

S641

535

9486

531

S642

S643

S644

451

532

533

534

S645

S646

S647

544

542

541

S648

S649

S650

549

548

550

S651

S652

S653

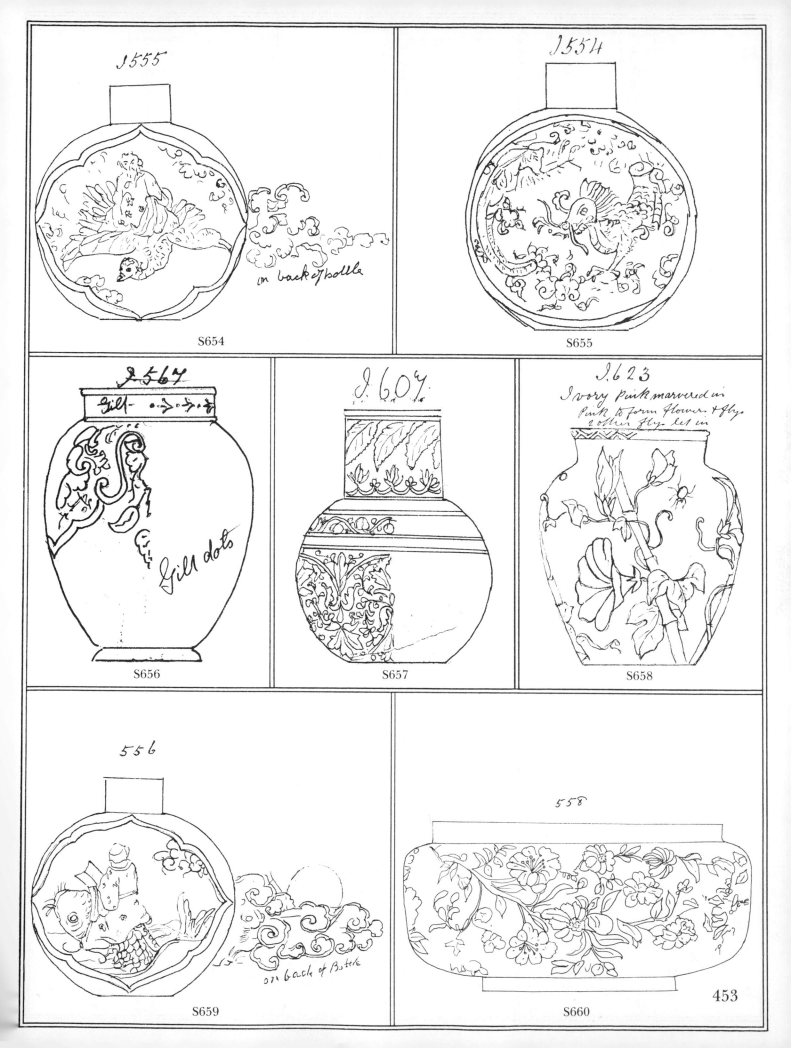

1555

on back of bottle

S654

1554

S655

1567

Gill

Gill dots

S656

1607

S657

1623

Ivory pink marvered in
Pink to form flower & fly.
2 other fly let in

S658

556

on back of Bottle

S659

558

1554

S660

453

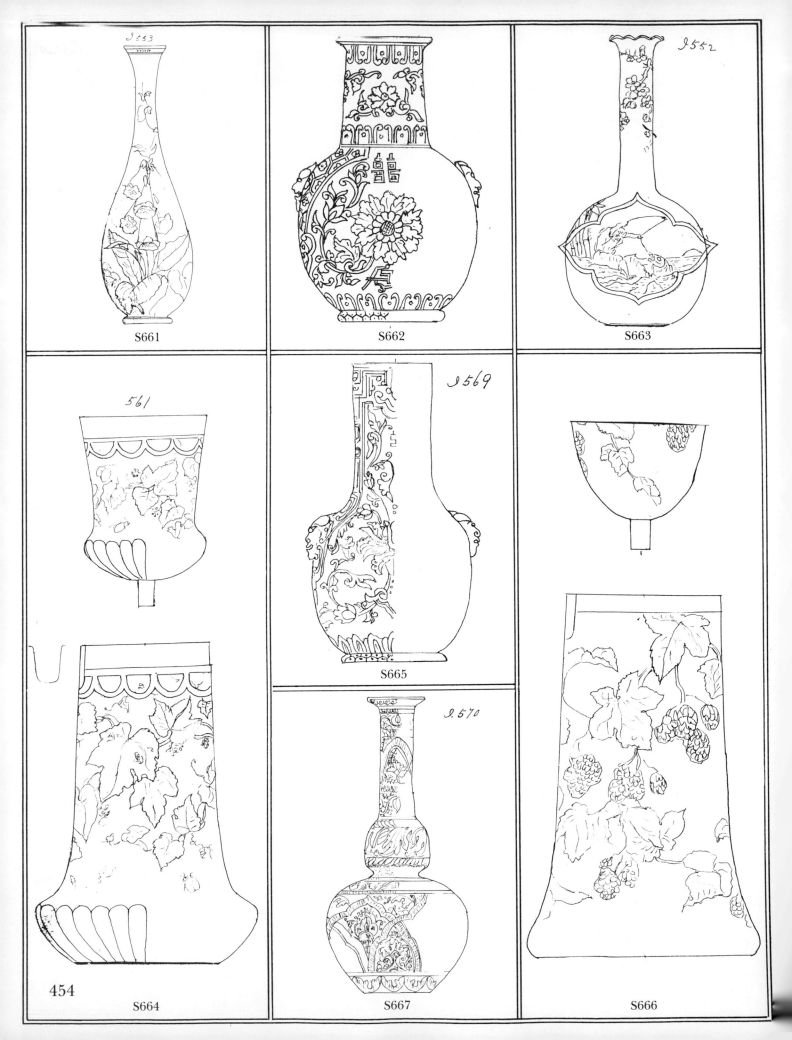

S661

S662

S663

561

S665

S664

S667

454

S666

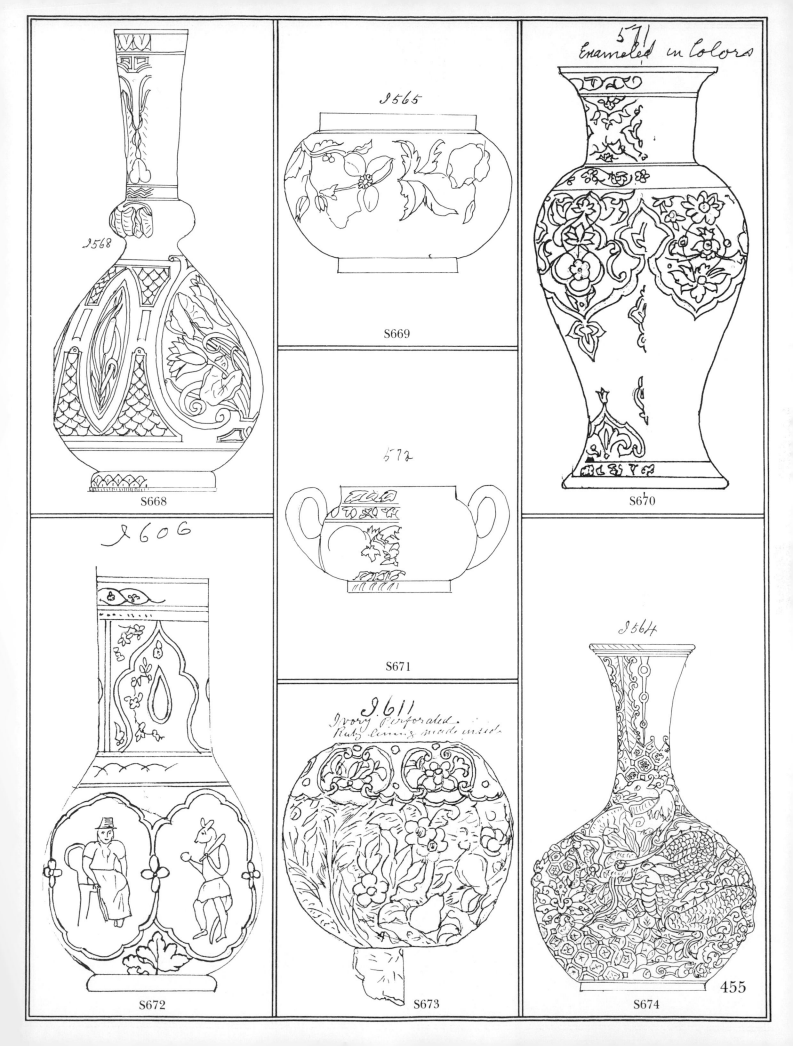

9568

S668

9565

S669

572

S671

571 Enameled in Colors

S670

9606

S672

9611
Ivory. Perforated.
Ruby lining made inside

S673

9564

455

S674

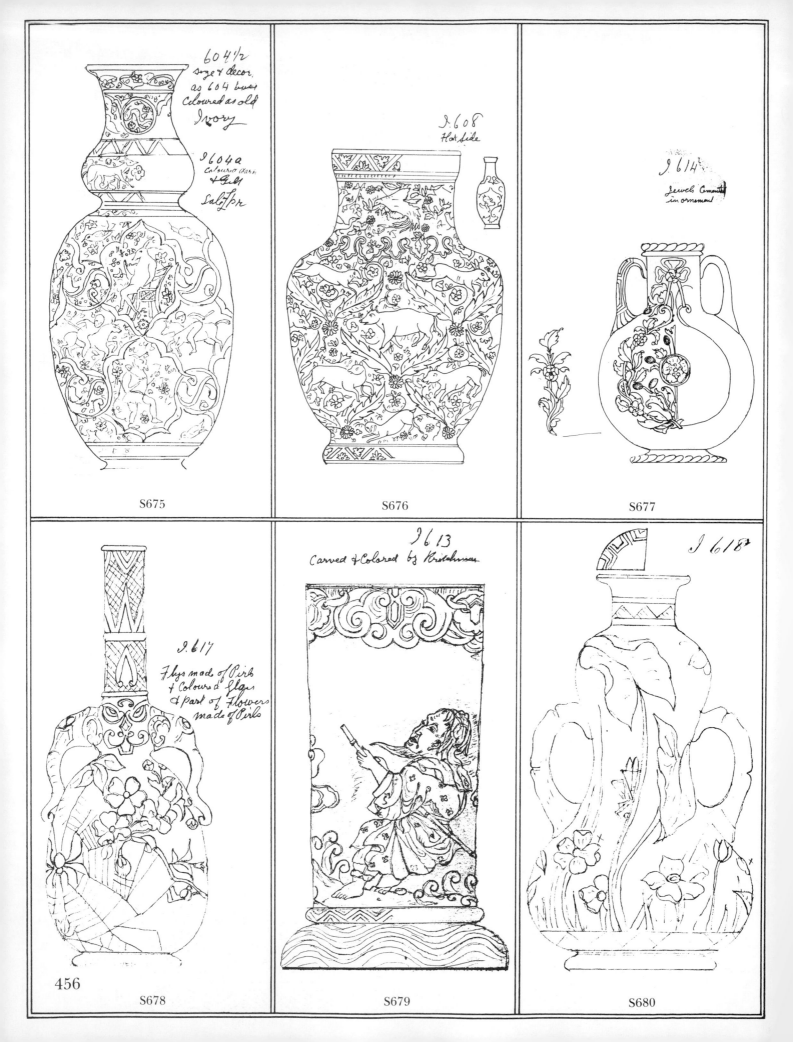

604½
size & decor.
as 604 but
Coloured as old
Ivory

9604a
Coloured dark
& Gilt
Sal 7/pr

S675

9608
Flat Side

S676

9614
Jewels Cemented
in ornament

S677

9617
Flys made of Pirls
& Coloured Glass
& part of Flowers
made of Pirls

S678

9613
Carved & Colored by Krotchman

S679

9618

S680

456

S.620

Fly, air Bubbles
+ Balls let in mad.
colours Slap + Pears

S.621

S.622

S681

S682

S683

S.615

S.616

Fish + fly
made of Purple + R—

x Figures for side of Vases

S684

S685

457

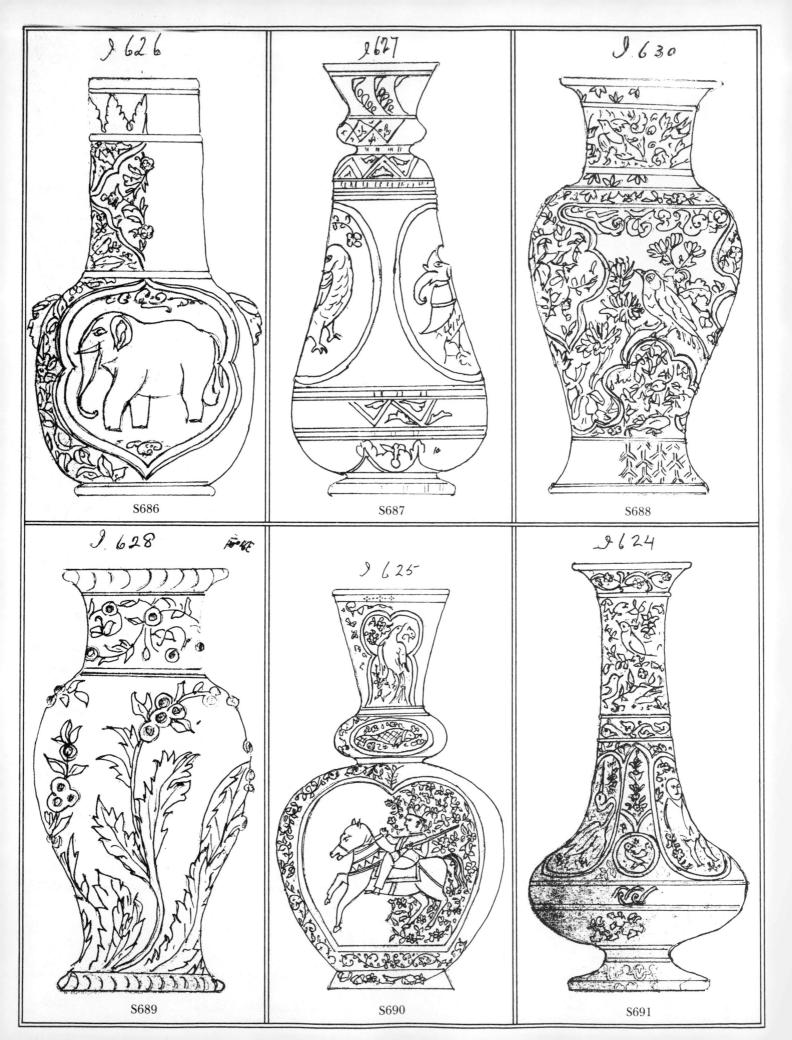

S686 S687 S688

S689 S690 S691

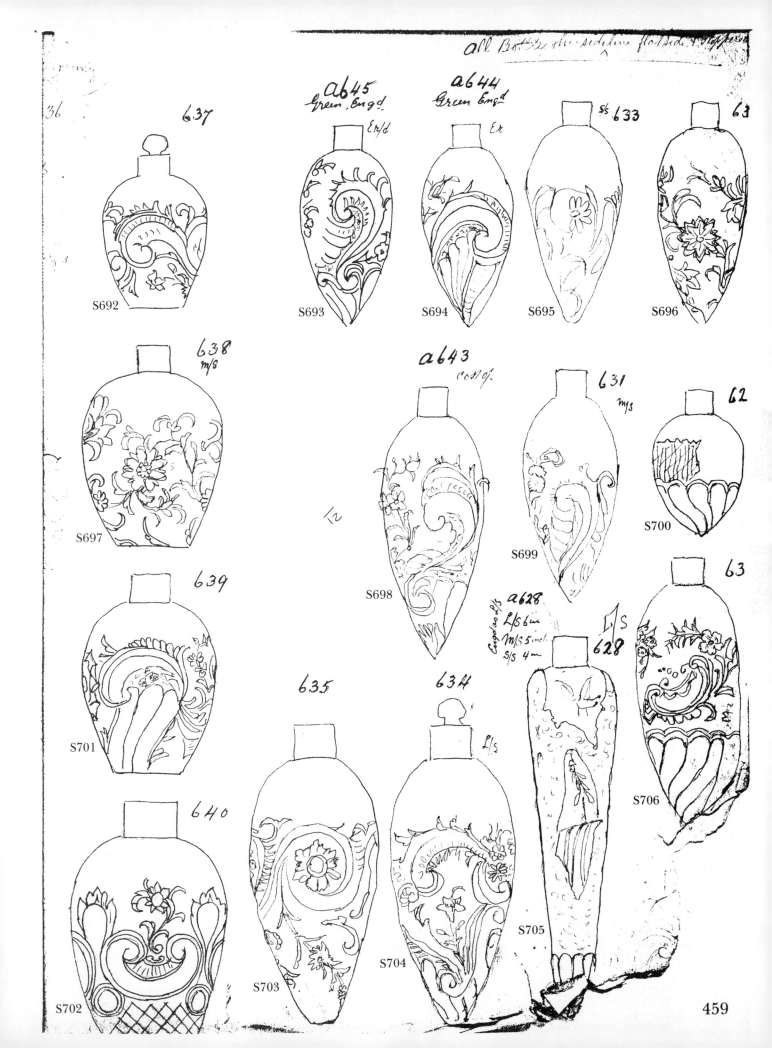

36

637

S692

a645
Green Eng'd
Eng'd
S693

a644
Green Eng'd
Er
S694

s/s 633
S695

63
S696

638
m/s
S697

a643
con of
S698

631
m/s
S699

62
S700

639
S701

635
S703

634
L/s
S704

a628
Engd no p/s
L/s 6in
m/s 5 incl
s/s 4in
L/S
628
S705

63
S706

640
S702

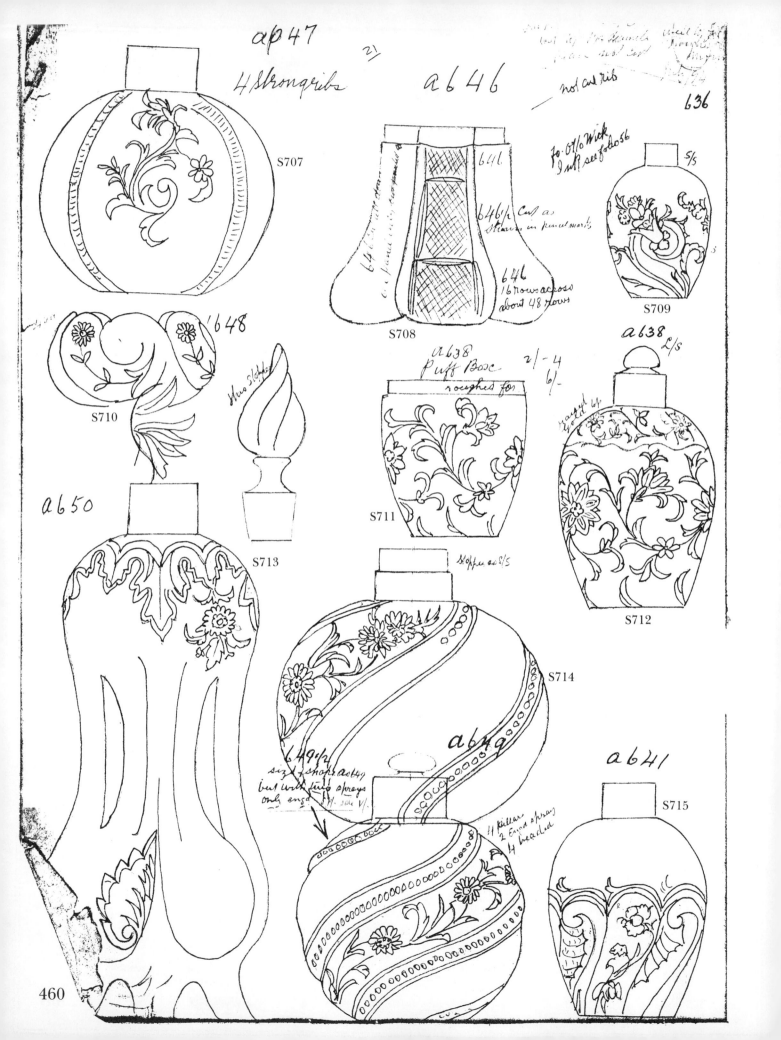

ap47

21

4 Strong ribs

a646

not cut rib

636

S707

646

646½ Cut as
shewn in pencil marks

70 0¼% Wick
I will see follo 56

5/s

S709

646
16 rows across
about 48 rows

S708

1648

a638
Puff Box
roughes for

2/- 4
6/-

a638 L/s

rouched by
gold

this Stopper

S711

S710

a650

S713

Stopper as S/s

S712

S714

b49½
size + shape as b49
but with two sprays
only enga FM. see V.

ab49

4 pillar
2 Enva sprays
4 beaded

a641

S715

460

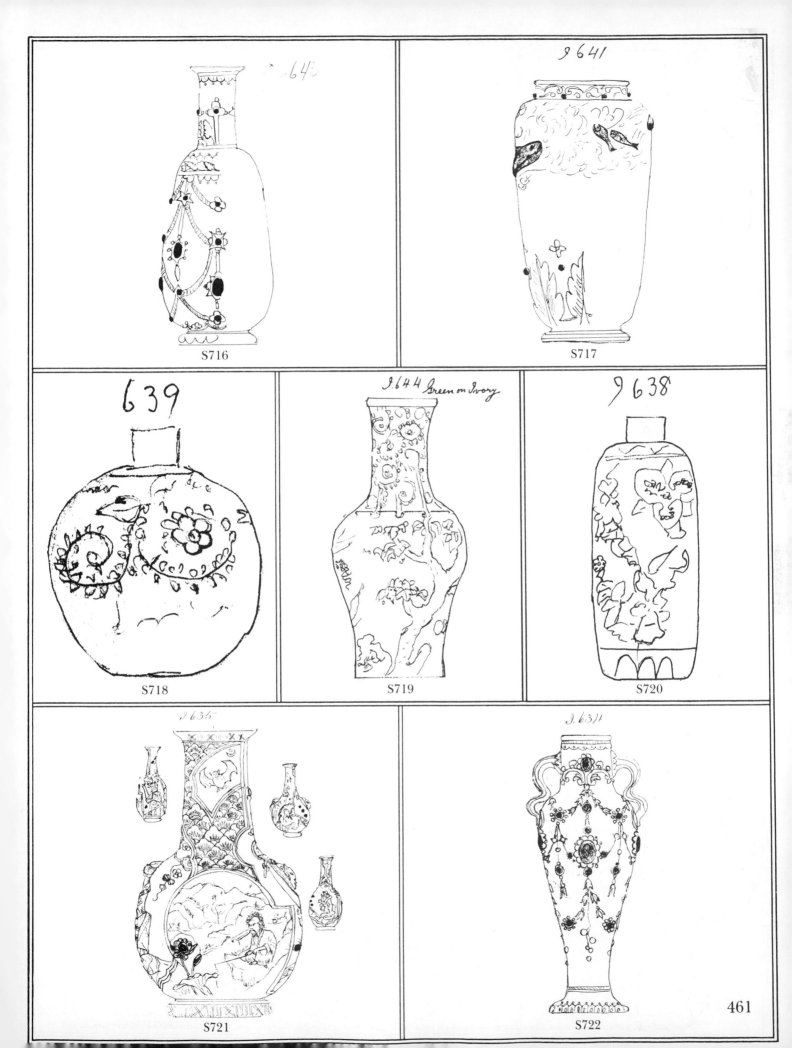

S716

9641

S717

639

S718

9644 Green on Ivory

S719

9638

S720

9635

S721

9634

S722

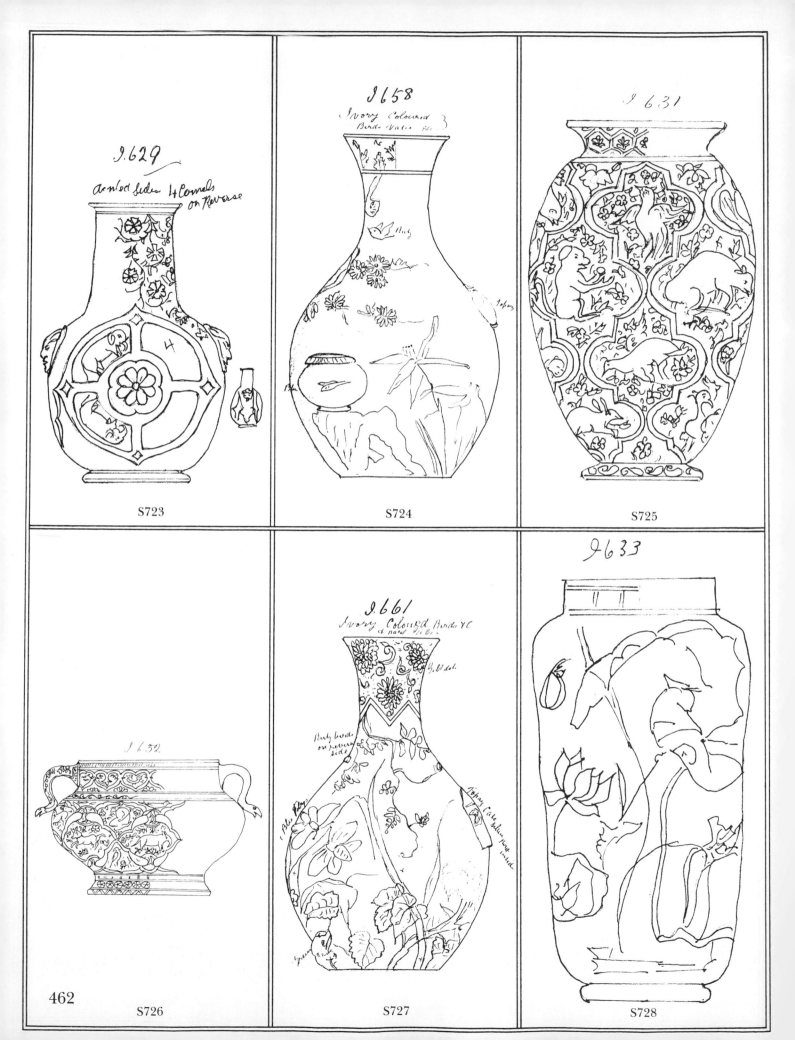

9.629

Arched Sides 4 Camels
on Reverse

S723

9.658

Ivory Coloured
Birds Vase &c

S724

9.631

S725

9.632

S726

9.661

Ivory Coloured Birds &c
& narw bell.

G.W. del.

S727

9.633

S728

462

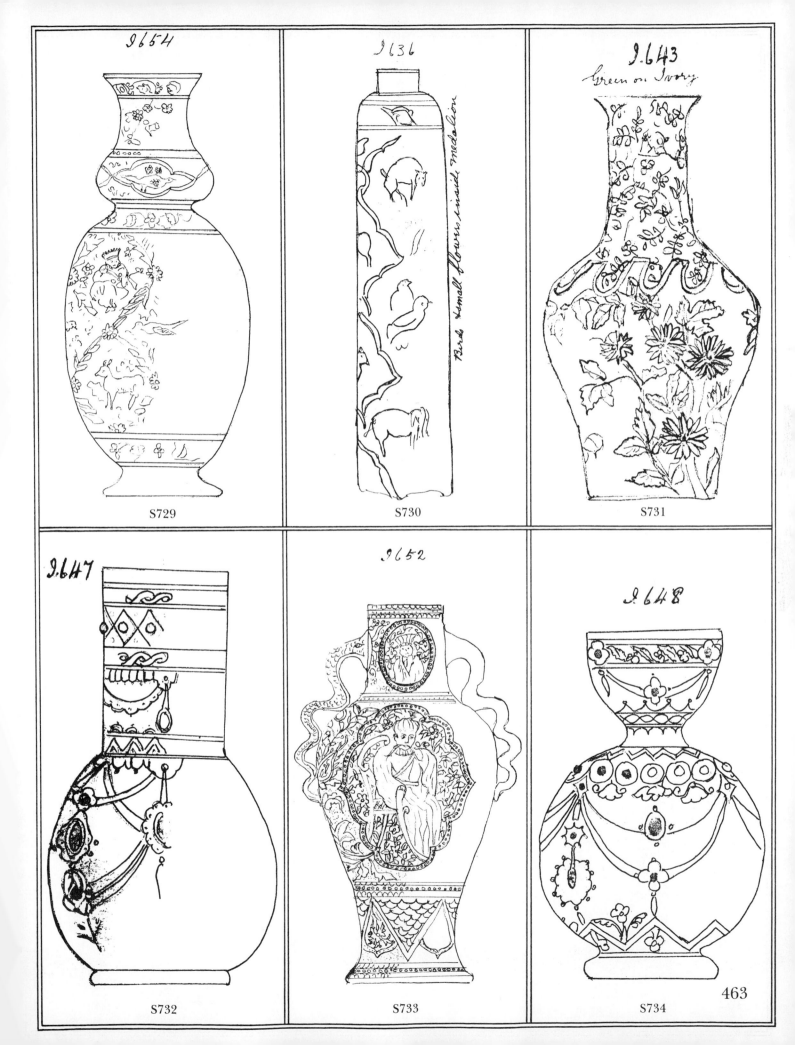

9654

S729

9636

Birds small flowers inside medalion

S730

9.643

Green on Ivory

S731

9.647

S732

9652

S733

9648

S734

463

S735

S736

S737

S738

S739

S740

S741

464

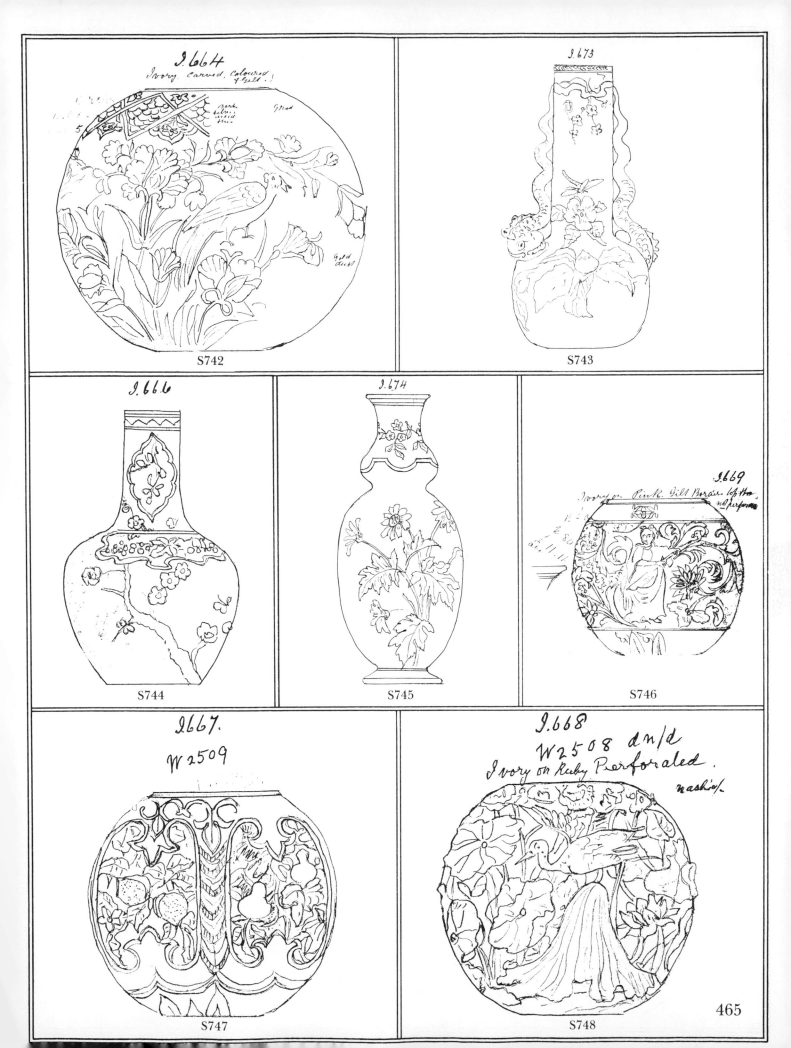

S742

S743

S744

S745

S746

S747

S748

465

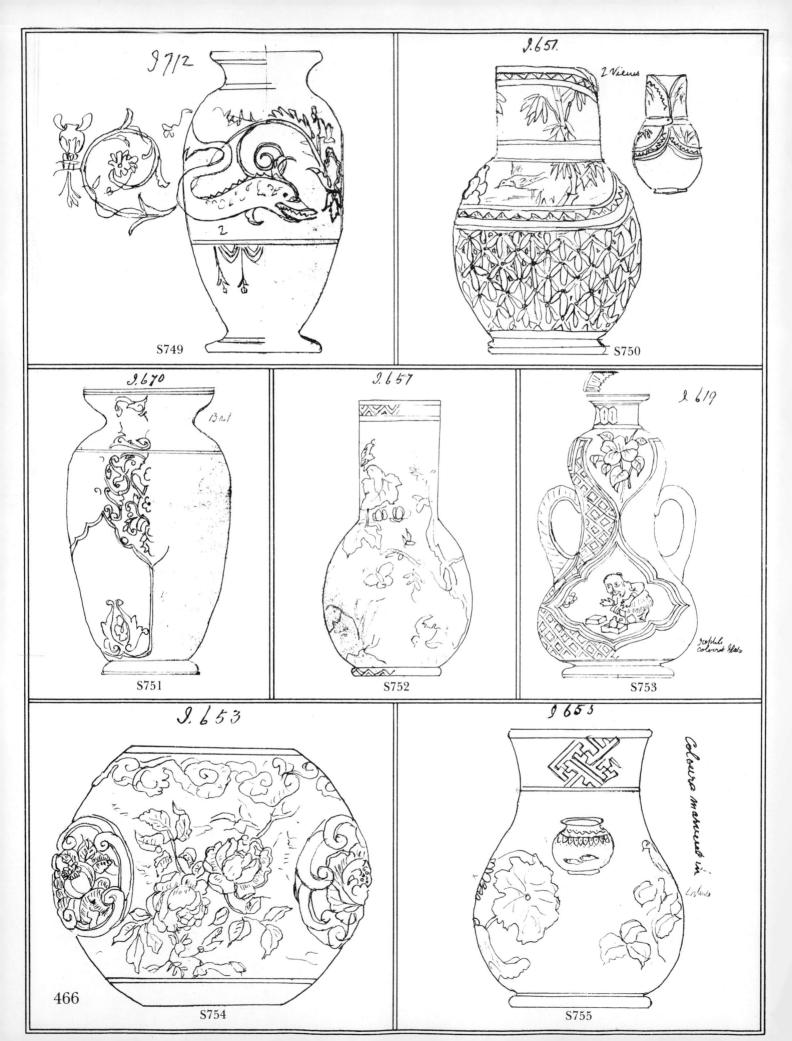

9 7/2

S749

9.651.

2 Vienus

S750

9.670

Bn1

S751

9.657

S752

9.619

Grapfele
coloured Glatz

S753

9.653

466

S754

9.655

colours marcus in

Lestens

S755

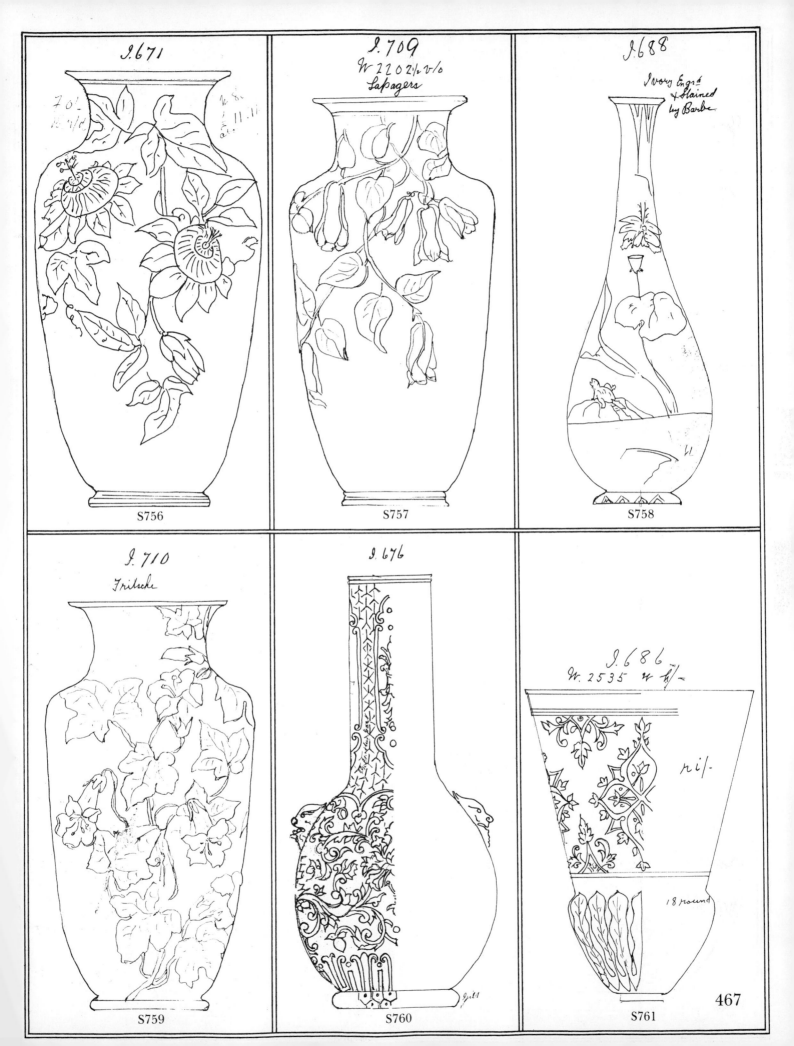

J.671

7 0/-
/2 s/d   2 8/-
                          d. 11.11

S756

J.709
W 2202½ v/o
Lapagers

S757

J.688

Ivory Eng'd
& Stained
by Barbe

S758

J.710

Fritsche

S759

J.676

S760

J.686
W. 2535 4 h/-

n i/-

18 round

S761

467

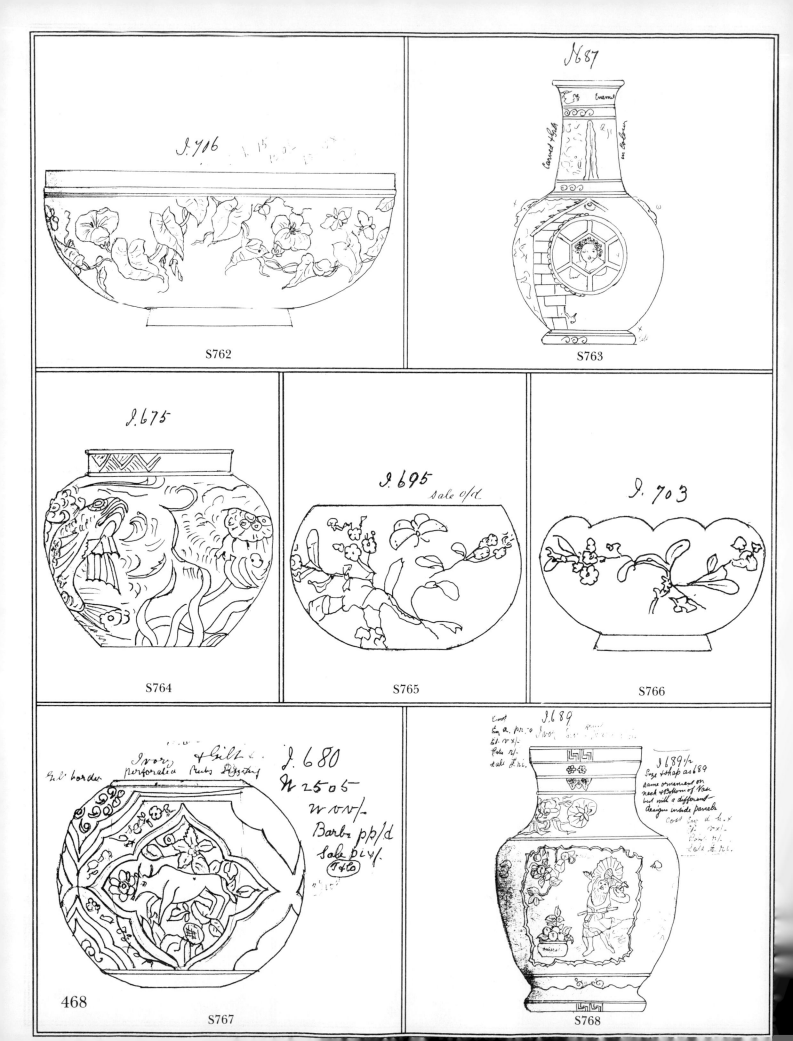

J.716

S762

N87

S763

J.675

S764

J.695   sale o/d

S765

J.703

S766

Gilt' border   Ivory + Gilt +   J.680
    Perforated parts slipping   W 2505
        W v v/-
        Barb pp/d
        Sale b i v/.
        T+Co

468

S767

Cost   J.689
Eng a. pr. o   Ivory
£1. v x/-
Polis v/-
Sale £ri.

J.689½
Size +shap as 689
Same ornament on
neck +Bottom of Vase
but with a different
design inside panels
    Cost Eng d h. x
    V- v x/-
    Polis v/-
    Sale £ xi.

S768

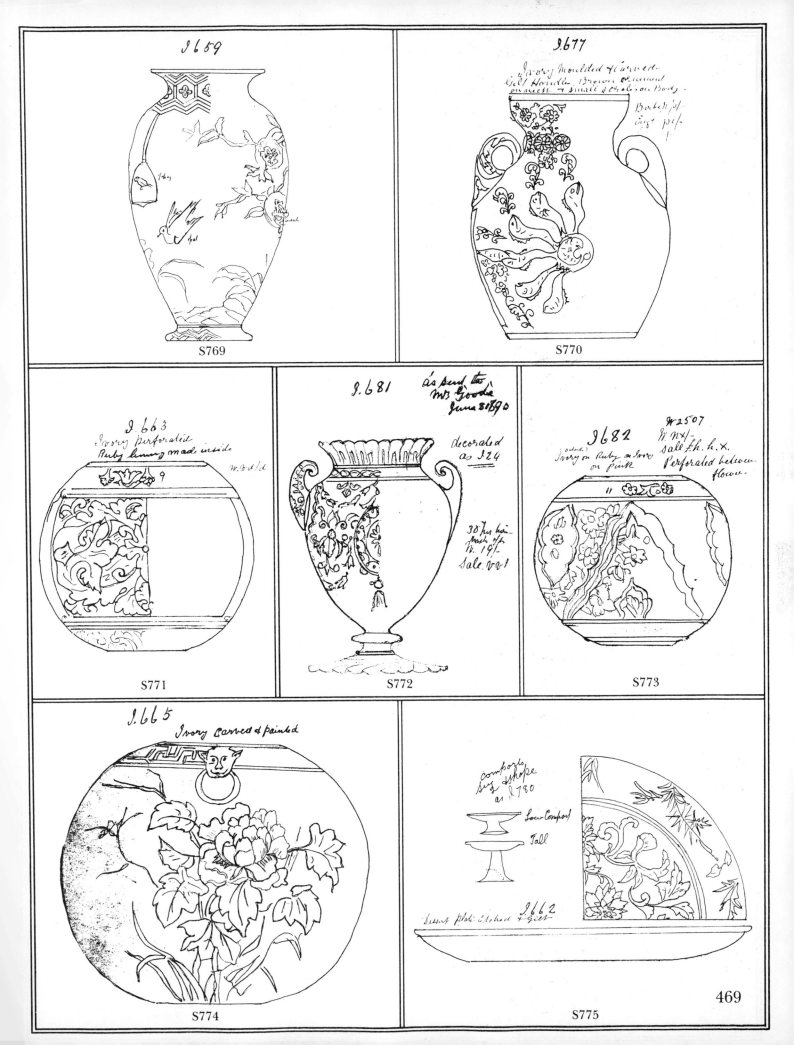

9659

S769

9677

Ivory Moulded & Carved
Gilt Handle, Brown Ornament
on neck & small scrolls on Body.

Bottle of
type psf.

S770

9663

Ivory perforated
Ruby lining made inside

W Bold

9

S771

9681

As sent to
Mrs Goode
June 3 1890

decorated
as 924

38 hrs bis
mak off
W. 19/-
Sale V=1

S772

9682

(ordered)
Ivory on Ruby on Ivory
on Pink

W2507

W nx/-
sale f.h. h. X.
Perforated between
Flowers

11

S773

9665

Ivory Carved & painted

S774

comports
sug shape
as 9780

Low Comport
Tall

Dessert plate etched & gilt

9662

S775

469

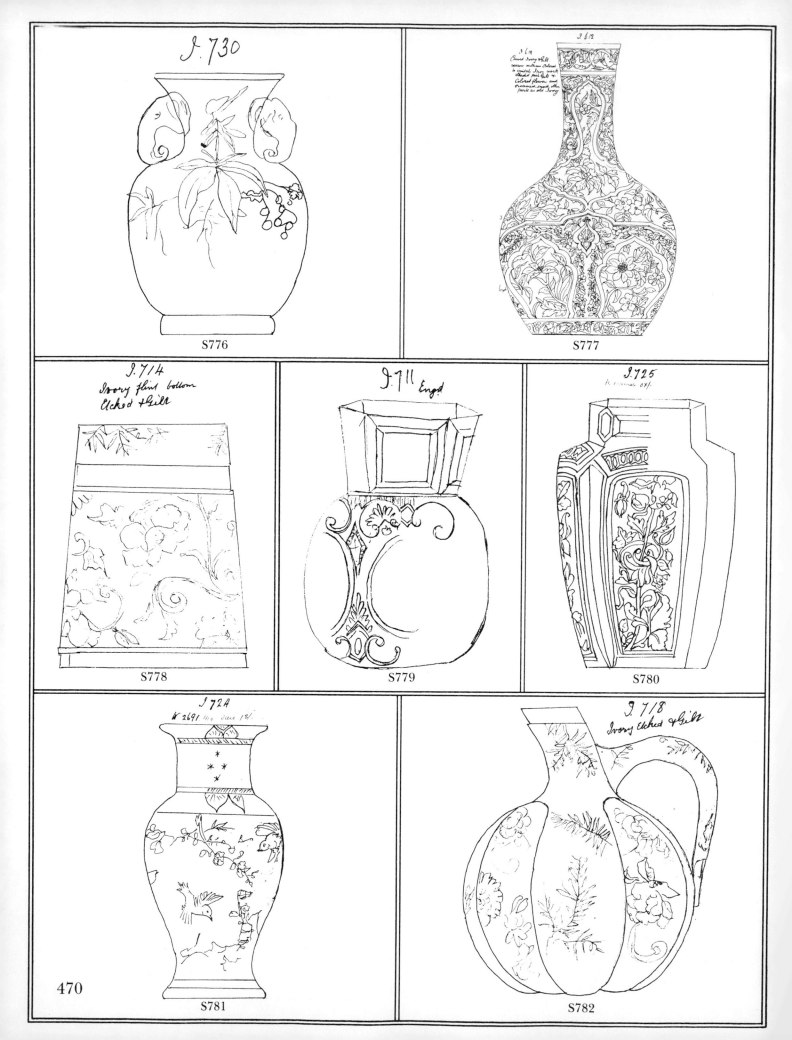

S.730

S776

S777

S.714
Ivory flint bottom
Etched & Gilt

S778

S.711 Eng.d

S779

S.725

S780

S.724
N 2691

S781

S.718
Ivory Etched & Gilt

S782

470

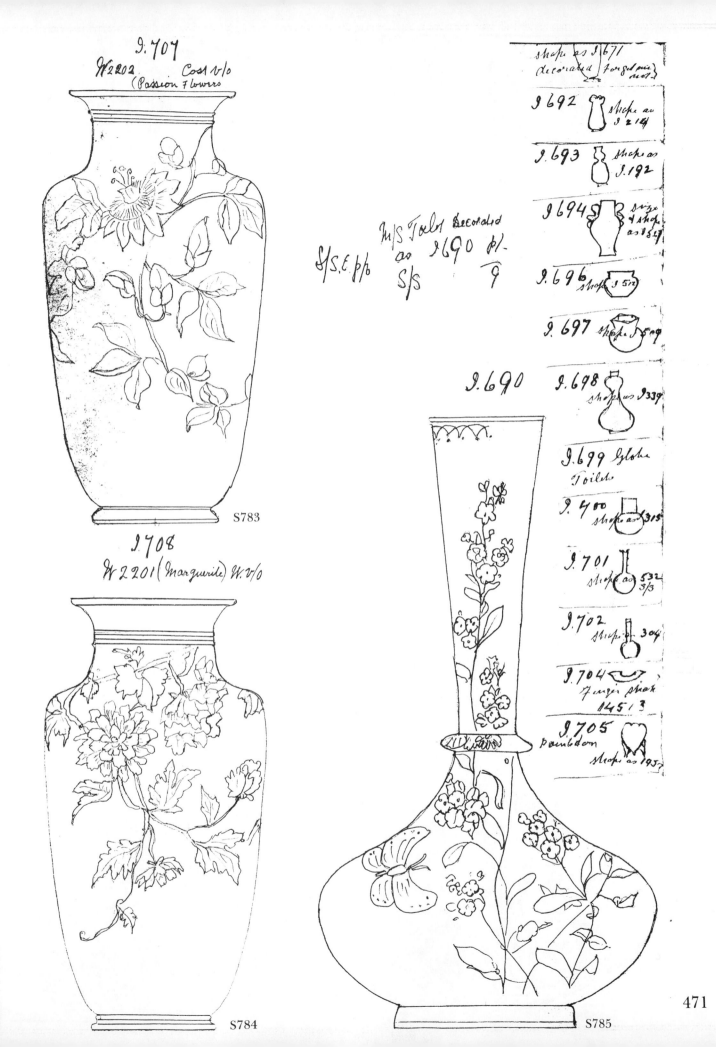

9.707
W2202   Cost 1/0
(Passion Flowers

S783

9.708
W2201 (Marguerite) W.2/0

S784

shape as 9671
decorated forget me not

9.692   shape as 9.214

9.693   shape as J.192

9.694   size & shape as 854

9.696   shape J.512

9.697   shape J.509

9.698   shape as 9.339

9.699   Globe Toilet

9.700   shape as 315

9.701   shape as 532 3/3

9.702   shape as 304

9.704   Finger shape 14513

9.705   Dandelion shape as 195

9.690

S/S.E.p/o   M/s Toilet decorated as 9690 Pl-
S/S   9

471

S785

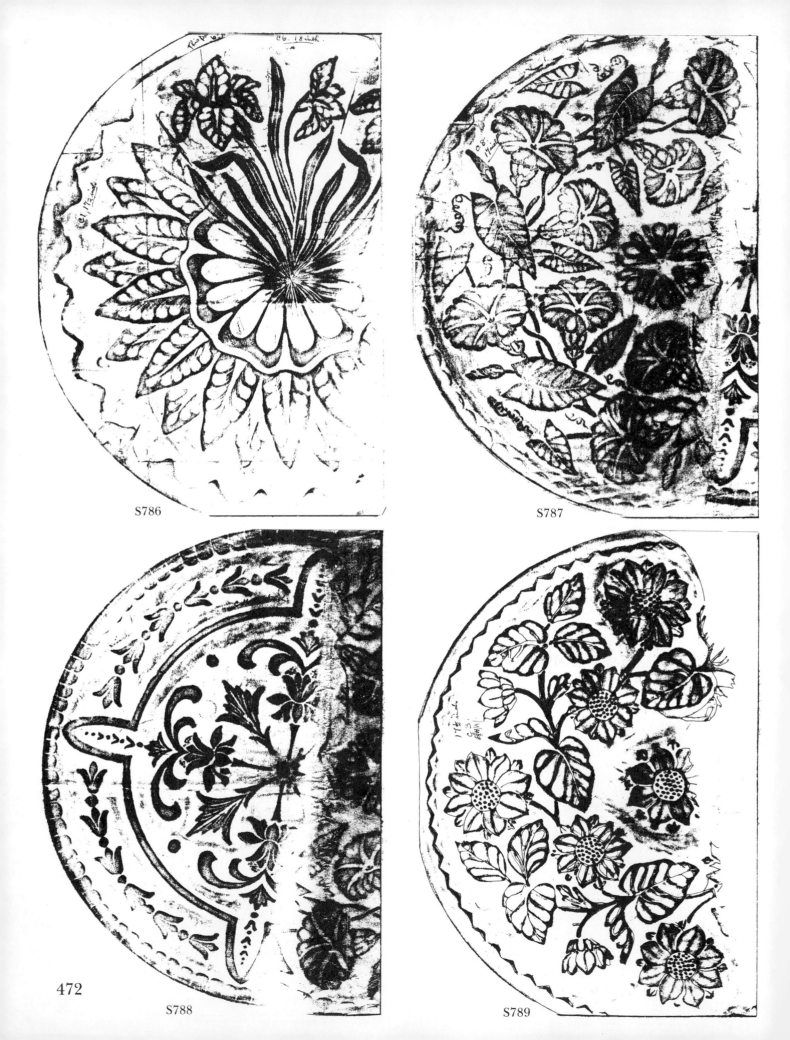

S786

S787

472

S788

S789

MUSEUMS

ALFRED UNIVERSITY MUSEUM, Alfred, New York, established 1900, offers art education, design glass, painting, photography, printmaking, and sculpture. Robert C. Turner, head of the division of art and design.

BIRMINGHAM CITY MUSEUM AND ART GALLERY, Birmingham, England, collection of cameo glass, including the Elgin vase by John Northwood.

CHRYSLER MUSEUM OF ART AT NORFOLK, Mowbray Arch and Olney Road, Norfolk, Virginia, founded 1926. Walter P. Chrysler, Jr., president and director; Nancy Merrill, curator. Hours April through November, 10:00 A.M. to 5:00 P.M.; December through March, 12:00 noon to 5:00 P.M. Collections include arts from Egypt, Greece, Rome, Near East, Africa, the Orient, pre-Columbian America, and paintings and sculptures of all periods. Ancient to modern glass, furniture, decorative arts, textiles, costumes, jewelry, silver, and artifacts.

CINCINNATI ART MUSEUM, Eden Park. Millard F. Rogers, Jr., director. Open 10:00 A.M. to 5:00 P.M. Collections include paintings, American prints and drawings, Chinese bronzes, pottery, and a collection of early American glass.

CORNING MUSEUM OF GLASS, Corning, New York. Thomas S. Buechner, director. Dwight Lanmon, vice director, collections. Hours July and August, 8:30 A.M. to 5:00 P.M.; September through June, 9:30 A.M. to 5:00 P.M.; November through May, closed on Mondays.

Established in 1951 to present to the public the entire story of glass, its history, art, science, and actual manufacture. Collection is most comprehensive; over 14,500 items, dating from 1500 B.C. to the present, dealing with glass. Library has 15,000 volumes for reference, rare books, color slides, periodicals, microfilms, and photographs.

CURRIER GALLERY OF ART, 192 Orange Street, Manchester, New Hampshire. David S. Brook, director. Melvin E. Watts, curator. Open 10:00 A.M. to 4:00 P.M., closed on Mondays. Established 1915 by the will of Mrs. Hannah M. Currier, and endowed; building opened in 1929. Collections of American painting and sculpture, eighteenth century to the present. Fine American decorative art from the seventeenth to the twentieth century; furniture, textiles. A highlight is the Sophie and Albert Murray collection of glass.

DUDLEY ART GALLERY, Dudley, England. Charles Hajdamach, keeper of glass and fine arts. Roger Dodsworth, assistant. Collection of English art glass and cameo glass, photographs, library of glass, original manuscripts, pressed glass, blown glass goblets.

GREENFIELD VILLAGE AND HENRY FORD MUSEUM, Dearborn, Michigan. Open weekdays 9:00 A.M. to 5:00 P.M. Established in 1929 as a general museum of American culture and history for educational purposes.

Collections include decorative arts, folk art, transportation, rare book collections, manuscripts, and photographs. Henry Ford archives contain some 14 million documents.

HAWORTH ART GALLERY, Accrington, Lancashire, England.

HESSISCHEN LANDESMUSEUM, Darmstadt, West Germany

HOUSTON ANTIQUE MUSEUM, 201 High Street, Chattanooga, Tennessee. Open Tuesday through Saturday 10:00 A.M. to 4:30 P.M., closed Mondays. Established in 1961 with a collection, willed to the city of Chattanooga by Mrs. Houston, containing porcelains, 15,000 pitchers, and all types of fine art glass.

KUNSTMUSEUM, Dusseldorf, West Germany, undoubtedly houses the finest and most comprehensive collection of art nouveau glass in Europe, composed primarily of the private collection of Professor Doctor Helmut Hentrich. It is located at Dusseldorf Strasse 65, and is a must for any traveler who can find the time to visit this important museum.

METROPOLITAN MUSEUM OF ART, Fifth Avenue at 82nd Street, New York City, founded in 1870. Museum library contains 200,000 books, 1,200 periodical titles, photograph and slide library. The departments are numerous, including American paintings and sculptures, an American wing, arms and armor, ancient and Near Eastern art, a costume institute, Egyptian art, Greek and Roman art, Islamic art, medieval art, primitive art, prints, twentieth-century art. Chairman of the board is C. Douglas Dillon; president, William Macomber; director, Phillipe de Montebello.

MILAN HISTORICAL MUSEUM, INC., 10 Edison Drive, Milan, Ohio, two miles south at Exit #7 from the Ohio Turnpike, just east of Toledo, Ohio. Main building of the museum offers many rooms and collections, including the Robert Mowry Glass Collection now numbering over 1,500 pieces and listed in the top ten of the nation. There are more than 500 examples of fine early pressed glass, and English and American cut and etched glass. One case is attributed to Sandwich glass. The art-glass wing houses the art nouveau glass. Open during April, May, September, October, 1:00 P.M. to 5:00 P.M., June, July, August, 10:00 A.M. to 5:00 P.M.; Sayles Home Annex, May through October 1:00 P.M. to 5:00 P.M. Newton Memorial Arts Building, May through October 1:00 P.M. to 5:00 P.M.

MORSE GALLERY OF ART, Rollins College, Winter Park, Florida

MUSÉE DES ARTS DÉCORATIFS, Paris, France. Established in 1863 to adapt beauty to industry, financed by city and state appropriations. Collections include decorative art, architecture, home décor of the French Middle Ages, Oriental art, tapestry collection, art nouveau glass.

MUSEUM OF FINE ARTS, Boston, Massachusetts

MUSEUM FUR KUNST AND GEWERBE, Hamburg, West Germany

MUSEUM OF MODERN ART, New York, New York

PILKINGTON GLASS MUSEUM, England, is one of the finest private industrial museums in Europe. Opened as an integral part of the new Pilkington head office complex at Prescot Road, St. Helens, in 1964, the museum is designed to illustrate the evolution of glassmaking techniques, as well as how the product has been used since Phoenician times. Open weekdays from 10:00 A.M. to 5:00 P.M., the museum is located on A 58, within easy reach of Manchester, Liverpool M 6, M 61, and M 62.

ROCKWELL-CORNING MUSEUM, Baron Steuben Place, Market Street, Corning, New York. Collections of Stevens & Williams glass, over 4,000 examples of Steuben glass, toys, and western paintings and bronzes by

Frederic Remington and Charles Russell. Collection formed by its founder, Robert Rockwell. Kristin A. Amylon, assistant director of collections.

SMITHSONIAN INSTITUTION, 1000 Jefferson Drive, S.W., Washington, D.C., was founded in 1846, for the "increase and diffusion of knowledge among men" by a bequest to the United States from James Smithson. The presiding officer (ex-officio) is the President of the United States. Chancellor, Warren E. Burger, Chief Justice of the United States. Volumes in the library number over 950,000. Glass donated by leading companies of the United States from the early inception of the museum. Home of the Dennis Pegasus vase by Northwood. Smithsonian performs fundamental research, publishes results of studies, explorations, and investigations, preserves for study and reference about 65 million items of scientific, cultural, and historical interest.

STEVENS & WILLIAMS WORKS MUSEUM, Brierley Hill, England

STOURBRIDGE COUNCIL HOUSE MUSEUM, Stourbridge, England

TOLEDO MUSEUM OF ART, Monroe Street at Scottwood Avenue, Toledo, Ohio. Open weekdays, 9:00 to 5:00; Sundays and Mondays, 1:00 to 5:00. Closed all national holidays. Convenient parking adjacent to the museum. The museum collection, consisting entirely of original works of art, is internationally known. It traces the history of art from ancient Egypt to the twentieth century. Included are over 700 American and European paintings. An extensive glass collection is featured. Founded in April 1901 by Edward Drummond Libbey, who originally brought the glass industry to Toledo. A fine contemporary collection of glass is additionally featured, and a periodic exhibition of current artists with suitable awards is nationally recognized. Their library has 30,000 volumes for reference, and 40,000 photographic slides.

VICTORIA AND ALBERT MUSEUM, Cromwell Road, S.W., London, England. Open 10:00 A.M. to 6:00 P.M. Established in 1852. Collections of fine and applied arts of all countries, periods, and styles, including Oriental art. Library contains 400,000 volumes.

VIRGINIA MUSEUM OF FINE ARTS, Richmond, Virginia

WALTERS ART GALLERY, Baltimore, Maryland

BIBLIOGRAPHY

American Pottery Gazette, July 1905, page 19; December 1907, page 19; January 1908, page 20.

Ancient Vases from the Collection of Sir Henry Englefield, Bart., drawn and engraved by Henry Moses. Fifty-one plates of which twelve are now first published. London: H. G. Bohn, 4 York St., Covent Garden, MDCCCXLVIII.

Antiques Magazine, July 1935; September 1936, "Cameo Glass," Homer Eaton Keys; November 1937, Cameo Glass, Ruel P. Tolman; March 1963; June 1954, page 72; July 1955, page 73.

ARWAS, VICTOR. *Glass—Art Nouveau to Art Deco.* London: Academy Editions, 1977.

BEARD, G.W. *Nineteenth Century Cameo Glass.* Newport, Monmouthshire, England: Ceramic Book Co. 1956.

BULFINCH, THOMAS. *Bulfinch's Mythology.* New York: The Modern Library, Random House.

BUTTERWORTH, L. M. ANGUS. *British Table and Ornamental Glass.* London: Leonard Hill Books, Ltd., 1956.

The Works of Antonio Canova. London, 1876.

Country Life, February 1954, page 357; December 1951.

Connoisseur, September 1907, page 3, No. 10; September 1909, page 2.

CORNING MUSEUM OF GLASS. *English Nineteenth Century Cameo Glass.* Corning, New York.

DILLON, EDWARD M.A. *Glass.*

ELVILLE, E.M. *Paperweights and Other Glass Curiosities,* London: Spring Books, 1954.

ELVILLE, E.M. *English and Irish Cut Glass 1750–1950*.

EVERARD, BARBARA, AND MORLEY, BRIAN D. *Wild Flowers of the World*.

GANDY, WALTER. *The Romance of Glassmaking*.

GARDNER, PAUL V. *The Glass of Frederick Carder*. New York: Crown Publishers, Inc., 1971.

GENT, J.W. *Systema Horticulture or the Art of Gardening*. London, 1683.

GROVER, RAY AND LEE. *Art Glass Nouveau*. Rutland, Vt., and Tokyo, Japan: Charles E. Tuttle Co., 1967.

GROVER, RAY AND LEE. *Carved and Decorated European Art Glass*. Rutland, Vt., and Tokyo, Japan: Charles E. Tuttle Co., 1970.

GUTTERY, D. R. *From Broad Glass to Cut Crystal*. London: Leonard Hill Books, Ltd., 1956.

HADEN, H. J. *Notes on the Stourbridge Glass Trade*. Libraries and Arts Committee, Brierley Hill, England, 1949.

HAJDAMACH, C.R. *English Rock Crystal Glass, 1878–1925*. Catalog by Dudley Art Gallery, 1976.

HAYNES, D. AND L. *The Portland Vase*. London: Trustees of the British Museum, 1964.

HAYNES, E. BARRINGTON. *Glass Through the Ages*. Baltimore, Maryland: Penguin Books, 1948.

HONEY, W.B. *Glass—A Handbook and a Guide to the Museum Collection*. London: Victoria and Albert Museum, 1946.

Journal Society of Glass Technology, 1949.

The Lady, June 1899, page 954.

LEMPRIÈRE, J. *Classical Dictionary*. New York: E.P. Dutton & Co., Inc., 1949.

Madame, June 1899, page 196.

MANKOWITZ, WOLF. *Wedgwood*. London: B.T. Batsford, Ltd., 1953.

NEWMAN, HAROLD. *An Illustrated Dictionary of Glass*. Thomas and Hudson.

NORTHWOOD, JOHN. "Stourbridge Cameo Glass," *News and Reviews of the Society of Glass Technology*, 1949.

NORTHWOOD, JOHN II. *The Reproduction of the Portland Vase*.

NORTHWOOD, JOHN II. *John Northwood*. Stourbridge, England: Mark and Moody Ltd., 1958.

Paris International Exibition, 1878.

PELLATT, APSLEY. *Curiosities of Glassmaking*. London: David Bogne, 86 Fleet Street, MDCCCXLIX.

PHILLIPS, ROGER. *Wildflowers of Britain*.

Pottery Gazette, January 1, 1895; June 1, 1894; January 1, 1896.

REVI, ALBERT CHRISTIAN. *Nineteenth-Century Glass*. Camden, New Jersey: Thomas Nelson & Sons, July, 1967.

478

RICHTER, WALTER. *The Orchid World.*

SILVERMAN, PROFESSOR ALEXANDER. *Monograph on Joseph Locke—Art of Glass, 1969.* Ludgate Hill, London: Smith Greenwood and Co. Ludgate Hill, 1969.

SYNGE, ROY HAY AND PATRICK M. *The Dictionary of Garden Plants.*

THORPE, W.A. *English Glass.* Libraries and Arts Committee, Brierley Hill, England, 1949.

TRIPP, EDWARD. *Crowell's Handbook of Classical Mythology.* New York: Thomas Y. Crowell Co.

WAKEFIELD, HUGH. *Nineteenth Century British Glass.* New York: Thomas Yoseloff, 1961.

WEISS, GUSTAV. *The Book of Glass.* New York: Praeger Publishers, 1971.

WILKINSON, R. *Hallmarks of Antique Glass,* London: Richard Madlery Ltd., 1968.

WILLS, GEOFFREY. *Victorian Glass.* Transatlantic Arts, Inc., England, 1977.

WOODWARD, H.W. *Art, Feat, and Mystery.* Stourbridge, England: Mark and Moody Ltd., 1975.

WOODWARD, H.W. *The Glass Industry of the Stourbridge District.*

WOODWARD, H.W. *The Literature of Glass.*

WOODWARD, H.W. *One Hundred Years of Royal Brierley Crystal.*

WOODWARD, H.W. *Stourbridge Glass.*

Index

Figures in italics indicate illustration numbers. C refers to color plate. S applies to sketch number.

480

481